The Futures of Reparations
in Latin America

Genocide, Political Violence, Human Rights Series

Edited by Alexander Laban Hinton, Nela Navarro, and Natasha Zaretsky

For a complete list of titles in the series, please see the last page of the book.

The Futures of Reparations in Latin America

Imagination, Translation, and Belonging

EDITED BY PIERGIORGIO DI GIMINIANI, HELENE RISØR,
AND KARINE VANTHUYNE

Rutgers University Press

New Brunswick, Camden, and Newark, New Jersey, and London and Oxford

Rutgers University Press is a department of Rutgers, The State University of New Jersey, one of the leading public research universities in the nation. By publishing worldwide, it furthers the University's mission of dedication to excellence in teaching, scholarship, research, and clinical care.

978-1-9788-4439-1 (cloth)
978-1-9788-4438-4 (paper)
978-1-9788-4440-7 (epub)

Cataloging-in-publication data is available from the Library of Congress.
LCCN 2025022454

A British Cataloging-in-Publication record for this book is available from the British Library.

rutgersuniversitypress.org

In Memoriam Paula Vásquez Lezama (1969, Caracas–2021, Paris)

Contents

**The Futures of Reparations
in Latin America**

Introduction

• •

The Futures of Reparations in Latin America

PIERGIORGIO DI GIMINIANI,

HELENE RISØR, AND

KARINE VANTHUYNE

"Verdad, justicia, y reparación" ("Truth, justice, and reparation"). In Latin America, these are inseparable concepts. Together, they form the core of the most prominent slogan used by human rights organizations seeking accountability for crimes against humanity committed during the Cold War–era military dictatorships. More recently, these demands have expanded to address the enduring legacies of slavery, Indigenous dispossession and genocide, and environmental destruction. Several state-led transitional justice programs are named after this slogan, reflecting how demands for justice are often pursued through both grassroots activism and state-led initiatives, which frequently intersect and overlap. Each of the three notions stands as a necessary condition for the others. Reparations are essential for uncovering the truth about past violence and achieving justice for its victims. Their significance in Latin America's histories of democratization can be traced to the implementation of transitional justice systems following the return to democratic governance in many countries during the 1980s and 1990s.

Driven by this momentum, the past three decades in Latin America have seen an unprecedented wave of reparations addressing historical injustices.

1

These efforts have targeted Indigenous and Afro-Latin communities, victims of state repression, and those affected by environmental harm caused by both private and state enterprises. Reasons, subjects, and methods of reparation vary enormously. Reparations concern acts of remembrance for victims of political violence, including memorials and truth commissions (Crenzel and Allier 2016; Drinot 2009; Feldman 2021; Hite 2013; Popkin and Roht-Arriaza 1995; Sodaro 2017; Zaretsky 2021); social-therapeutic interventions in postconflict contexts (Frazier 2007; Lira 2010; Mora-Gámez and Brown 2019; Ronsbo 2015; Theidon 2007); compensation and health remediation for victims of pollution and environmental damage (Johnston 2010; Li 2015; Zourhi et al. 2017); strategies of remediation directed at Afro-Latin communities in both urban and rural areas that are victims of forced relocation and displacement (Collins 2015; Silberling 2003); land redistribution policies for Indigenous groups affected by colonial displacement or slavery (Araujo 2017; Di Giminiani 2018); and more recently, refugees with histories of forced relocation during conflict (Meertens and Zambrano 2010). As violence and injustice stemming from processes of state building and modernization in Latin America are inherently intersectional, reasons, subjects, and methods of reparation require attention to overlaps and differences.

The history of reparations in Latin America is marked by the enduring legacy of state terror and the ensuing project of democratization following the end of the military dictatorships and civil wars in the 1970s and 1980s. Democratization remains an ongoing and incomplete process. The region's new democracies continue to grapple with the risk of a resurgence of totalitarian governments, often emerging as anti-elite political projects. Reparations unfold in contexts marked by enduring authoritarian cultures (see Araujo and Beyer 2013), epitomized by the popular cry for iron-fist governance not only against criminality, particularly drug traffickers (Goldstein 2004; Risør 2010), but also in the control and marginalization of communities and groups through high incarceration rates (Aedo and Faba 2022; Weegels 2020). Recent popular uprisings, such as those in Chile (2019) and Colombia (2021), highlight a growing disenchantment with the unfulfilled promises of democratization. These movements call for a more inclusive democracy that genuinely protects minorities and fosters peaceful coexistence while also prompting critical reflection on the limitations of the neoliberal reforms that have shaped contemporary democratic governance across much of the region. In the past decades, we have witnessed how processes of rewriting constitutions in countries such as Colombia, Ecuador, Bolivia, and, most recently, Chile also unfold as powerful, albeit contested, expressions of recognition and reparation. Two additional historical phenomena help explain the distinct nature of reparations in Latin America. First, the ideology of *mestizaje* is an underlying influence in public debates on reparations for Indigenous and Afro-Latin communities. Mestizaje posits the emergence of a national identity in Latin America that arose from Indigenous, Black, and European miscegenation (see Cornejo-Polar 1997; Wade 2005). While mestizaje entails the acknowledgment of Indigenous and Black heritages, it is also a particular modernist paradigm that questions the continuity of Indigenous societies in the present, diminishes claims of difference from national majorities or dominating elites, and ignores ongoing racism and racial inequalities. Imaginaries of national unity in Latin America have long been inspired by the ideology of mestizaje, which often serves as an obstacle to advancing reparations claims addressing colonial dispossession and violence.[1] Second, neoliberalism is the other historical umbrella under which reparations are designed and implemented across the region. Despite the cyclical resurgence of antineoliberal political projects leading to the rise of postneoliberal governments in many countries in the region, neoliberalism continues to hold a strong influence in the restructuring of state actions based on principles of financial management rather than ethics and justice (Silva 2009). The influence of neoliberalism on transitional justice is evident in compensation systems that prioritize individual subsidies for health, education, and agriculture over collective reparations, such as initiatives targeting marginalized communities.

In Latin America, a region marked by overlapping histories of political and ethnic violence alongside state-led reconciliation efforts, reparation emerges as a central framework for fostering hopes and aspirations of democratic coexistence. Although Latin America is now one of the most democratic regions in the world, citizens' expectations for meaningful democratic participation and justice are still largely unmet (see Munck and Luna 2022). This is particularly evident in the protection of civil and human rights during cycles of social unrest as well as in addressing the ongoing violence and discrimination faced by women, Indigenous, and Black populations. Across the region, support for democracy is suffering serious backlashes. In 2023, only 48 percent of the continent's population supported democracy compared to 63 percent in 2010, and an increasing number of people declared themselves indifferent as to whether they live in a democratic or authoritarian state (Latinobarómetro 2023). The reasons for this decline in support of democracy are manifold and depend on the particularities of national histories. When thinking about politics and practices of reparation, it is necessary to consider how they unfold within and speak to this overall context of ongoing democratization and the vulnerabilities of democracy in the region. Latin American societies struggle not only with coming to terms with state violence and colonial dispossession in the past, which resurface and mark social life, but also with the arduous work needed to strengthen their democratic culture. Latin American postdictatorship democracies are also disjunctive (Caldeira and Holston 2000), meaning that the political institutions have democratized while the civil components remain weak: Citizens continuously experience violations of their social and legal rights. While the region has democratized, it remains notoriously violent (Arias and Goldstein 2010), as new injustices and atrocities continue to take place, mostly among the same groups and populations that have historically been subject to violence and dispossession in the first place. Past and present harms intersect across generations.

Reparation plays a key role in Latin America's recent history of democratization. Without reparations, justice remains an unattainable ideal. As the promises of democratization—particularly the inclusion of historically marginalized groups in the new democratic societies at the turn of the twentieth century—have often led to dissatisfaction, reparations are increasingly seen as the most effective path to justice, even when their impact is largely symbolic: It is justice nonetheless. In Latin America, the promises of reparation are double. They are not solely aimed at addressing past harm; they are also essential for building a more inclusive democracy. They prompt the imagination of new forms of coexistence, offering durable solutions to the persistent and often resurfacing consequences of historical injustice. The talks of reparation that cyclically reemerge in the public debate remind us that democracy is not a system or rule but rather an ongoing process with precarious achievements. Everyday and vernacular forms of democracy are shaped by the often unpredictable consequences of institutionalized processes and by forms of repair unfolding at the edges of state power.

Reparations prompt us to think about the enduring legacy of the past, but they are also powerful forms of future work. In this book, we explore how reparation programs and demands are shaping various political landscapes in Latin America, expanding the possibilities for thinking about democracy and justice in the future. We offer insight into how environmental harm is remediated—or not—in Peru and Guatemala, how repair through judicial archives and other forms of memory can be achieved in Chile and Argentina, how psychological traumas from experiences of war are treated in El Salvador, and how the restoration of Indigenous land ownership unfolds in Bolivia. Reparations originate in national and local histories, which are, in many cases, hardly comparable. Yet taken together, the cases of reparations that we will explore reveal that the significance of reparations in contemporary Latin American politics lies not only in their debated effectiveness for victims but, more importantly, in their generative potential to inspire new ways of imagining and practicing justice, both within and beyond the state.

The centrality of reparations in the recent history of democratization in Latin America contrasts with the elusive definition of this concept. What constitutes a reparation is a matter of controversy, deeply influenced by personal and collective experiences of harm as well as the political context in which restorative justice is conceptualized and implemented. This definition is shaped by the ongoing processes of violence, exclusion, and assimilation (Rojas and Shaftoe 2021). Reparations are inevitably controversial in how they define harm, which can be intergenerational and interpersonal, rooted in class, ethnic, and political conditions as well as intimate individual experiences. This scenario is not unique to Latin America but is at the core of reparation talks worldwide.

Defining reparations is not easy. Early references to this notion are found in the context of peace treaties in which invading armies that lost the war were compelled to pay compensations for the harm they generated. The Hague Convention of 1907 was the first instance of the development of an international framework for war reparations (see Ferstman et al. 2009). Following the atrocities of the Second World War, the institutionalization of the United Nations, and the rise of universal human rights in the second half of the twentieth century, reparations have been increasingly defined as legal constructs targeting populations affected by genocide and crimes against humanity. In recent decades, the scope of reparation politics has significantly expanded. Collective claims for reparations now extend beyond transitional justice in postconflict societies to encompass conflict resolution for environmental disputes and anti-racist struggles led by Indigenous people and Black communities in countries all over the Americas, where histories and present realities remain marked by colonialism and slavery. In cases of colonial violence and dispossession, the moral legitimacy of restorative justice is based not on harms inflicted upon individuals in the past but on the intergenerational effects of colonialism (Thompson 2002, 9). Even though talks of slavery reparations have acquired attention in several countries in the last two decades, claims for reparations for colonial dispossession or slavery are not entirely new. During the era of slavery, enslaved and freed people in the Americas and the Caribbean rarely used the term *reparation*, but many "evoked it by using synonyms such as redress, compensation, indemnification, atonement, repayment, and restitution" (Araujo 2017, 1) in correspondence, public speech, or judicial claims. They thus "showed how conscious they were of having been victims of an injustice" and therefore "owed financial and material restitutions" (Araujo 2017, 2).

Johnston (2009) provides a general definition of reparation, describing it as "any action or process that seeks to repair, make amends, or compensate for gross violations of fundamental human rights" (9). Reparations always extend beyond the legal realm, manifesting as social constructs through which grassroots movements seek long-term remedies for violence and exclusion by demanding accountability for past and ongoing injustices (10). For this reason, reparations are never exclusively material. Symbolic reparations, such as the commemoration of tragic events or the establishment of truth commissions and archives, promise a new form of coexistence enabled by public acknowledgment of the injustice and the moral imperative of learning from and therefore not repeating the mistakes of the past (see Hamber and Wilson 2002). The elusiveness of reparations stems from not only the assessment of harm and its just compensation but also the closure that they can offer. The questions of when reparations can be considered complete and who has the authority to decide when it is time to move on from the past highlight the temporal indeterminacy of reparations. In official discourses, such as those associated with Indigenous multicultural policies, past injustices are recognized as traumatic events that, once subject to reparations, can be forgotten. However, for subjects of reparation, closure of the past is often neither possible nor desired. Restorative justice "may be signified but is not exhausted by a particular reparations program or reparative gesture like a public apology" (Walker 2006, 379). More often than not, governmental aspirations of closure inevitably clash with the need for continuing attention to the often unexpected and ongoing consequences of past violence. This dynamic explains why, in contexts of both mistrust and hope, people navigate complex processes by simultaneously appealing to state authorities and international courts for justice and reparation while also working within community settings to pursue justice and repair beyond the state's reach. As Faulk and Brunneger remind us, in Latin America "non-governmental organizations, organizations from across the political spectrum, and public protests may all appeal to ideas of 'justice'—environmental, social, racial, global, economic, and so on—and only in some cases are legal channels (i.e., the criminal or civil 'justice' systems) seen as the first, most appropriate, or only avenue for enacting change" (2016, 3).

How are economic and political values assigned to past suffering? What is accomplished by the state and by victims through reparation policies? How is the imagination of new forms of nationhood and the environment governed through demands or state actions of reparation? How are they contested by both victims and perpetrators? Many are the questions surrounding reparations today. In this volume, we tackle them by paying particular attention to the anticipatory effects of reparations. The various cases and forms of reparation discussed in this book demonstrate how the forward-looking potential of reparations can reshape understandings of state power, its critique, and its influence on contemporary ideas and experiences of democracy in Latin America. Even though restorative politics remains deeply concerned with historical factuality, recent perspectives on reparations have increasingly shifted attention from the role they play in framing collective pasts to the often unintended effects of reparations on the future (Aguilar Díaz 2011; Di Giminiani 2018; Li 2015; Lyons 2018; Rauhut 2018; Theidon 2010; Vanthuyne 2014). Taiwo (2022, 5) suggests that reparations are "construction projects" that, beyond government-led strategies of redistributive justice, have the potential to reactivate political processes of world making, such as those imagined by anti-colonial and antiracist movements.

In this book, we advance a definition of reparations that emphasizes their processual nature and often unpredictable results. Reparations, we argue, are best understood as a set of material and ideological practices through which multiple futures are imagined and anticipated, past harm is translated into symbolic or material acts of repair, and emergent forms of belonging to the nation or other social collectivities are forged. Contributions to this volume explore three processes significant to the analysis of reparation politics: (1) the imagination of pasts, presents, and futures set in motion by the promises of reparations among both government actors and targeted beneficiaries; (2) the translation of past damages and ongoing suffering into government interventions and/or social responsibility programs of private enterprises; and (3) the reconfiguration of contested forms of belonging that emerge from the implementation of reparation policies.

Imagination, translation, and belonging are core elements of reparation projects. Reparations are driven by the imagination of future political horizons that emerge through and beyond them while simultaneously sustaining that vision. They unfold as contested processes of translation, prompting new forms of belonging that are experienced through radically diverse perspectives. The argument exposed in this book, we believe, provides a framework for analyzing and understanding reparations across the globe. At the same time, it draws inspiration from the unique insights into reparations that a focus on Latin American politics can offer. In particular, imagination, translation, and belonging constitute the core of reparation politics in the three intersecting contexts of repair—postconflict and postdictatorship transitional justice, colonial dispossession and genocide, and environmental harm—that characterize current debates on justice and democracy in Latin America. Even when mobilizing different expertise, affects, and political dynamics, these three areas of reparation reveal a shared underlying logic, similar ambivalent consequences, and a way of thinking about democracy inherent to Latin America. Ethnographic heuristics, such as those employed by contributors to this volume, are particularly effective in revealing the future-oriented potential of reparations. They highlight the generative possibilities of divergent understandings and embodied experiences of harm, hope, democracy, and ultimately, reparations. Before delving into specific cases of reparation, let us, in the remainder of this introduction, explore in greater detail how imagination, translation, and belonging operate within and through reparations.

Imagination: Linking Past Trauma and Future Justice

The rearticulation of past trauma is a central problematic in transitional justice (Fassin 2008; Laplante and Theidon 2007; Ross 2003; Vanthuyne and Falla 2016; Wilson 2003) insofar as it dynamically recasts memories about the past and their enduring effects in the present. Social demands for repair and government programs of reparation prompt new and varied ways of framing past violence in the present and futures that can be envisioned after reparations. The dynamic link between past trauma and justice articulated through reparations, we propose, is best captured by the idea of imagination. While it retains a certain speculative potential, imagination is not a synonym for fantasy. In line with its etymological association with the term *image* (*imago*), imagination concerns the casting and circulation of images through which time and space are represented. The association between imagination and politics is central to the role that institutions play in evaluating divergent claims, such as those concerning reparations. Among social scientists (see Spencer 1997), the term *political imagination* is understood as "the act of identifying with and reacting to political affairs as much as the concrete processes through which the conceptual horizons of social thinking are established, contested, and occasionally subverted" (Di Giminiani 2018, 20).

The term *imagination* plays a significant role in public debates on reconciliation, particularly in reference to the future that follows reparations and transitional justice as a whole. In exploring the imaginative potential and effects of reparation politics in Latin America, we approach imagination as a contested social process in which institutions and political actors engage from different standpoints. The idea of the political imaginary differs from imagination insofar as it is often treated by social scientists as a determinist force for the emergence of political practices and ideas. Rather than a condition for political action, imagination is the result of conflictive and overlapping acts of imagining sustained by different technologies of government. As proposed by Sneath et al. (2009, 6), technologies of imagination consist of all those social and material means by which particular imaginings are generated. These technologies are rarely conducive to consensual forms of imagination. In the context of reparation politics, some of the most frequent—and thus disputed—technologies of imagination stem from archives and museums, which are responsible for representing pasts that need to be repaired. While archives and museums are government technologies particularly adept at producing official images of the past and future, these forms of reparation prompt imaginations that often go beyond their intended purpose.

One of the consequences of official projects of reparation is the situating of events in a discrete, finite past, encouraging the imagination of a future in which past sufferings are left behind. As shown in several chapters of this book, this possibility is captured by the trope of *deuda histórica*, or historic debt (see Han 2012; Paz y Miño Cepeda 2004). Across Latin America, governments articulate their actions as fostering inclusiveness and democratization on the basis of the image of a debt to be paid back to marginalized subjects, such as the urban poor, Indigenous, and Black peoples. By imagining past injustices as a debt to be paid by the state, victims and their suffering are publicly acknowledged and transformed into matters of concern for all of society. At the same time, debt can be extinguished such that past violence is no longer considered to exist in the present. This outcome of reparations is notably visible in postcolonial governmental projects of national reconciliation, where the promise of launching a new era of coexistence for Indigenous groups as well as colonizers is predicated upon the idea that colonization was a single event that took place in the past rather than an enduring framework for experiencing racial hierarchy (Simpson 2016; Wolfe 1999). Critiques of postcolonial processes of reconciliation show how truth commissions contribute to the imagination of peaceful intergroup relations in the future but fail to acknowledge Indigenous sovereignty as an enduring and necessary form of reparations (Corntassel and Holder 2008). As Mbembe reminds us, a major concern of any democracy is to stifle awareness of the latency of violence at its very foundation, such as the role of colonial dispossession in their creation (2019, 23). By selectively remembering specific forms of violence, reparations can fail to recognize the structural conditions of ongoing inequalities and marginalization that remain long after initial harms.

In this volume, we approach reparations as temporally loaded techniques of governance, capable of framing past trauma both as concluded events and as ongoing processes. This ambivalence explains the inevitably disputed nature of reparations, marked by both government aspirations for closure and grassroots hopes for justice to come. Since the 1990s, the potential for governments to use reparations as a means to conclude discussions of past violence and injustice has been widely debated. This period marked a shift in human rights discourse from an active, often revolutionary pursuit of justice to the more humanitarian, and arguably less ambitious, goal of ensuring the nonrepetition of genocidal violence. As argued by Meister (2010), human rights are increasingly conceptualized as a defensive and pragmatic set of humanitarian practices aimed at rescuing victims from forms of political violence widely recognized as intolerable by the international community. In this contemporary dominant humanitarian discourse, "a moral consensus on evil is both necessary and sufficient to put it in the past; once this happens, resuming old political struggles can be repudiated as a potentially catastrophic effort to go backward" (14). In liberal democracies, the imagination of future justice is frequently shaped more by the desire to prevent any possible return of evil than by a search for redistributive justice.

The dominant position of human rights as a defense against the repetition of past evil explains why reparations frequently consist of ritualistic acts of closure. Rituals are key features of state power in general (see Abélès 1988; Hansen and Stepputat 2001; Lomnitz 1995). Across different national contexts, rituals of remembrance share structural features and languages inspired by global human rights discourses, but they are also malleable to national politics and pressures from political actors involved in the transitional justice process (Wilson 2003, 383; see also Hinton 2010; Lefranc 2008; Ross 2003; Sodaro 2017). The question of the effectiveness of symbolic reparations is central to debates across Latin America on museums and commemorative sites (see Milton and Ulfe 2011). Even though these sites are bound to generate controversial exclusions in the narratives they convey, they can effectively highlight the unresolved nature of past violence (Feldman 2021, 78–79). As with rituals in general, reparations of this type can also contribute to the consolidation of a liminal stage between past and present in which the memory of past violence can be unsettling but also conducive to new ways of imagining social justice (Zaretsky 2021, 11). Among activists and scholars, historical narratives produced by memorial sites, truth commissions, museums, and archives are inevitably subject to critical interpretations, emphasizing the unfinished nature of reparations in contrast with governmental representations of these projects as reconciliatory moments of closure (see Bernasconi 2019).

Through various technologies of imagination, reparations aim to counter past and present perceptions of the subjects of violence by affirming their human dignity, political resistance, and other attributes that were denied through the experience of harm. Zaretsky argues that imagination "can generate certain ways of conceiving of human belonging and difference—of generating those 'constellations of meanings' that can then produce violence; in the aftermath, imagination can also be important as a response to that violence" (2021, 100). Although implemented by states to this end, reparations rarely achieve the desired goal of exhausting the past, as they raise questions on the very legitimacy of the state, such as how nation building should be remembered and by whom (Povinelli 2002, 154). The ambivalence of reparations as both state projects of reconciliation and tools for encouraging forward-looking political action explains their ability to undermine the consolidation of official imaginations of the past and future. Reparation projects frequently act as "hope-generating machines," a term coined by Monique Nuijten to indicate the state's ability to capitalize on citizens' expectations (2003). As contributions to this book show, government promises of reparations are key tools used by the state to capture hope and thus postpone the realization of justice in an indeterminate future. However, hope is not always synonymous with inaction. Hope can animate and even guide actions in the future (Miyazaki 2006). As Krøijer reveals, a vision of the future is any affective act through which the indeterminable is given form (2010, 149). The futures imagined through reparations are the result of concrete practices intended to create the conditions for future transformations. As such, the imaginative power of reparations is closely linked to their democratic potential in the forging of new notions of equality and civility and in their decolonizing potential, which can materialize in future commitments to continue to reflect critically on coloniality as an overarching framework in which governmental reparations are thought of and implemented (Figueroa 2015, 46).

The idea of reparations as contested technologies of imagination appears in several chapters in this volume. Bernasconi's historical inquiry into the archive built by the Comité de Cooperación para la Paz (Cooperation Committee for Peace, 1973–1975) and its successor, the Vicaría de la Solidaridad (Vicariate of Solidarity), in Chile illustrates how archives of political violence are not only tools to legitimize claims for reparation in the aftermath of violence but also forms of repair in and of themselves. By making visible the profound sense of social isolation and disorientation engendered through state terror, nonofficial archives can contribute to the reconfiguration of spaces of oppression as spaces of imagination, from which alternate ways of living grounded in the remembrance of what and who was lost can be imagined in the future.

Chapter 2 demonstrates how rehabilitation programs may uncover the imagination of a past that cannot be defined in any singular way and a future in which there remains an ongoing threat of possible violence. In rural El Salvador, massacres during the civil war (1979–1992), recent killings by the maras gangs, and discrimination against Indigenous villagers by members of the local elite are all traumatic experiences brought together in self-making processes engendered by rehabilitation programs. By drawing on his experience as a coordinator of one such program, Ronsbo shows how these memories of past trauma do not converge into a linear narrative but rather emerge as an arrangement of life trajectories characterized by repetition, interwoven experiences, and the return of violence and its memory in everyday lives.

Translation: Assigning Value to the Incommensurable

A second thematic focus of this volume concerns the concept of translation. This notion, according to Gal (2015, 226), has been a "very fruitful metaphor in anthropology." From its very beginnings, translation has been integral to the discipline as both a practical consideration for conducting fieldwork and, epistemologically, a tool for comparison. The anthropological reflection on the asymmetries of translation that arose in the 1980s led not to its rejection but rather to "a growing interest in the analytical potentiality of incommensurability and mistranslation" (Di Giminiani and Haines 2020, 3). Today, anthropologists not only ask "what we can know, how we can know it, and how we can make it known?" (Hanks and Severi 2014, 3) but also scrutinize the processes and politics involved in making different worlds "commensurate" (Povinelli 2001) or "legible" (Scott 1998) to corporate or state bureaucracies, raising the at times questionable role anthropologists play in such translations (West 2005).

Anthropological interest in translation is more than a heuristic tool. We follow anthropological takes on translation here to show how translations are ubiquitous in social life (Hanks and Severi 2014), including in the field of reparations. State or corporate compensation programs generally involve the assignment of economic and political value to historical and contemporary injustices. In the process, ravaged Indigenous territories are converted into land subsidies (Di Giminiani 2018; Jaramillo 2011; Van Meijl 2012) and environmental damage into infrastructure projects, such as new houses or villages (Cepek 2018). Translating in this way and through different value regimes is bound to produce unintended consequences (Li 2015; Nelson 2015). While some economic translations, when accepted by recipients, remain individualized with minimal collective impact (Slyomovics 2014), others involve negotiations on the nature of past events and the translation of moral values among perpetrators, victims, and their descendants (Doughty 2015; Mallard 2019; Torpey 2006). Considering what forms of commensuration are used in designing and administering reparation programs and understanding their practical and political effects are central concerns in any critical engagement with actual reparations.

Given the predominant role of property in liberal governance, past violence is most often translated into material forms of compensation rather than the restoration of social life before the violence took place (Meister 2010). Several factors explain the predominant material basis of reparations, among which the impossibility of fully assessing the original conditions of a prior social life seems central. Yet the limitations of materialist approaches that seek to quantify harm into monetary values remain a critical issue in political debates on reparations. Should the wrongs of slavery be redressed by retroactively treating the work as unpaid wage labor? If so, should we also consider the compound interest that would have accrued (Robinson 2000)? And should we not also include in our calculations the many additional losses that Black people suffered from their abduction, trafficking, enslavement, and mistreatment? And what about moving from a loss-based to a gain-based model of reparative justice, which would focus instead on how much whites have benefited from slavery (Meister 2010)?

In 2001, the U.N. World Conference Against Racism, Racial Discrimination, Xenophobia, and Related Intolerance recognized slavery and the Atlantic slave trade as crimes against humanity, giving a new strength to the now transnational movement demanding redress for these grave historical injustices (Araujo 2017). Yet to this day and despite the growing resonance of Black Lives Matter, no former slave society in the Americas has paid restitution to the descendants of slaves. The wrongs of slavery, however, like any other historical injustice, cannot be adequately redressed through a purely economic transaction. Marcel Mauss's *The Gift* was written during his involvement in French debates over the design of reparation policies following World War I (Mallard 2019). While the French government was focused on securing its fair share of indemnities from the German state, Mauss argued against conceptualizing reparations as debt payments, suggesting instead to view them as gifts or exchanges through which social actors (re-)create bonds between the past and future. For Tsing (2013), the processes of economic translation involved in designing and administering financial schemes of compensation necessarily imply a betrayal. Consider, for example, the translation of the destruction of Mayan Q'eqchi's sacred corn (*loqlaj ixim*) fields during the Guatemalan government's scorched-earth policy (1981–1983) to "material damages" (Viaene 2010). Loqlaj ixim are conceptualized as gifts from Mother Earth insofar as they "bring something personal with them, . . . serving as a continual reminder of the need for reciprocation." When loqlaj ixim becomes a commodity, by contrast, it is disengaged from its "makers"—the humans and more-than-humans involved in producing and consuming it (Tsing 2013, 22). The "commodity fetishism" (see chapter 8, this volume) behind assessing the price tag that the destruction of loqlaj ixim causes alienates it from its constitutive social relations. Yet as chapters in this volume show, economic translations are the basis of most reparation programs.

Drawing on her examination of the social practices and forms of social power that are used in Australia to administrate Aboriginal land claims to address colonial violence, Povinelli (2001) identifies "public reason" as playing a key role in "how the incommensurateness of liberal ideology and practice is made to appear commensurate" (328) to radical alterity. Any analysis of the violence further inflicted—for example, on Mayan Q'eqchi' by reducing the destruction of their loqlaj ixim (sacred corn) fields to "material damages"—is "deflected to the horizon of good intentions, and more immediately, as a welcomed part of the very process of liberal self-correction itself" (Povinelli 2001, 328). Prospective beneficiaries of state or corporate payouts may refuse such a betrayal by denouncing them as "blood money" (Slyomovics 2014, 26) or radically opposing them by demanding instead that their loved ones be "brought back alive" (Moon 2012, 193). As Moon explains, the Mothers of the Plaza de Mayo in Argentina did not believe that their disappeared relatives were still alive. Rather, they rejected the trade-off of compensation for truth, accountability, and justice—that is, "a full explanation of the circumstances surrounding their disappearance, acknowledgement of responsibility, and punishment of those responsible" (194). However, money, as Cattelino reminds us (2009), is fungible. While the per capita dividends that Florida Seminoles receive from tribal gaming revenues tie them to the settler state's market economy, it simultaneously unties them from it, reinforcing in this way their political authority and autonomy. By making Indigenous practices understandable to state and corporate actors involved in reparation processes, anthropology has oftentimes inadvertently reinforced colonial or capitalist forms of domination instead of working to disrupt them (Nadasdy 2003; West 2005). Yet through political actions and everyday gestures that are recalcitrant to universalizing interpretations, Indigenous people are able to "build and sustain relationships which disrupt the State's [and corporations'] attempts to 'command and control' the terms upon which ... [they] interact with the lands, waters and atmospheres within ... [their] reach" (Todd 2018, 62). To avoid further reinforcing the modern/colonial myth of our universality—the deeply ingrained presupposition that there is "only one world in the world at any one time" (Povinelli 2011)—we center our analysis in this volume on what has historically refused, and continues to refuse, to be eliminated or domesticated by colonialism or capitalism in reparation politics.

Like all processes of translation, reparation politics are first and foremost characterized by indeterminacy and, as such, not only may lead to "silencing, failure, and erasure" but can also be "generative of new meanings, conversations, and relationships" (Di Giminiani and Haines 2020, 9). The indeterminacy of what exactly is to be repaired is evident in the reparation of environmental harm. An ecological stance to reparation entails that repairing an environmental harm should not only focus exclusively on its impact on human collectivities but also address the possibility of restoring those more-than-human relationships conforming the environment in which human collectivities dwell. As suggested by Papadopoulos, Puig de la Bellacasa, and Tacchetti, "The coupling of ecological relations with reparations could . . . indicate a move beyond top-down, individualized and abstracted interventions, towards processes of repair of material relations in their complex embeddedness in communities" (2023, 2). Social science studies of toxicity, for instance, have invited us to rethink environmental remediation processes, given the nonlinear, unpredictable, and cumulative effects of toxicants, which Western science fails to fully acknowledge (Balayannis 2019; Fortun 2001). While some actors may resign themselves to living in toxic environments, others engage in care work of their surroundings that can be understood as acts of self-repair (Lyons 2018; Tironi 2018), given the well-documented tendency of transnational corporations or states to avoid any sort of liability. Recent developments in some jurisdictions may be turning the tide. With the aim of paving the way for reparations for environmental damage, elements of nature have been granted legal rights. In Colombia, for instance, Decree 4633 of 2011 "establish[es] specific measures for assistance, attention, integral reparation and restitution of territorial rights for Indigenous communities and groups" who were victimized by the internal armed conflict and identifies "territories" as rights subjects (Ruiz Serna 2017). Following Spivak (1988), Izquierdo and Viaene (2018, 5) ask whether territories "can speak when human beings go to the Special Jurisdiction of Peace." For them, while territories are able to express their feelings from Indigenous perspectives, this is not recognized in the human rights and transitional justice fields: "So, to what extent will judges be able to listen to and accept . . . [them] in their analysis?" (Izquierdo and Viaene 2018, 5). We see here how "controlled equivocation" (Viveiros de Castro 2004), the misunderstandings that arise when two interlocutors are not aware that they are not talking about the same issues, may lead to the redomestication, instead of the meaningful recognition, of Indigenous "ontological disagreements" (De la Cadena 2015). Yet the outcomes of these encounters remain unknown.

The limits and potentials of translation in the politics of reparation are central to Ulfe's analysis of remediation practices in Peru. Ulfe illustrates how the incommensurability of damage concerns both the victim-subjects of suffering and the objects of reparation. In a context where damage is pervasive but elusive to demarcation, such as an oil spill or mutual acts of political violence in Peru, "the boundaries between being or not being a victim are certainly permeable" (chapter 3, this volume). In such a context, the state is destined to fail to adequately translate sufferings into reparations. Yet attempts at translation still matter. As shown in chapter 3, translation is a process intimately intertwined with processes of belonging, since the limits and frustrations of translating past violence in remediations are pivotal to the collective articulation of multiple and overlapping political subjectivities that have little to do with the self-perception of victims and more to do with the creation of active agents of future transformations.

Chapter 8, which discusses the failed implementation of the World Bank and the International Finance Corporation's policies regarding resettlement, echoes these lines of analysis. Drawing on a case study of the forced resettlement of Indigenous sheepherders living in the high pasturelands of Peru, the author calls the process through which "particular, usually Indigenous, socionatural assemblages" are reduced into "quantifiable economic Western categories," producing an "illusion of commensuration." Financial institutions' guidelines were not in and of themselves to blame, Salas Carreño argues. Rather, it is the logic of capital and the state's complicity in enforcing it that led to the imposition of an "accelerated resettlement process" and the breaking apart of complex assemblages of "agricultural plots, pasturelands, crops, sheep, some cows, horses, and other animals and humans." Many of these networks were able to quickly reconfigure themselves, not because of the mining companies' compensation checks, but as a result of the enduring local gift economy. In Peru, as in Guatemala (see chapter 5, this volume), reparation politics are inscribed in a broader history of state actions and inactions that reproduce discrimination against rural Indigenous communities.

Drawing on an ethnography of an alternative form of justice, the Mixed Tribunal of Indigenous Native Peasant Justice in Bolivia, chapter 6 also demonstrates the extent to which the three most common domains of reparations politics—political violence, colonial injustices, and socioenvironmental conflicts—not only coexist but are tightly entangled in Latin America. Given the impossibility of translating complicated histories of colonial injustices into manageable wrongs that can be easily addressed by state action, the tribunal was unable to establish who the rightful users of the territory were. Nonetheless, Kennemore and Copa suggest that by encouraging the two communities to transcend their differences based on a common history of colonial oppression and contemporary experience of exploitation in the state justice system, the tribunal may have allowed them to collectively reimagine their future belongings in ways that would repair (put an end to) state, corporate, and colonial-caused divisions.

Belonging: Becoming at Home in a Violent World

Our third thematic focus is belonging, a term that typically has a positive connotation. After all, who wouldn't want to belong? We might strive toward an experience of belonging as "a state of being from which well-being is derived; a relation that makes us feel good about our being and being-in-the-world; a relation that is fitting, right or correct" (Miller 2003, 218). But to belong in smaller or larger relationships is neither positive nor negative per se, and we cannot always choose whether or not we belong. Our lifeworld comes into being intersubjectively in our coexistence with others. Human existence is, as Jackson

(2012) underscores, an interexistence where we struggle to become and find fulfillment. Often, we can find ourselves self-estranged in a world of (post)conflict, damage, and injustice. Our sense of belonging is, in other words, never stable but constantly evolving. To belong, we argue, also involves reconciling and reinterpreting the past to make future coexistence possible. Therefore, to belong to the world unavoidably raises ethical concerns as to how to live a moral life, in particular under difficult, uncertain, or even dangerous conditions (Kleinman 2007). The study of reparation underscores the arduous work required to coexist and generate bonds across social, cultural, and political differences, particularly during the aftermath of state violence and genocide or in the midst of the ongoing struggle and injustice that often characterizes Latin American societies. Belonging is a boundary-drawing exercise because we continuously define which human and nonhuman subjects rightfully belong to specific sites and social contexts. Even when boundaries are inevitably porous and subject to transformation, processes of boundary making, whether violent or not, always entail processes of othering. In our optics, belonging is always political. People's claims for reparation are a call for recognition and justice, and through them, they redefine who constitutes worthy members of the community and subjects of care, sometimes pushing the boundaries of the polis and redefining the meaning of proper citizenship, internal relations, and hierarchies among members.

Practices of belonging unfold on different scales, from the intimate task of situating ourselves in the social world—for instance, through (re)narrations of the past (Jackson 2005)—to the larger, often state-sponsored public rituals and performances that work to establish feelings of commonality and shared memories and history. Through our position, we weave ourselves into larger social collectives and nations and become embedded in moral obligations. The analysis of practices of belonging underscores how individual, communal, and state efforts intersect and conflict. Certainly, investments in belonging to different communities are not equal, as they rely on class-based, gendered, and racialized hierarchies. Tine Gammeltoft (2018, 77) argues that belonging "indexes fragile, uncertain, and often highly contingent human efforts to be part of something larger." Belonging can involve the painful and continuous work of placing ourselves within (or eventually contesting) the social world and, in this process, how our subjectivity, including our political subjectivity, is molded.

In postconflict societies, these thorny contingencies are salient. Belonging and becoming (re)embedded in moral obligations in worlds fraught with painful memories, divisions, and enduring injustices are ongoing tasks. According to Das (2007), restorative politics unavoidably address the issue of what it means to inhabit a world that has been destroyed. How can we flourish and feel at home in worlds that are fraught with injustice, conflict, and violence? By situating the analysis of reparations within individuals' and local communities' everyday efforts to rebuild relationships after mass violence, we can see how belonging becomes a process of restoring kinship ties and making them viable again after a betrayal (Das 2007). Similarly, Buch Segal's (2015) analysis of how the wives of Palestinian detainees in Israeli prisons exert immense emotional efforts to fulfill their expected roles as "exemplary" citizens in the Palestinian national narrative of struggle and resistance illustrates the "costs" of belonging in a world that is not of our choosing.

People's belonging is expressed and experienced according to notions of kinship, ethnicity, gender, social hierarchies, class, and so on. In heterogeneous societies and particularly in postconflict contexts, these overlapping categories of belonging can easily translate into different forms and expressions. If we understand that definitions and feelings of belonging are a political exercise, we should also recognize that the copresence of different groups and peoples—that is, those living together separately—does not necessarily constitute coexistence, which requires some level of mutual engagement (Thiranagama 2018, 359). Linking these notions to restorative politics, we suggest that reparation demands can be seen as both attempts to restore the social fabric and tools for social transformation, as people or groups (who might be copresent on unequal terms) demand further integration, recognition, and dignity. In Latin America, these questions are relevant to Indigenous peoples who often experience copresence as unequal subjects in the liberal state and must relegate their "difference" to the private sphere. Indigenous claims for reparation speak to wider discussions of what forms of citizenship and statehood are required if we are all to coexist and flourish.

Patricia Richards and Millaray Painemal (chapter 7, this volume) raise similar concerns. Their presentation of the life history narratives of Mapuche women elders discloses lives informed by the intersections of racism, sexism, classism, and colonialism, revealing harms that have accrued at multiple levels. Yet they also provide a record of the women's everyday forms of resistance, creativity, and survival, despite a state that fails to recognize them and others who do not acknowledge their full humanity. Richards and Painemal ask what these narratives—recalling Mapuche women's lives as individuals, members of their communities, and part of a sovereign people—teach us about reparations. In temporal terms, they invite us to consider reparation, not as a matter of assessing past harms but rather as a way to consider the ongoing effects of colonialism. In so doing, reparations become forces for making Indigenous futurities possible within the (decolonial) state.

Chapter 5 also addresses the (un)finished nature of Indigenous citizenship in postcolonial, postgenocide, extractivist Guatemala. By considering personal accounts of involvement in a grassroots movement claiming reparations from a mining corporation and the Guatemalan government, Vanthuyne explores how the politics of becoming an antimining activist bring to light the fundamentally precarious nature of Indigenous belongings. She examines the ways in which political communities are mended and unraveled anew, as subjects injured by corporate or state actors mobilize to claim reparations, and offers much-needed insight into the daily efforts and personal costs required to sustain such movements.

As these accounts indicate, practices of belonging are directly related to state and citizen formation, even when people's relationship to the state is highly ambivalent and even experienced as oppressive. The present volume engages the insights generated by a broader anthropological scholarship on state-citizen relations (e.g., Das and Poole 2004; Hansen and Stepputat 2001) and democratization processes in Latin America (Ellison 2018; Postero 2007, 2017; Schavelzon 2012). As Ghasan Hage (2002) writes in relation to Australia, political belonging is not a given simply because someone holds formal citizenship. To fully belong as citizens and feel a moral obligation toward the state, people must feel mutually recognized by it. These insights are highly relevant in the Latin American context and not only regarding Indigenous or Black populations. The continent is marked by long democratic transitions such as Chile's (Alexander 2009; Navia 2010), which require coexistence among victims and perpetrators. As Teresa Caldeira and James Holston (2000) have argued, this region's democracies tend to be disjunctive, meaning that political rights, such as the right to vote, have not necessarily been accompanied by substantial social rights. This reality is also reflected among the impoverished, where senses of belonging, both to the larger nation-state and to their crime-ridden communities, tend to be disjunctive (Risør and Arteaga 2018). To an important extent, reparation politics is a response that seeks to revert or at least ameliorate the effects of this reality.

Restorative politics create sociopolitical scenarios that allow people to imagine their belonging within the nation-state. In this sense, they are not so different from those of the censuses, maps, and museums that Benedict Anderson (1983) famously identified as techniques that allowed the state to create the nation and that helped otherwise geographically scattered communities and diverse ethnic groups to imagine themselves as belonging to a national collective. Just as the census creates a series of categories of different people who all come to belong to the nation, reparation practices offer a distinctive place within the nation, and hence state recognition, to collectives that have been subjected to state violence and historical disregard. States engage in restorative practices in order to make coexistence in the present possible. From the perspective of the state, symbolic and material reparations for state violence and wrongdoing work to effectively restore people's formal and moral status as citizens and help diverse populations reimagine national belonging. Reparation politics can therefore be seen as a form of governance that works to create governable citizens, and when we analyze reparation politics as a form of recognition, we are reminded that these processes can be deceitful. The downside of state recognition is that this very process forces people to become "legible" in the eyes of the state and adopt forms of life and cultural practices that no longer challenge social order or the limits of the liberal state (Povinelli 2001, 2002). A similar contradiction is identified by Helene Risør (2018) in her analysis of how victims of human rights violations in Chile are recognized as such but at the same time expected not to defy the political order that protects the economic privileges of their former perpetrators.

That said, it would be a mistake to exclusively conceive of reparation politics as a top-down relationship between the state and its citizens. People engage with these processes for a variety of reasons, and collectives are often highly involved in these practices yet defy the characterization of victims as passive recipients of state or corporate endowment (Jensen and Ronsbo 2014; Welker 2014). By prompting normative ideals of civic coexistence (Trnka and Trundle 2017), reparations spur novel discourses and practices of belonging to the nation, leading to profound identity changes among both victims and perpetrators. The victims' narratives can thus be understood as a cry for recognition and as a transformative technology through which survivors reinscribe themselves into the nation not only as victims (which is often the only category that is available to them) but also as agents of resistance and even heroes (Theidon 2010). Reparation politics also help define the face of the nation, both symbolically and literally, as people of color, Indigenous, and LGBTQ+ communities are granted explicit recognition. And while the reparation of past wrongdoings does not prevent states from continuously committing new acts of state violence and discrimination, it can provide people and social organizations with a set of rights they can use to denounce and condemn these acts. Through reparation politics, new hierarchical relations structured around different moral positions are articulated, such as the emergence of powerful political actors endowed with guilt and a moral imperative to repair past injustices (Benson 2016; Sundar 2004). Restorative practices are open-ended processes that allow people to continuously review and assess past and ongoing harm according to the shifting social, economic, and political context (Clifford 2013). Thus, although reparations are used by state and corporate actors to legitimize their role in postconflict societies, through demands for reparations, grassroots political actors can also forge forms of collective belonging that contest dominant discourses (Johnston 2009, 13).

Chapter 4 addresses such complex and disputed forms of belonging in her depiction of the long histories of state violence and demands for reparation in Argentina. As claimed by Zaretsky, the temporality of reparation is twofold: It concerns the framing of violent events from the past into an ongoing narrative about justice and democracy yet to come, and it also creates expectations about the future whose realization remains close and yet out of reach. The liminal state created by the ethical demand to hold onto the past while envisioning a new future is not simply an impasse. It can be the effective grounds from which Argentineans with similar and yet different histories of violence and injustice can creatively reframe new ways of belonging beyond national identity and be capable of rewriting the very conditions of being part of the nation.

Conclusion: Reparations Today

While this book was in progress, public debates on reparations in Latin America took new directions. A wave of protests with different origins but shared anti-elite feelings, have reverberated across the region since 2019: protests led by Indigenous organizations in Ecuador against austerity measures in 2019; a national strike in Colombia against corruption and a controversial tax reform introduced by Ivan Duque's government in 2021; clashes in Venezuela following Nicolás Maduro's second inauguration in 2019 between supporters and opponents of the regime demanding democratization; and protests in Chile in 2019, known by the media as estallido social (social outburst), originating in response to a rise in the metro fare in Santiago and the so-called neoliberal model in general.[2] The causes of unrest are numerous and linked to specific contingencies in each country, including corruption, economic precariousness, and authoritarian rule. The optimism of the early 2000s, sustained by economic growth, now feels particularly distant, a sentiment further animated by the uncertainties and sufferings of the social, health, and economic crises caused by the COVID-19 pandemic.

The protests were accompanied by a resurgence of police brutality, systematic human rights violations, and government-driven conspiratorial narratives about foreign intervention and internal enemies—evoking for many Latin Americans the memories of Cold War–era dictatorships and civil wars. Human rights infringements during social unrest include deaths, torture, sexual abuse, unlawful detentions, and injuries, including eye loss from the use of rubber bullets by police forces. Legal cases against state brutality remain open, and many of them are unlikely to find justice soon. In this context, new victim categories and organizations have emerged, and both "old" and new organizations are actively demanding official investigations and reparations. As for reparations in general, the future of their demands lies largely in political contingencies that will shape the political landscape for years to come. The establishment of new truth commissions and reparation programs will depend equally on the capacity of the victims' organizations to endure and persist with their claims, public opinion, and the conformation of legislative and executive branches. The resurgence of human rights violations and renewed public debates on reparations compel us to consider the ethical and political implications of viewing reparation as a forward-looking process with unintended consequences—an inquiry that this volume seeks to explore. A critical reflection on the effects of reparations can shed new light on the broader historical processes of democratization in Latin America. Democratic institutions are not as robust as they could be, and weak political culture persists throughout the continent, leading to the strengthening of authoritarianism (see Economist Intelligence Unit 2021, 47–51). However gloomy the scenario appears, we should not forget that over the last few decades, this region has also seen an unprecedented emergence of experimentations with democratic participation and social inclusion that have inspired political observers and policymakers from other continents.

Through a focus on reparation, in this book we revisit state-citizen relations in Latin America and engage in a necessary public debate about the "state of the democratic state" in the continent. As noted by Ellison (2018), democracy holds different meanings to different people and groups, particularly when it comes to understanding what constitutes a democracy with substantial civil, social, and economic rights for all citizens (see Marshall 1950). Democracy and citizenship therefore should not be taken—at least not exclusively—as a priori categories. Democracy must instead be studied as an emic category in constant and emergent movement and as a form of governance that is kept alive, challenged, or expanded through specific interests, including transnational market forces (Paley 2001). Grounded notions of citizenship can emerge from local histories and traditions of sociopolitical organization (see Lazar 2008; Risør 2016). A critical engagement with the effects of reparation might reveal how social coexistence is maintained and made precarious through different actions constitutive of restorative democracies. At a time when many are questioning the consistency between progressive democracy and the economic model of most Latin American countries, reparations might tell us a lot about how democracy could look in the future.

Notes

1   The most robust conceptual alternative to mestizaje is the model of political governance known as *plurinacionalidad* (plurinationality), which posits rights of autonomy as well as political participation for Indigenous First Nations. This model has acquired public relevance in the design of new constitutions, as with the 2009 Constitution of Bolivia (see Schavelzon 2012) and, in 2021, the failed constitutional process in Chile (see Pairican 2022).
2   For more on the Chilean social outburst, see Aedo et al. (2023).

References

Abélès, Marc. 1988. "Modern Political Ritual: Ethnography of an Inauguration and a Pilgrimage by President Mitterrand." *Current Anthropology* 29 (3): 391–404.
Aedo, Angel, Oriana Bernasconi, Damián Martínez, Alicia Olivari, Fernando Pairican, and Juan Porma. 2024. "Multitude and Memory in the Chilean Social Uprising." *South Atlantic Quarterly* 123 (1): 192–202.
Aguilar Díaz, Miguel. 2011. "Entre diálogos y repatriaciones: Reparación colonial por la memoria y preservación de Machu Picchu." *Antípoda: Revista de Antropología y Arqueología* 12:211–234.
Alexander, William L., ed. 2009. *Lost in the Long Transition: Struggles for Social Justice in Neoliberal Chile.* New York: Rowman & Littlefield.
Anderson, Benedict. 1991. *Imagined Communities: Reflections on the Origin and Spread of Nationalism.* London: Verso.
Araujo, Kathya, and Nelson Beyer. 2013. "Autoridad y autoritarismo en Chile: Reflexiones en torno al ideal-tipo portaliano." *Atenea* 508:171–185.

Balayannis, Angeliki. 2019. "Routine Exposures: Reimaging the Visual Politics of Hazardous Sites." *GeoHumanities* 5 (2): 572–590.

Benson, Peter. 2016. "The Crime of Innocence and the Depths of Sorriness: Notes on Apologies and Reparations in the United States." *Cultural Dynamics* 28 (2): 121–141.

Bernasconi, Oriana. 2019. "Introduction: A Civilian Response to State Terror." In *Resistance to Political Violence in Latin America: Documenting Atrocity*, edited by Oriana Bernasconi, 1–12. New York: Palgrave Macmillan.

Caldeira, Teresa, and James Holston. 2000. "Democracy and Violence in Brazil." *Comparative Studies in Society and History* 41 (4): 691–729.

Cattelino, Jessica R. 2009. "Fungibility: Florida Seminole Casino Dividends and the Fiscal Politics of Indigeneity." *American Anthropologist* 111 (2): 190–200.

Cepek, Michael. 2018. *Life in Oil: Cofán Survival in the Petroleum Fields of Amazonia*. Austin: University of Texas Press.

Clifford, James. 2013. *Returns: Becoming Indigenous in the Twenty-First Century*. Cambridge, Mass.: Harvard University Press.

Collins, John F. 2015. *Revolt of the Saints: Memory and Redemption in the Twilight of Brazilian Racial Democracy*. Durham, N.C.: Duke University Press.

Cornejo-Polar, Antonio. 1997. "Mestizaje e hibridez: Los riesgos de las metáforas." *Apuntes: Revista iberoamericana* 63 (180): 341–344.

Corntassel, Jeff, and Cindy Holder. 2008. "Who's Sorry Now? Government Apologies, Truth Commissions, and Indigenous Self-Determination in Australia, Canada, Guatemala, and Peru." *Human Rights Review* 9 (4): 465–489.

Crenzel, Emilio A., and Eugenia Allier. 2016. *Las luchas por la memoria en América Latina: Historia reciente y violencia política*. Mexico: Bonilla Artigas Editores.

Das, Veena, and Deborah Poole. 2004. "State and Its Margins. Comparative Ethnographies." In *Anthropology in the Margins of the State*, edited by Veena Das and Deborah Poole, 3–33. Santa Fe: School of American Research Press.

De la Cadena, Marisol. 2015. *Earth Beings: Ecologies of Practice Across Andean Worlds*. Durham, N.C.: Duke University Press.

Di Giminiani, Piergiorgio. 2018. *Sentient Lands: Indigeneity, Property, and Political Imagination in Neoliberal Chile*. Tucson: University of Arizona Press.

Di Giminiani, Piergiorgio, and Sophie Haines. 2020. "Introduction: Translating Environments." *Ethnos* 85 (1): 1–16.

Doughty, Kristin. 2015. "Law and the Architecture of Social Repair: Gacaca Days in Post-Genocide Rwanda." *Journal of the Royal Anthropological Institute* 21 (2): 419–437.

Drinot, Paulo. 2009. "For Whom the Eye Cries: Memory, Monumentality, and the Ontologies of Violence in Peru." *Journal of Latin American Cultural Studies* 18 (1): 15–32.

Economist Intelligence Unit. 2021. "Democracy Index 2021: The China Challenge." Economist Intelligence. Accessed December 2, 2022. https://www.eiu.com/n/democracy-index-2021-less-than-half-the-world-lives-in-a-democracy/.

Ellison, Susan Helen. 2018. *Domesticating Democracy: The Politics of Conflict Resolution in Bolivia*. Durham, N.C.: Duke University Press.

Fassin, Didier. 2008. "The Humanitarian Politics of Testimony: Subjectification Through Trauma in the Israeli-Palestinian Conflict." *Cultural Anthropology* 23 (3): 531–558.

Faulk, Karen A., and Sandra Brunnegger. 2016. "Introduction: Making Sense of Justice." In *A Sense of Justice: Legal Knowledge and Lived Experience in Latin America*, edited by Sandra Brunnegger and Karen Faulk, 1–24. Stanford, Calif.: Stanford University Press.

Feldman, Joseph. 2021. *Memories Before the State: Postwar Peru and the Place of Memory, Tolerance, and Social Inclusion*. New Brunswick, N.J.: Rutgers University Press.

Ferstman, Carla, Mariana Goetz, and Alan Stephens. 2009. Introduction to *Reparations for Victims of Genocide, War Crimes and Crimes Against Humanity: Systems in Place and Systems in Making*, edited by Carla Ferstman, Mariana Goetz, and Alan Stephens, 7–19. Leiden: Martinus Nijhoff.

Figueroa, Yomaira C. 2015. "Reparation as Transformation: Radical Literary (Re)Imaginings of Futurities Through Decolonial Love." *Decolonization: Indigeneity, Education & Society* 4 (1): 41–58.

Fortun, Kim. 2001. *Advocacy After Bhopal: Environmentalism, Disaster, New World Orders*. Chicago: University of Chicago Press.

Frazier, Leslie Jo. 2007. *Salt in the Sand: Memory, Violence, and the Nation-State in Chile, 1890 to the Present*. Durham, N.C.: Duke University Press.

Gal, Susan. 2015. "Politics of Translation." *Annual Review of Anthropology* 44:225–240.

Gammeltoft, Tine M. 2018. "Belonging: Comprehending Subjectivity in Vietnam and Beyond." *Social Analysis* 62 (1): 76–95.

Hage, Ghassan. 2002. "Citizenship and Honourability: Belonging to Australia Today." In *Arab-Australians Today: Citizenship and Belonging*, edited by Ghassan Hage, 1–15. Melbourne: Melbourne University Publishing.

Hamber, Brandon, and Richard A. Wilson. 2002. "Symbolic Closure Through Memory, Reparation and Revenge in Post-Conflict Societies." *Journal of Human Rights* 1 (1): 35–53.

Han, Clara. 2012. *Life in Debt: Times of Care and Violence in Neoliberal Chile*. Berkeley: University of California Press.

Hanks, William F., and Carlo Severi. 2014. "Translating Worlds: The Epistemological Space of Translation." *HAU: Journal of Ethnographic Theory* 4 (2): 1–16.

Hansen, Blom Thomas, and Finn Stepputat. 2001. "Introduction: States of Imagination." In *States of Imagination: Ethnographic Explorations of the Postcolonial State*, edited by Thomas Blom Hansen and Finn Stepputat, 1–38. Durham, N.C.: Duke University Press.

Hinton, Alexander. 2010. "Introduction: Toward an Anthropology of Transitional Justice." In *Transitional Justice: Global Mechanisms and Local Realities After Genocide and Mass Violence*, edited by Alexander Hinton, 1–22. New Brunswick, N.J.: Rutgers University Press.

Hite, Katherine. 2013. *Politics and the Art of Commemoration: Memorials to Struggle in Latin America and Spain*. London: Routledge.

Izquierdo, Belkis, and Liselotte Viaene. 2018. "Decolonizing Transitional Justice from Indigenous Territories." *Peace in Progress* 34:1–9.

Jackson, Michael. 2005. "Storytelling Events, Violence, and the Appearance of the Past." *Anthropological Quarterly* 78 (2): 355–375.

Jackson, Michael. 2012. *Lifeworlds: Essays in Existential Anthropology*. Chicago: University of Chicago Press.

Jaramillo, Pablo. 2011. "Post-Multicultural Anxieties? Reparations and the Trajectories of Indigenous Citizenship in la Guajira, Colombia." *Journal of Latin American and Caribbean Anthropology* 16 (2): 335–353.

Jensen, Steffen, and Henrik Ronsbo, eds. 2014. *Histories of Victimhood*. Philadelphia: University of Pennsylvania Press.

Johnston, Barbara R. 2009. "Waging War, Making Peace: The Anthropology of Reparations." In *Waging War, Making Peace: Reparations and Human Rights*, edited by Barbara Johnston and Susan Slymovics, 11–30. London: Routledge.

Johnston, Barbara R. 2010. "Chixoy Dam Legacies: The Struggle to Secure Reparation and the Right to Remedy in Guatemala." *Water Alternatives* 3 (2): 341–361.

Kleinman, Arthur. 2007. *What Really Matters: Living a Moral Life Amidst Uncertainty and Danger*. Oxford: Oxford University Press.

Krøijer, Stine. 2010. "Figurations of the Future: On the Form and Temporality of Protests Among Left Radical Activists in Europe." *Social Analysis* 54 (3): 139–152.

Laplante, Lisa J., and Kimberly Theidon. 2007. "Truth with Consequences: Justice and Reparations in Post-Truth Commission Peru." *Human Rights Quarterly* 29:228–250.

Latinobarómetro. 2021. "Informe Latinobarómetro 2021." Accessed June 28, 2022. https://www.latinobarometro.org/lat.jsp.

Lazar, Sian. 2008. *El Alto, Rebel City: Self and Citizenship in Andean Bolivia*. Durham, N.C.: Duke University Press.

Lefranc, Sandrine. 2008. "La justice transitionnelle n'est pas un concept." *Mouvements* 1:61–69.

Li, Fabiana. 2015. *Unearthing Conflict: Corporate Mining, Activism, and Expertise in Peru*. Durham, N.C.: Duke University Press.

Lira, Elizabeth. 2010. "Trauma, duelo, reparación y memoria." *Revista de estudios sociales* 36:14–28.

Lomnitz, Claudio. 1995. "Ritual, Rumor and Corruption in the Constitution of Polity in Modern Mexico." *Journal of Latin American Anthropology* 1 (1): 20–47.

Lyons, Kristin. 2018. "Chemical Warfare in Colombia, Evidentiary Ecologies and Senti-Actuando Practices of Justice." *Social Studies of Science* 48 (3): 414–437.

Mallard, Grégoire. 2019. *Gift Exchange: The Transnational History of a Political Idea, Cambridge Studies in Law and Society*. Cambridge: Cambridge University Press.

Marshall, T. H. 1950. *Citizenship and Social Class, and Other Essays*. Cambridge: Cambridge University Press.

Mbembe, Achille. 2019. *Necropolitics*. Durham, N.C.: Duke University Press.

Meertens, Donny, and Margarita Zambrano. 2010. "Citizenship Deferred: The Politics of Victimhood, Land Restitution and Gender Justice in the Colombian (Post?) Conflict." *International Journal of Transitional Justice* 4 (2): 189–206.

Meister, Robert. 2010. *After Evil: A Politics of Human Rights*. New York: Columbia University Press.

Merry, Sally Engle. 2003. "Human Rights Law and the Demonization of Culture (and Anthropology Along the Way)." *Polar* 26:55–76.

Miller, Linn. 2003. "Belonging to Country—a Philosophical Anthropology." *Journal of Australian Studies* 27 (76): 215–223.

Milton, Cynthia E., and María Eugenia Ulfe. 2011. "Promoting Peru: Tourism and Post-Conflict Memory." In *Accounting for Violence*, edited by Ksenija Bilbija and Leigh A. Payne, 207–234. Durham, N.C.: Duke University Press.

Miyazaki, Hirokazu. 2006. *The Method of Hope: Anthropology, Philosophy, and Fijian Knowledge*. Stanford, Calif.: Stanford University Press.

Moon, Claire. 2012. "'Who'll Pay Reparations on My Soul?': Compensation, Social Control and Social Suffering." *Social & Legal Studies* 21 (2): 187–199.

Mora-Gámez, Freddy, and Steven D. Brown. 2019. "The Psychosocial Management of Rights Restitution: Tracing Technologies for Reparation in Post-Conflict Colombia." *Theory & Psychology* 29 (4): 521–538.

Nadasdy, Paul. 2003. *Hunters and Bureaucrats: Power, Knowledge, and Aboriginal-State Relations in the Southwest Yukon*. Vancouver: University of British Columbia Press.

Navia, Patricio. 2010. "Living in Actually Existing Democracies: Democracy to the Extent Possible in Chile." *Latin American Research Review* 45 (4): 298–328.

Nelson, Diane M. 2015. *Who Counts? The Mathematics of Death and Life After Genocide*. Durham, N.C.: Duke University Press.

Nuijten, Monique. 2003. *Power, Community and the State: The Political Anthropology of Organisation in Mexico*. London: Pluto Press.

Pairican, Fernand. 2022. *La vía política Mapuche: Apuntes para un estado plurinacional*. Santiago: Paidós.

Paley, Julia. 2001. *Marketing Democracy: Power and Social Movements in Post-Dictatorship Chile*. Berkeley: University of California Press.

Paz y Miño Cepeda, Juan J. 2004. *Deuda histórica e historia inmediata en América Latina*. Quito: Editorial Abya Yala.

Popkin, Margaret, and Naomi Roht-Arriaza. 1995. "Truth as Justice: Investigatory Commissions in Latin America." *Law & Social Inquiry* 20 (1): 79–116.

Postero, Nancy G. 2007. *Now We Are Citizens: Indigenous Politics in Postmulticultural Bolivia*. Stanford, Calif.: Stanford University Press.

Postero, Nancy G. 2017. *The Indigenous State: Race, Politics, and Performance in Plurinational Bolivia*. Berkeley: University of California Press.

Povinelli, Elizabeth A. 2001. "Radical Worlds: The Anthropology of Incommensurability and Inconceivability." *Annual Review of Anthropology* 30:319–334.

Povinelli, Elizabeth A. 2002. *The Cunning of Recognition: Indigenous Alterities and the Making of Australian Multiculturalism*. Durham, N.C.: Duke University Press.

Povinelli, Elizabeth A. 2011. "Routes/Worlds." e-flux. Accessed August 11, 2022. https://www.e-flux.com/journal/27/67991/routes-worlds.

Rauhut, Claudia. 2018. "Caribbean Activism for Slavery Reparations: An Overview." In *Practices of Resistance in the Caribbean*, edited by Wiebke Beuhausen, Miriam Brandel, Joseph T. Farquharson, Marius Littschwager, Annika McPherson, and Julia Roth, 137–150. London: Routledge.

Risør, Helene. 2010. "Twenty Hanging Dolls and a Lynching: Defacing Dangerousness and Enacting Citizenship in El Alto, Bolivia." *Public Culture* 22 (3): 465–485.

Risør, Helene. 2016. "Closing Down Bars in the Inner City Centre: Informal Urban Planning, Civil Insecurity and Subjectivity in Bolivia." *Singapore Journal of Urban Geography* 37 (3): 330–342.

Risør, Helene. 2018. "Civil Victimhood: Citizenship, Human Rights and Securitization in Post-Dictatorship Chile." *Anthropological Theory* 18 (2–3): 271–295.

Risør, Helene, and Ignacia Arteaga. 2018. "Disjunctive Belonging and the Utopia of Intimacy: Love, Friendship and Violence Among Urban Youth in Neoliberal Chile." *Identities: Global Studies in Culture and Power* 25 (2): 228–244.

Robinson, Randall. 2000. *The Debt: What America Owes to Blacks*. New York: Dutton.

Rojas, Hugo, and Miriam Shaftoe. 2021. *Human Rights and Transitional Justice in Chile: Memory Politics and Transitional Justice*. London: Palgrave Macmillan.

Ronsbo, Henrik. 2015. "A Republic of Remedies: Psychosocial Interventions in Post-Conflict Guatemala." In *The Clinic and the Court: Law, Medicine and Anthropology*, edited by Ian Tobias Kelly and Akshay Khanna, 265–295. Cambridge: Cambridge University Press.

Ross, Fiona C. 2003. *Bearing Witness: Women and the Truth and Reconciliation Commission in South Africa, Anthropology, Culture, and Society*. London: Pluto Press.

Ruiz Serna, Daniel. 2017. "Territorio como víctima: Ontología política y las leyes de víctimas para comunidades indígenas y negras en Colombia." *Revista Colombiana de Antropología* 53 (2): 85–113.

Schavelzon, Salvador. 2012. *El nacimiento del Estado Plurinacional de Bolivia: Etnografía de una Asamblea Constituyente*. La Paz: Plural Editores.

Scott, James C. 1998. *Seeing like a State: How Certain Schemes to Improve the Human Condition Have Failed*. New Haven: Yale University Press.

Segal, Lotte Buch. 2015. "The Burden of Being Exemplary: National Sentiments, Awkward Witnessing, and Womanhood in Occupied Palestine." *Journal of the Royal Anthropological Institute* S1:30–46.

Silberling, Louise S. 2003. "Displacement and Quilombos in Alcantara, Brazil: Modernity, Identity, and Place." *International Social Science Journal* 55 (175): 145–156.

Silva, Eduardo. 2009. *Challenging Neoliberalism in Latin America*. Cambridge: Cambridge University Press.

Simpson, Audra. 2016. "Consent's Revenge." *Cultural Anthropology* 31 (3): 326–333.

Slyomovics, Susan. 2014. *How to Accept German Reparations*. Philadelphia: University of Pennsylvania Press.

Sneath, David, Martin Holbraad, and Morten Axel Pedersen. 2009. "Technologies of the Imagination: An Introduction." *Ethnos* 74 (1): 5–30.

Sodaro, Amy. 2017. *Exhibiting Atrocity: Memorial Museums and the Politics of Past Violence*. New Brunswick, N.J.: Rutgers University Press.

Spencer, Jonathan. 1997. "Post-Colonialism and the Political Imagination." *Journal of the Royal Anthropological Institute* 3 (1): 1–19.

Spivak, Chakravorty Gayatri. 1988. "Can the Subaltern Speak?" In *Marxism and the Interpretation of Culture*, edited by Cary Nelson and Lawrence Grossberg, 271–313. London: Macmillan Education.

Sundar, Nandini. 2004. "Toward an Anthropology of Culpability." *American Ethnologist* 31 (2): 145–163.

Taiwo, Olúfẹ́mi O. 2022. *Reconsidering Reparations*. Oxford: Oxford University Press.

Theidon, Kimberly. 2004. *Entre Prójimos: El conflicto armado interno y la lógica de reconciliación en Perú*. Lima: Instituto de Estudios Peruanos.

Theidon, Kimberly. 2007. "Transitional Subjects: The Disarmament, Demobilization and Reintegration of Former Combatants in Colombia." *International Journal of Transitional Justice* 1 (1): 66–90.

Thiranagama, Sharika. 2018. "The Civility of Strangers? Caste, Ethnicity, and Living Together in Postwar Jaffna, Sri Lanka." *Anthropological Theory* 18 (2–3): 357–381.

Thompson, Janna. 2002. *Taking Responsibility for the Past: Reparation and Historical Injustice*. Cambridge: Polity.

Tironi, Manuel. 2018. "Hypo-Interventions: Intimate Activism in Toxic Environments." *Social Studies of Science* 48 (3): 438–455.

Todd, Zoe. 2018. "Refracting the State Through Human-Fish Relations: Fishing, Indigenous Legal Orders, and Colonialism in North/Western Canada." *Decolonization* 7 (1): 60–75.

Torpey, John. 2006. *Making Whole What Has Been Smashed: On Reparations Politics*. Cambridge, Mass.: Harvard University Press.

Trnka, Susanna, and Catherin Trundle, eds. 2017. *Competing Responsibilities: The Ethics and Politics of Contemporary Life*. Durham, N.C.: Duke University Press.

Tsing, Anna. 2013. "Sorting Out Commodities: How Capitalist Value Is Made Through Gifts." *HAU: Journal of Ethnographic Theory* 3 (1): 21–43.

Turchin, Peter. 2016. *Ages of Discord: A Structural Demographic Analysis of American History*. Chaplin: Beresta Books.

Van Meijl, Toon. 2012. "Changing Property Regimes in Maori Society: A Critical Assessment of the Settlement Process in New Zealand." *Journal of the Polynesian Society* 121 (2): 181–208.

Vanthuyne, Karine. 2014. *La présence d'un passé de violences: Mémoires et identités autochtones dans le Guatemala de l'après-génocide*. Québec: Presses de l'Université Laval/Hermann.

Vanthuyne, Karine, and Ricardo Falla. 2016. "Surviving in the Margins of a Genocide Case in the Making: Recognizing the Economy of Testimony at Stake in Research on Political Violence." *Journal of Genocide Research* 18 (2–3): 207–224.

Viaene, Lieselotte. 2010. "Life Is Priceless: Mayan Q'eqchi' Voices on the Guatemalan National Reparations Program." *International Journal of Transitional Justice* 4 (1): 4–25.

Viveiros de Castro, Eduardo. 2004. "Perspectival Anthropology and the Method of Controlled Equivocation." *Tipití: Journal of the Society for the Anthropology of Lowland South America* 2 (1): 3–22.

Wade, Peter. 2005. "Rethinking Mestizaje: Ideology and Lived Experience." *Journal of Latin American Studies* 37 (2): 239–257.

Walker, Margaret. 2006. "Restorative Justice and Reparations." *Journal of Social Philosophy* 37 (3): 377–395.

Welker, Marianne. 2014. *Enacting the Corporation: An American Mining Firm in Post-Authoritarian Indonesia*. Berkeley: University of California Press.

West, Paige. 2005. "Translation, Value, and Space: Theorizing an Ethnographic and Engaged Environmental Anthropology." *American Anthropologist* 107 (4): 632–642.

Wilson, Richard Ashby. 2003. "Anthropological Studies of National Reconciliation Processes." *Anthropological Theory* 3 (3): 367–387.

Wolfe, Patrick. 1999. *Settler Colonialism and the Transformation of Anthropology: The Politics and Poetics of an Ethnographic Event*. London: Cassell.

Zaretsky, Natasha. 2021. *Acts of Repair: Justice, Truth, and the Politics of Memory in Argentina*. New Brunswick, N.J.: Rutgers University Press.

Zhouri, Aandréa, Raquel Oliveira, Marcos Zucarelli, and Max Vasconcelos. 2017. "The Rio Doce Mining Disaster in Brazil: Between Policies of Reparation and the Politics of Affectations." *Vibrant: Virtual Brazilian Anthropology* 14 (2): 1–21.

1

On Insurgent Knowledge
and Affiliative Powers

• •

Human Rights Violations,
Civil Society Archives, and
Forms of Repair

ORIANA BERNASCONI

In the last decades, the analysis of practices and policies of reparation for mass
human rights violations in Latin America has primarily been associated with
state actions through the framework of transitional justice (de Greiff 2006).
Under the social and political objectives of truth, justice, memory, and nonrepetition, transitional justice refers to the institutional mechanisms and strategies
employed primarily by the state to retrospectively address past harm, mark new
eras, and lay the foundations for democratic and peaceful coexistence (Skaar,
García-Godos, and Collins 2017).[1] Thus, the notion of reparation in Latin
America has a pronounced legal emphasis, involving a series of economic,
administrative, and symbolic actions through which past harm is acknowledged, responsibility is assumed, and compensation is offered.

In Chile, fifty years ago, civil society organizations documented the human
rights violations committed by the state during the military dictatorship led
by General Augusto Pinochet (1973–1990). This documentation was part of a
courageous movement of peaceful resistance that involved collective actions of

denunciation of atrocity, legal defense, and social assistance of affected citizens. By exploring the archive of the leading human rights organization that confronted Chile's dictatorship in the 1970s and 1980s, this chapter explores practices of reparation by civil society. Based on a multisited analysis of documents and interviews with creators, managers, and users of the archive of the Comité de Cooperación para la Paz (Cooperation Committee for Peace, 1973–1975; herein Comité) and its successor, the Vicaría de la Solidaridad (Vicariate of Solidarity, 1976–1992; herein Vicaría), I ask, How do human rights archives instigate and expose reparation? What forms of repair are these?

An inquiry into an archive's capacity to participate in reparation processes requires a specific view of these types of sociotechnical artifacts. Within the prevailing legalistic view of documents as sources of information and of the archive as the institutional domicile storing and conserving such documentary collections (Da Silva and Jelin 2002; Groppo 2006; Nazar 2021; Weld 2014), the interest in archival documentation generally focuses on its testimonial, probative, historical, and pedagogical content.

The works of Derrida (1995) and Foucault (2003) have paved the way for an alternative approach to the archive. Derrida has noted that two distinct forces come into play in the production of an archive: first, an institutive, creative, innovative, and disruptive force that identifies and enunciates; second, a conservational force that excludes, repeats, and organizes. If the performative dimension of an archive's practices is linked to its institutive powers by which "the archive endows to what we can say—and to itself—its forms of appearance, its forms of existence and coexistence, its system for accumulating historicity and disappearance" (Foucault 2003, 221), the preservationist force is associated with the tasks of defining an order, standardization, and safeguarding the archive.

Expanding this conceptualization, the analysis of the instituting-performative and conservative-preservationist powers of a Chilean human rights archive will show how it mobilizes and inscribes practices of contestation, resistance, and care that engender forms of individual, collective, and public repair we need to consider if we want to fully understand how societies cope with and heal their wounded worlds. Reading the human rights archive from the viewpoint of reparation will allow me to propose that its force cannot be reduced to its enunciative capacities. Rather, I will argue that such capacities are intimately linked with the archive's *affective* and *affiliative powers*. To propose this argument, I will draw on David Eng's work. Discussing reparation in Cold War Asia, Eng (2010) offers the idea of "affective reparation" as an alternative to conceptions based on political theory. If the latter "seek to write history into a definitive past," leaving harms in the past, the former "does not delineate such a finite process" but rather presents a way of "working through" (196) the present based on affective correspondences, providing the means of reconnecting disconnected words and things. Following this line of thought, the analysis of a civil society human rights archive will allow me to expand the notion of reparation provided by the framework of transitional justice to think of it as a political and affective concern of a collective (Eng 2010; Sosa 2015), less as a delineation of the past orchestrated by the state and more as an achievement of human beings *working through* the present. More specifically, analyzing archival practices and artifacts, I will claim that this *working through* is associated with the *becoming* of new collectives, the production of insurgent knowledge, the constitution of the present, and the anticipation of the future. Inspired by Arendt, Butler, Taylor, Rancière, and Das, I will argue that the archive contributes to the production of a *space of appearance* for the wounded subjects, a space composed by "the organization of the people as it arises out of acting and speaking together" (Arendt 2015, 223), out of recognizing each other and themselves, and out of inscribing pain as the reality of state terror. Furthermore, I will show that far from being relegated to oblivion, fifty years later, that *appeared reality* remains latent in the archive, awaiting future connections between things and words in the hope of finding "vicarious audiences" and affiliations (Sosa 2014) to sustain the space of appearance and, with it, the archive's disruptive power.

Furthermore, following archival artifacts in different political contexts— during the oppressive regime, in the transition to democracy, and in the future—the chapter will connect three temporalities that are often considered separately in the literature, showing how political practices of state violence resistance of one generation are recovered in memory practices by the next generations.

Stimulated by the lines of exploration of reparation projects proposed by this book's editors, my analysis focuses on three archival operations, which I call "making visible," "making common," and "forging futures." Through them, I argue that the human rights archives repair, on the one hand, through their institutive power, which contributes to making the reality of state terror visible through the voices of its victims and witnesses, restoring their identities and activating processes of identification and belonging that engender affiliations over time. In this light, I show how the act of recording the pain of fellow beings is a powerful way of collectively confronting harm and dispossession, in contrast to the individualized and depoliticized notion of reparation that stems from the trauma model and the victim paradigm. Documentation processes of this kind bear witness to how pain is written enduringly into those lives touched by state violence (Das 2015) but also shift the discussion on political violence "beyond the idea of scenes or trauma as purely scenes of repression and the unspeakability of pain" (2). On the other hand, the archive's conservational power repairs by sustaining a repertoire that documents the damage caused, as well as collective practices for confronting it, while safeguarding sources as open latencies that refer to other appropriations and future affiliations.

Thus, the question of reparation allows me to propose that the power of a human rights archive cannot be reduced to its enunciative capacities. Rather, I argue that such capacities are intimately linked with the archive's *affective* and *affiliative powers.* Therefore, the chapter contributes to this volume's discussion by "amplifying the inherently political capacity of affects" (Lara et al. 2017, 35) and connecting temporalities, generations, and communities around a sociomaterial device—the archive.

The chapter begins by describing the emergence, role, and characteristics of the human rights archives created during the dictatorship in Chile. Next, I explain my approach to these archives and to reparation practices, to then analyze how the Vicaría archive instigated and exposed repair through its work during the regime, in its aftermath, and in the future. To conclude, I reflect on the forms of repair associated with the human rights archive.

State Terrorism and the Documentation of Human Rights Violations

On September 11, 1973, the armed forces seized power in Chile. A military coup deposed the government of the first socialist president democratically elected in the continent, ending the revolutionary project underway in this Latin American society. In a matter of hours, repression extended throughout the country, with thousands of men and women arrested and taken into detention. Those targeted, as well as their families, turned to churches for help and guidance. Religious leadership of different faiths came together in an urgent attempt to restore peace. Only twenty days after the coup d'état, they founded two interfaith offices that they thought would be temporary: the Comité Nacional de Refugiados (National Committee for Refugees), which sought to give refugee status and assistance to those who required it, and the Comité to collaborate in the "reestablishment of peace based on justice, . . . assuming the suffering of others as our own" (1973, 2).

Shortly afterward, the Comité expanded its work throughout the territory with support from dioceses of the Catholic Church (Precht 1998). More than forty thousand people requested legal assistance in the first two years of their work. The direct repression against nuns, priests, and laity who worked for the Comité and explicit orders from Pinochet forced its closure in December 1975. However, the following month, its functions were resumed by the newly formed Vicaría, an entity of the Catholic Church created by the pope at the request of the Archbishop of Santiago. In its offices on the Plaza de Armas, the main square in the heart of the capital city, between 1976 and 1992, the Vicaría sought "to provide legal assistance to those individuals or families affected by the exceptional legal situation that has emerged in Chile since September 11, 1973; to promote respect and give full validation to the principles proclaimed by the Universal Declaration of Human Rights; and to coordinate actions with other institutions" (González 1981, cited in Del Villar et al. 2019, 85).

In the years to come, similar organizations followed, such as the Christian Churches' Social Assistance Foundation, founded in 1975 to support political prisoners and their processes of exile and return to the country; the Association of Relatives of Detained-Disappeared, founded at the Comité headquarters in 1974; the Foundation for the Protection of Children Damaged by States of Emergency, formed in 1979 to assist returning exiles and provide social assistance and mental and physical health care to more than twelve thousand children who were relatives of victims; and the Corporation for the Promotion and Defense of the Rights of the People, created in 1980 to assist the persecuted and their families by fighting against impunity, mainly through legal and psychosocial assistance.[2]

Through this unprecedented system of human rights organizations, Chilean civil society offered legal, health, psychological, social, economic, and educational assistance to those affected by detention, torture, politically motivated dismissal from their jobs or places of study, and exile. They searched persistently for the disappeared detainees, sought truth and justice for the men and women politically executed, and made use of diverse legal resources in the defense of persecuted people. They systematically compiled and classified evidence of military abuses, identified patterns of repression, and produced statistics. They published reports and books about these situations and their evolution over time as well as magazines and pamphlets that informed people about the larger social, economic, and political reality the country was living through. Despite defamation of these organizations, constant threats, and reprisals against their workers, the Comité and the Vicaría successfully protected and preserved their documentary collections throughout the entire dictatorship period.

Thus, unlike in other Latin American countries that faced severe human rights violations against their citizens, after the military coup led by General Pinochet, Chilean civil society was capable, albeit not without great cost, of setting up and sustaining a system of assistance and denunciation that endured the seventeen years of dictatorial rule (1973–1990). Collectively, these organizations can be said to have enabled the rise of the Chilean human rights movement, which has been key in the international political history of human rights.[3]

At the center of the Comité and the Vicaría's unprecedented endeavor, an archive was built, little by little, by a series of artifacts that inscribed and denounced state terrorism as it unfolded. The archive is composed of various types of information (textual, visual, and oral), including national and international reports; press records; official documents from the state administration, the armed forces and its intelligence services, international organizations, and foreign countries; testimonies from witnesses, survivors, and deserters; drawings, letters, and poems written by political prisoners in captivity; and identity documents and letters from public figures representing the fields of politics, the arts, international relations, churches, and human rights activism, supporting the organization's actions. Additionally, there are over one hundred standardized forms for registering and processing information, including anthropomorphic forms with data on the physical characteristics and medical histories of the disappeared, which later helped identify human remains.

Today, the archive's legal collection contains more than 85,000 unique documents, over 45,000 individual case files chronicling state repression and the assistance provided for each person. The press archive contains more than 650,000 clippings, organized chronologically and by topic. The archive also houses periodic reports published monthly and annually with systematizations of the information on human rights abuses, as well as the three hundred issues of the magazine *Solidaridad* published between 1976 and 1990 and distributed for free by the churches. The audiovisual archive brings together collections of photographs taken by the Vicaría's own photographers, along with images, films, and documentaries that depict the reality of life under the dictatorship. The archive includes administrative and medical records related to the victims and their family members who received assistance, which remain confidential.

In January 1993, FUNVISOL (Fundación de Documentación y Archivo de la Vicaría de la Solidaridad) was created "to hold, preserve and manage the documents and audiovisual archive of the Vicaría de la Solidaridad and its predecessor the Comité para la Paz, as part of the historical memory of the country and of the Catholic Church, making them available to civil society as instruments that might assist in the path toward reconciliation and the construction of a society founded on truth, justice and respect for human rights."[4]

Indeed, since the dictatorship's defeat at the polls in 1988, the documentation of the Chilean human rights archives has been used extensively and systematically as a source of information and evidence by truth commissions, in judicial processes concerning crimes against humanity (see Hau, Lessa, and Rojas 2019), in sociohistorical research, and in practices of memory. Because the archives produced in later phases—in particular, the work of the two truth commissions organized by the transitional state—are not publicly accessible, the documentation gathered by human rights organizations continues to be the main source of public information on the systematic human rights violations perpetrated in the period.

On Archive and Reparation

Human rights archives are essential resources for transitional justice processes and procedures.[5] They play a critical role in recognizing the harm caused by these abuses, contributing to the establishment of the truth, facilitating victim reparations, serving as evidence in criminal prosecutions, and supporting educational practices related to past atrocities.[6] Victims, their relatives, lawyers, justice ministers, truth commissions, and memorial sites heavily rely on these collections of records that document systematic state-led abuses of power through violence.

Through collaborative and interdisciplinary research that analyses the relationship between documentation, state violence, and resistance, I have contributed to developing a different perspective on these archives.[7] This approach views the archive as a complex construct encompassing material, human, technological, and political elements, each with multifaceted expressions. At times, it manifests as an institutional entity; at other times, it takes the form of practices, objects, or repertoires; it can also represent potentiality or serve as an index. From this standpoint, the human rights archive is understood as a political project, an intellectual technology, an informational infrastructure, an affective device, and a system of discursive order. Over time, it evolves into a technology of history and an archaeological site (Bernasconi 2023). The archive is an open-ended, incommensurable, and heterogeneous assemblage. As Michel Foucault asserts in *The Archaeology of Knowledge*, "In its totality, an archive is indescribable and unshapeable in the present context" (2003, 221).

As a technology of history, the archive serves multiple functions beyond merely collecting documents from a specific era, along with their subjects, themes, and producers. It provides fragmentary evidence of the cultural repertoires of those times and the power struggles in which they were embedded. The archive captures not only what could be articulated but also what remained unspoken, highlighting the exclusions and silences inherent in its formation. It reflects the social imaginaries associated with recorded discourse, the conflicting narratives surrounding the events documented, and both individual and collective responses to historical trauma. Furthermore, it reveals how history is constructed and situates these memory technologies within that process (Trouillot 2005). Additionally, from an archaeological perspective, the archive facilitates the exploration of archival objects and practices by offering insights into the artifacts, operations, and processes that mediate documentation and preservation.

Making Visible

Wording Violence

In the Comité, the Vicaría, and the other human rights organizations that emerged through the long Chilean dictatorial rule, those who listened and tried to shoulder the pain of others were young professionals and volunteers, lay and religious, of different political affiliations who had experienced such things as politically motivated dismissal from their jobs, the detention of a son, or the disappearance of a partner. Daniela Sánchez was the first social worker to arrive at the Comité in October 1973, less than a month after the coup. "We were in our twenties, and our life project was cut off. It was a very ideological, very political project," she explains to me. Rather than an extemporaneous attempt to delineate a space from the past to house that pain, the organization and its archive emerged as a move *forward*, a response to those reached by violence, and a standing with and commitment to them (Taylor 2020). It arose out of a sense of solidarity and resistance and as a means to keep human beings responsive to moral standards and responsible to each other (Walker 2006).

The daughter of a doctor, María Luisa Sepúlveda's first job as a social worker was in a community health service in Santiago. Shortly after the coup, she was fired. Her father-in-law and her brothers-in-law were arrested. In the initial days when states of exception made it impossible to travel through the city, she obtained information on executions and torture. She had expected the coup and that President Allende would be overthrown, but she had never imagined how massive the repression would be. And she could not ignore it. At just twenty-six years of age, she joined the Comité in 1974, not expecting the dictatorship to last long or that she would play a leadership role in the country's main human rights organization, which she herself would close down once its work had been completed. Nor did she imagine rereading testimonies as a member of a truth commission or that she would sit on the board of a memory museum. "The other day, I was thinking about what my great motivation was," she says when recalling her initial days with the Comité. "For some, it was justice; for others, transformation, but for me, it was to alleviate the pain. I was devastated by pain. And we felt very useful. Somehow it was a privileged space from which to resist what we were experiencing."

In May 1976, when her father, Victor Díaz, the deputy secretary general of the Communist Party of Chile, was arrested, Viviana Díaz was twenty-five years old. She recalls that following the illegal event, "The first information we received over the phone was that we had to go to the Vicaría de la Solidaridad." Victor Díaz had gone into hiding on the day of the coup, twenty months earlier. In 1976, the Communist Party leadership was dismantled and exterminated, and several of his colleagues had been detained before her father. With his abduction, fear enveloped and isolated Viviana's family from the rest of the world. "No one could go to our home," she recalls. Viviana remembers arriving at the Vicaría to a "door that open[ed] and a place of listening in that difficult moment." "There are people who, to this day, if they run into me on the street, want to talk about it," María Luisa adds. "About the space that we had in the middle of that brutality. It was a space where you could speak whatever you wanted, you could comment, you could listen to people's fears. None of this was recorded most of the time, but I think it had a lot of value."

When the lives of fellow humans are taken, the archive becomes a place of inscription of acts of enunciation and listening, an abode for affirming gestures, a house that protects "documentary noise" (Vicente 2019) from obstinate and often precarious signs that whisper what is happening. In line with Veena Das's propositions based on Wittgenstein's language games, I suggest that in the context of a systematic policy of state violence, the archive becomes a means through which different forms of pain find *a home* in language (2007, 57).

Black Holes of Humanity

According to Derrida (1995), there would be no drive to create archives without the possibility of forgetfulness. Political violence, especially when perpetrated by the state, faces the menace of denial and impunity imposed by the perpetrators' power and their circuit of complicity. Under such circumstances, denial and impunity can easily lead to oblivion and ignorance.

Human rights archives that are built while political violence is exercised do not emerge for the purpose of recording history or memory, although they contribute to both. Rather, they arise as affective, cognitive, and political resources to approach unnarratable atrocities and encourage action. For the Comité and the Vicaría, the "archive drive" (Derrida 1995) represents an early impulse in the midst of uncertain, chaotic, painful days. In those initial months, registering the pain of others was a means for finding the whereabouts of detainees and, somehow, freeing them from further suffering, as explained by María Luisa: "The victim's testimony was not yet central. The central thing was to locate the missing people, save lives, and protect those that were in danger so that they would not be taken." This required that there be "elements to assess the person's security situation and take corresponding measures."

The recording of information was key for that assessment. "There was a rationality behind the recording of data that at that time had nothing to do with history. It had to do with effectiveness, with what we could do for the individual and the international denunciations," she adds. Daniela Sánchez continues, "If you came to tell me that last night, they had taken your partner from your home in [the working-class neighborhood of] La Legua, we also wanted to know if the same thing had happened at the house next door, and at the next one over too. And [we found] that once it happened in La Legua, it would happen in another neighborhood nearby. By December [1973], we were aware of the existence of repressive intelligence and that the episode would travel from one place to another."

In her memoirs, the Vicaría attorney Carmen Hertz writes, "We made files for each victim, for each disappeared person . . . with more information including: a photograph, the account of the detention, the victim, his full name, his profession, occupation, the full description of the circumstances of the detention and all the judicial and administrative procedures that had been made for that victim. The letters, the petitions, the appeals for protection, the complaints of alleged misfortune, everything, everything, everything . . . because everything was recorded in the Vicaría, including the responses of each authority regarding the disappeared persons. The victims become embodied" (2017, 160–161).

Hugo Vezzetti defines the *chupaderos* as "those pieces of Calvary that absorbed the disappeared detainees during the Southern Cone dictatorships" (2000, 16). The archive drive and the actions that it enabled represent attempts to rescue lives and vitalities from the centrifugal forces of those black holes of humanity. The act of inscription warded off oblivion; the archive's loquaciousness countered immobilization, fear, and a sense of powerlessness imposed by impunity. Identities that had vanished from the face of the earth were reincarnated through the conjunction of other presences and other political powers: the photos of their faces, their birth or marriage certificates, their diplomas, and the bodies of protesting family members who marched in the streets, chained themselves to the court building, and held hunger strikes (figure 1.1).

Insurgent Repertoire

Documentation processes and procedures are means to understand and apprehend violence while it occurs, helping make it an object of knowledge for intervention. Documentation can help distinguish different repressive practices, mediate their enunciation, and define the type of assistance required. Processes of nomination, categorization, definition, operationalization, and narrative composition, the compilation of lists, reports, statistics, and the creation of graphic representations enabling synoptic perspectives on various cases and the identification of repressive patterns, were also part of this information infrastructure. Translations from one artifact to another allowed for the circulation of "data" between modalities of enunciation (e.g., from oral to written) and between artifacts and genres (e.g., the translation of a testimony to a legal redress or a psychological diagnosis to an international denunciation).

The processing of these registries into information fueled actions from the organizations and the associations of victims and their relatives, including the production and dissemination of regular reports about how forms of repression were evolving and their characteristics; the filing of lawsuits in court, presenting denunciations before national and international law entities; the organization of affected people; the investigation of operative forms of repression in order to find the whereabouts of unlocated detainees; and providing information to the general public about the situation unfolding in the country.

As a result of this work, a repertoire of human rights abuses has emerged. I propose that this repertoire represents another form of reparation. Derrida suggests that "archivization produced as much as it recorded the event" (1995, 17), while Arfuch notes that the "constitution of the archive is also a constitution of meaning" (2008, 11). Consequently, this repertoire can be understood as a mechanism for exercising control over meaning, thereby fixing the value of specific terms (Foucault 1979, 219; see also Bernasconi 2019, 23). While the events are occurring, this repertoire arises from the voices and the experiences of those repressed and from the courageous resilience of a community that is forged in its defense, knowing that its strength lies in the power of being together and seizing every interstice of hope. This is a repertoire sustained by knowledge from below—an "insurgent repertoire" upheld by an oppressed community (Taylor 2020). Unlike state bureaucratic archives, this repertoire of enunciation

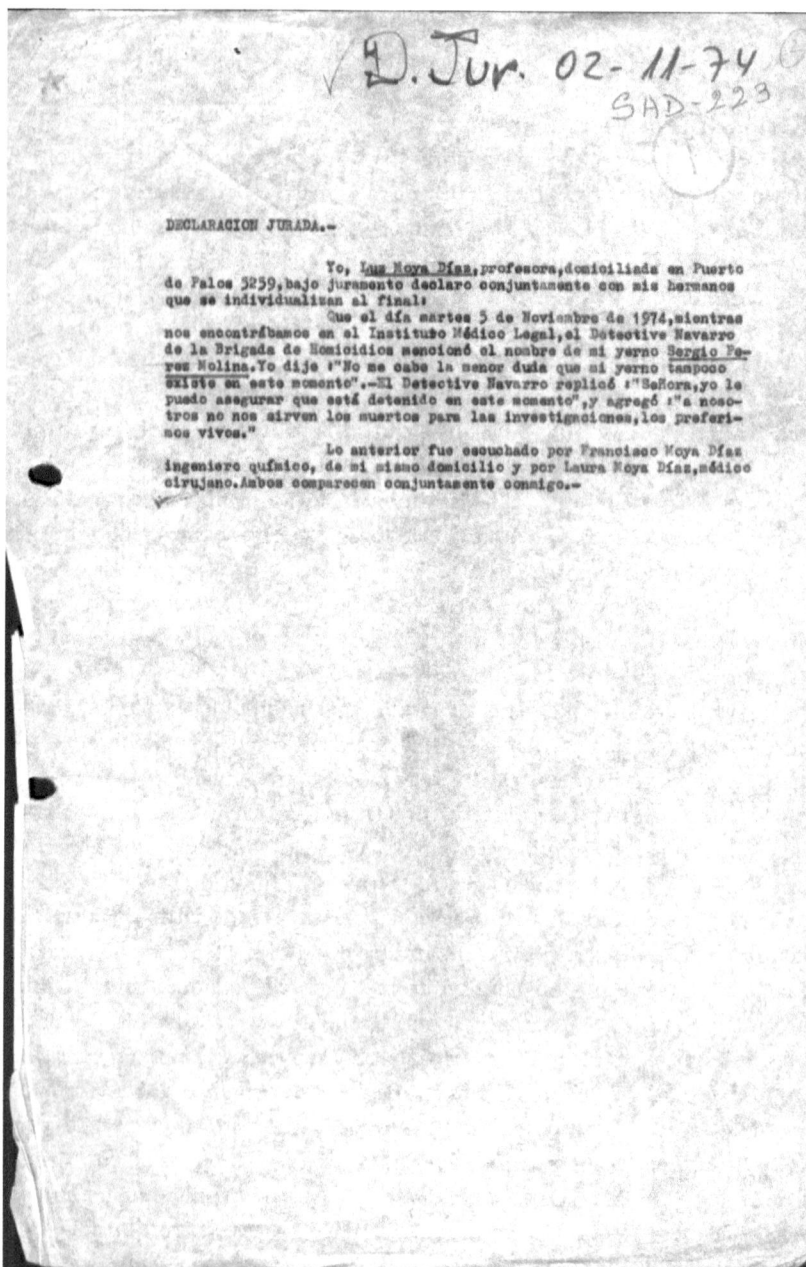

√ D. Jur. 02-11-74
SAD-223

DECLARACION JURADA.-

Yo, Luz Moya Díaz, profesora, domiciliada en Puerto
de Palos 5259, bajo juramento declaro conjuntamente con mis hermanos
que se individualizan al final:
Que el día martes 5 de Noviembre de 1974, mientras
nos encontrábamos en el Instituto Médico Legal, el Detective Navarro
de la Brigada de Homicidios mencionó el nombre de mi yerno Sergio Pérez Molina. Yo dije :"No me cabe la menor duda que mi yerno tampoco
existe en este momento".-El Detective Navarro replicó :"Señora, yo le
puedo asegurar que está detenido en este momento", y agregó :"a noso-
tros no nos sirven los muertos para las investigaciones, los preferi-
mos vivos."
Lo anterior fue escuchado por Francisco Moya Díaz
ingeniero químico, de mi mismo domicilio y por Laura Moya Díaz, médico
cirujano. Ambos comparecen conjuntamente conmigo.-

a

FIG. 1.1 Documentation on disappeared detainees: (a) marriage certificate of Mario Fernandez González, mine foreman, missing since November 26, 1973; (b) affidavit from 1974 concerning Sergio Pérez Molina, engineer, member of the Movement of the Revolutionary Left
(MIR), last seen in José Domingo Cañas detention center; (c) relatives of unlocated detainees
chained themselves to the court building in Santiago in 1979. *Source:* Vicariate of Solidarity
archive and documentation center.

007351   M 10

CERTIFICADO DE MATRIMONIO
EXCLUSIVO PARA ASIGNACION FAMILIAR

CERTIFICO: QUE EN LA CIRCUNSCRIPCION DE _____ Lota _____

DEL DEPARTAMENTO DE _____ Coronel _____ CON FECHA 13

DE _____ Mayo _____ DE 1991 _____ Y N° 181 _____ SE HALLA INSCRITO

EL MATRIMONIO _____ NOMBRES Y APELLIDOS DEL MARIDO

Mario Fernandez Gonzalez

NOMBRES Y APELLIDOS DE LA MUJER

Digna del Carmen Leiva Morales

FECHA DE LA CELEBRACION	DIA	MES	AÑO	HORA
	13	May	1991	9

OBSERVACIONES ANOTACIONES SUBINSCRIPCIONES

FECHA DEL CERTIFICADO _____ Lota _____ 13 May 1991

NELSON BENAVENTE BARRERA
Oficial del Registro Civil
e Identificación

b

ARCHIVO SOLIDARIDAD
TEMA: Desaparecidos Manifestacion 18-4-78
FECHA:
PUBLICADO:
FOTOGRAFO: L.N.
CAJA: 13-89

28

c

does not govern populations; rather, it actively resists necropolitics, defined as the subjugation of life to the power of death (Mbembe 2011). A repertoire that unfolds "at the edges of state power" (see introduction) and against it.

Space of Appearance

Each record of a repressive event contributed to inscribing the reality of violence, thus forcing the "impossible into the real," as Agamben puts it (1999, 148). Soon, the sheer volume of denunciations revealed a reality that dramatically contrasted with the picture painted by the regime. It laid bare the existence of a systematic policy of human rights violations perpetrated by the state against the population. This is the archive instituting power that helps create the *space of appearance* of state terror. It is the archive acting in the world.

Herein lies the political potential of archival documentary practices. If, as suggested by Rancière (2011), we think of politics not as the exercise or seizure of power but as the configuration of a specific space, the cutting of a particular sphere of experience, of objects posed as common, of subjects recognized as capable of designating these objects and of advocating for them, then the archive can be conceived of as a site of political contestation. Through systematic, elliptical, and always incomplete efforts *to know* what was happening, the archive became a tool for challenging the dictatorship over the regime of truth surrounding this horror.

Attorney Héctor Contreras, who directed the Disappeared Detainees Department of the Vicaría, recalls that in "the year 1979, after the hunger strike for the first time, the government was compelled to comment on national television. After all the lies they had always said about the disappeared persons, the spokesman conceded that they were willing to explore any avenue. That spurred us to create the famous '¿Dónde Están?' files." Figure 1.2 presents one such file that was sent to the government in one of hundreds of letters signed by the archbishop of Santiago, with all the information compiled thus far about every disappeared detainee known to the organization. "That was our way of telling the government that they had a serious avenue, a known case, to investigate," Contreras explains.

It seems to me that this is a form of reparation. It operates by acknowledging and denouncing violence and by displacing its subjects from the infamous images through which the dictatorship tried to present them: that of a beautiful woman victimized by a crime of passion, that of young guerrilla fighters betraying each other, that of a husband who left his family for his lover. It is the archive force allowing damaged lives to appear *as such*, rescuing vitalities from the "zone of nonbeing" (Fanon 1970), dignifying.

Thus, when it says "this is happening," the archive's "power of consignation" (Derrida 1995) mobilizes reparation in the form of the constitution of the present as a space of visibility for the truth of the tragedy (Rousso 2018). In Chile, long before the state officially recognized this truth through truth commissions

6

NAME	: ASTORGA NANJARI JOSE BRAULIO
IDENTITY CARD N.	: 1.239.528, of Santiago.
MARITAL STATUS	: Married.
DATE OF BIRTH	: 15th december of 1918.
AGE	: 55 years old at the date of detention.
ADDRESS	: 1670 Carrion Street.
OCCUPATION	: Carpinter and furniture maker.
POSITION	: Member of Communist Party of Chile.

FACTS of the CASE.

He was arrested on December 19, 1973 in his home around 20.30, in the presence of his spouse Florencia Gamboa Ugalde and his mother Carmen Nanjari Carvajal by two individuals in plainclothes who were armed. He was taken immediately to the Carabinero police precincts 17 and 18, of the Radio Patrol and Highways units, respectively, at the time located on Carrion Street, practically in front of the home of the affected individual. His mother and spouse are also witnesses to his transfer to the police stations. No arrest warrant was exhibited.

It is important to note that in the morning and afternoon of September 12, 1973 his home was raided by approximately twenty heavily armed Carabinero police officers, who did not exhibit a search warrant.

On March 19, 1974 Cesar Mendoza Duran, Carabinero General Director and member of the Governing Junta, through his attaché Lieut. Colonel Carlos Donoso Perez informed the affected individual's mother that: "According to the information obtained from Armed Forces Intelligence Service, it has been established that your son José Braulio was arrested and then released on December 26, 1973; his present

42

whereabouts are unknown, despite exhaustive procedures deployed to locate him".

Notwithstanding this information, to this date the whereabouts of Jose Braulio Astorga Nanjari are unknown.

LEGAL and ADMINISTRATIVE ACTIONS.

A habeas corpus writ was filed with the Santiago Court of Appeals on January 3, 1974, registered as N. 5-74. On January 26 of the same year, the 2nd Chamber of the Santiago Court of Appeals dismissed the petition.

The dismissal of this habeas corpus writ gave rise to (upon orders from the Santiago Court of Appeals) the initiation of an inquest concerning presumed misfortune by the 3rd Superior Criminal Court, proceedings that are registered at Rol. 115.828. On March 4, 1974 the Court ordered the inquest, and on August 17 of the same year, as certified on p. 6, exclusively based on the inquest report, the case was temporarily stayed "until greater and better investigative information arise."

However, on March 29, 1974 the Committee for Cooperation for Peace in Chile filed a class action habeas corpus motion on behalf of 131 people, including this affected person. Said motion is registered at Rol 289-74. On November 28 of the same year, the 6th Chamber of the Court of Appeals denied it. An appeal was filed with the Honorable Supreme Court, that on January 31, 1975 upheld the ruling to deny, ordering an inquest to investigate the destiny of the individuals of the habeas corpus who could not be located, including this Astorga Nanjari. It recommended that the Santiago Court of Appeals assign a Special Investigative Judge, assigned the case to Mr. Enrique Zurita.

On September 29, 1975 Judge Zurita recused himself from case 106.657, communicating the information to the Santiago

43

Military Court (II Division), which designated the 3rd Military Court to resume the investigation, registered as Rol 1.382-76.

On September 14, 1976 the Military Judge ruled to close the case and shelve the file.

Additionally, proceedings are pending and open with the 2nd Superior Criminal Court of Santiago, for presumed misfortune, proceedings that are registered as Rol 86-614.

Furthermore, the family members of the affected individual have undertaken various administrative initiatives to obtain information concerning the affected individual's situation. Such efforts include the following:

Twice they wrote to Carabineros Police General Director Cesar Mendoza Durán, who on one occasion replied that he had been arrested and then released; to the President of the Republic, from whom there has been no response; to the Interior Minister, on November 3, 1974, who replied through the director of the Ministry's Confidential Department, on the 7th of the same month and year, that: "Unfortunately inquiries have not been successful and the information presently available does not enable a concrete response concerning the whereabouts of Astorga Nanjari. Notwithstanding, should any information arise about this matter, you will be informed immediately." Also to the Inter American Human Rights Commission and the International Red Cross.

44

FIG. 1.2 File of José Astorga Nanjari, "¿Dónde Están?," Vicaría de la Solidaridad. *Source:* FUNVISOL.

and reparation laws and programs, reparation took the form of the affirmation of the experiences of the affected people. In the enunciation preserved in the archive, however, the language was not that of victimhood, as Erika Hennings recalls.

Erika and her husband, Alfonso Chanfreau, were members of the Movement of the Revolutionary Left (MIR). After Alfonso was detained in June 1974, in an attempt to break him, the security agents came for Erika. Both were placed in the Londres 38 space of detention (see figure 1.3) and were forced to witness the torture of the other until Alfonso's definitive disappearance, followed by Erika's release. In a recent interview with us, Erika stresses, "We were not victims. We were social activists, and very early on, we populated the registries of the Comité and the Vicaría with our voices, as witnesses." As Agamben points out (1999, 158), a witness is an actor whose authority stems from the ability to talk, driven by the inability of others to speak.

Against the devices of impunity, lies, and censorship, the archive attests, through the power of firsthand witnesses, to the harm that was inflicted and remains etched in the memory of those situations in which the detainees "were able to generate community and implement strategies to communicate with one another, identify and know each other, and if later released, give testimony and denounce what they had seen and heard," as stated by Juan, guide at Londres 38 Espacio de Memorias.

Making Common

Little by little, the documentation of individual realities allowed the human rights organization workers to identify patterns that unveiled the dictatorship's exceptionally cruel repertoire of criminal practices. "We did not lose the names or the facts. Because we were trying to get people to organize themselves," explains Daniela Sánchez. Victoria Baeza, a social worker with both the Comité and the Vicaría, adds, "We had been trained to work with the other, not for the other. The family members are protagonists of their own story." "We believed that role would give them strength," María Luisa recalls. Grouping cases by shared issues could "help people understand the problem they were experiencing, encouraging them to take an active role in searching for solutions, while also contributing to the development of solidarity in the face of those problems" (Vicaría de la Solidaridad 1977, 27). Putting words to or "wording" violence (Das 2007) may be regarded as a way of producing the time and space of *we*. Viviana Díaz recalls that during that fateful year of 1976, when Communist Party members were the targets of the repression, every single day, comrades arrived at the Vicaría whom she did not know, whose husbands or children had been detained. She explains that "the Vicaría, however, was careful not to immediately declare them disappeared, . . . so a transition group was formed. . . . An entire journey had to be undertaken: file appeals with the court, go to the National Detainee's Service, to the coroner's office to see if a body with the characteristics of your relative was there. . . . I will never forget when a comrade in the year '75 or maybe '74 asked me, 'How long have you been looking for him?' And I replied, 'Three months,' which for me was already a long time. 'And you?' I asked in return. 'I've been looking for him for a year and a half.'" Here, words and ears recognized common pain and concerns, identifying each other, sharing experiences, and envisaging paths of action.

FIG. 1.3 Translation of Erika Hennings's testimony of political imprisonment and torture (three pages) and image of the detention center where Erika and her husband, Alfonso, were kept. Affidavit given by Erika Hennings, November 23, 1990, concerning her detention and the detention and disappearance of her husband, Alfonso Chanfreau. Room of the former detention, torture, and extermination center Londres 38, Santiago. Recuperated as a site of memories. *Source:* Susana Ariasda Salazar, May 19, 2015.

Affiliations

The archive mobilizes and documents the formation of collective subjects and the emergence and use of a repertoire of collective actions of contestation, care, mourning, and resistance with which to confront damaged worlds by "being together" (Sosa 2014): searching for and identifying prisoners in hospitals, morgues, and detention centers; writing letters denouncing the situation to military officials, to the judiciary, or to international entities; producing press releases; taking court actions such as habeas corpus writs, denunciations of presumed misfortune, or criminal lawsuits for abduction; and protesting through marches, commemorative ceremonies, and hunger strikes such as those held in June 1977 and between May and June of 1979.

"We," says Victoria Baeza in reference to the social workers of the Vicaría, "accompanied them in this process. We were there along that road with them. When they had the hunger strike, we were there Saturday and Sunday." And they were even present when the family member could not be, as in the following recollection offered by Argentina Valenzuela, a social worker with the Comité and the Vicaría: "I remember a terrible case of the Pérez twins, a man and a woman, who were murdered in a confrontation. The entire family had to go into hiding. We went with a Comité lawyer and a priest to recover the bodies from the Legal Medical Institute and give them a dignified burial. We bought sheets for shrouds, coffins, burial sites, and we had them buried."

Rather than recording an individual and temporary psychic state, the archive provides glimpses of "the work of a community of social actors when facing shared experiences of loss" (Gatti 2015, 5), of their personal worlds written by pain (Das 2007). In this way, a lifelong *working through* (Eng 2010) of trauma in an expanded affiliative kinship (Sosa 2014) emerged in response to state violence. Borrowing from Diana Taylor in her reflection on different forms of resistance in Latin America, the archive safeguards an "ongoing *becoming* as opposed to a static being, participatory and relational, founded in mutual recognition" (Taylor 2020, 4). The archive safeguards affective correspondences, providing the means of reconnecting disconnected words and things (Eng 2010; Sosa 2015).

These affective correspondences were gradually achieved over the course of time and, in the 1980s, spilled over to encompass the majority of Chilean society in the public acknowledgment of the truth of victims and witnesses, despite efforts to distort and communicational orchestrations mounted by the dictatorship and the official communications media.

Remembering what is unacceptable is key to restoring a political community and imagining forms of shared coexistence and citizenship. The human rights archive has played a critical role in recovering that sense of belonging within this society. Extending Pilar Calveiro's reflections on the operations of state violence (2012), we may bear in mind that it is the historicity of an entire society subjected to an exceptional regime that these archives encompass, although always in an incomplete manner. In bringing together traces of the histories of those who were victimized, the archive speaks of and to the entire society of that era, revealing what it was like to live under a dictatorship. If, as Derrida affirms, "it is possible to think of participation and access to the archive, of its comprisal and interpretation, as indicators of a society's democratic base" (quoted in Pittaluga 2006, 17), the archive's vitality offers signs of the reconfiguration of the political fabric of the society that was torn apart by state violence.

Forging Futures

Alongside the national archival system, the Chilean human rights organizations emerged and still survive, ensuring the long-term preservation of records of the country's worst catastrophe. According to Giorgio Agamben (1999), a dead language is one that is unable to keep opposing preservation and innovation, the two forces that rule an archive's productive power. As inscription devices, the transitive capacity of archival documents allows them to "travel" across time and space to reach other processes and actors in the future. Consequently, the question concerning the future of the facts and experiences contained in the archive is whether it has the capacity to continue speaking to the present-day public and generate other affiliations through new appropriations. Unlike the Chilean transition's policy of "closing the subject" (Richards 2017), the archive's backbone lies in its ability to keep the past open. As a type of indomitable latency, the archive opens itself to new interpretations, refusing to close the door on the past.

Archive Imprint

As I described at the outset, since the end of the dictatorship, the FUNVISOL archive, as well as others that now compose a local human rights archive network, has been consulted extensively by diverse actors. Since 1994, when Villa Grimaldi in Santiago redefined itself as a site museum, the first site of memory in Latin America, the human rights archives have played an important role in the recovery and "refunctionalization" of spaces that were "alienated from their initial functions to be employed for [state] repression" (López and Guglielmucci 2019, 61) and make way for their appropriation, occupation, and public accessibility as memory sites. Human rights archives have contributed to the recognition of such repressive places, the interpretation of their vestiges, the identification of survivor and witness testimonial voices, and the design of the site's exhibition and visitor experience. As part of their heritage management, sites of memory often form testimonial and documentary archives. Thus, in these sites, "foundational" and new site-based human rights archives intersect. In this relation, we can observe the *archive's imprint*—its archaeological and citational power—acting on a series of reparation practices instantiated by survivors to create and sustain other *documentary infrastructure* through which the space where state violence once appeared is pluralized by practices of marking, commemoration, preservation, reflection, and dialogue.

When regarded as a technology of history, the human rights archive enables us not only to approach the past in order to repair it but fundamentally to imagine the future to be sustained. In this sense, extending Eng's arguments (2010), affective correspondences might motivate new relations between archival objects and future words (Das 2007). The archive safeguards histories that have not been memorialized or that may be memorialized in new ways. Such potential connections engender postsanguine filiations. Sociologist Rodrigo Suárez (2021) has explored what motivates young people like himself, born in the later years of the regime without biographical ties to the repression, to join an association for the recovery of a former detention center. Suárez encourages fellow organization members to delve into human rights archives, where they discover documents, previously unknown to them, about uncles, parents, or old friends who were affected by the dictatorship's repression. Over a period of years, Suárez holds conversations with them and shows how "the registries involve and foster connections" that redefine identities and belonging, allowing for the understanding of family cultures and encouraging kinship dialogues. Paula, one of his *compañeras*, did not attribute her initial motivation for joining the association years earlier to the fact that her father was a political prisoner. But after the process triggered by the documents, her motivation changed: "If now you ask me why, I would say it is because I am my father's daughter" (26). Affects modulate forthcoming implications in the order of the archive; indeterminate emotional forces expose new generations to this embodied relation with and through matter, evoking the gestures of previous users and amplifying the archive's political and affective repertoire. Expanding affiliative ties, the human rights archive continues to foster reparation processes.

Conclusions: Forms of Repair

Returning to the dictatorship years in Chile, this chapter explored the significant role of civil society's human rights archives in repairing the worlds damaged by state violence.

In the human rights field, the notion of reparation in Latin America is fundamentally attached to the actions of the state. It carries, then, a legal concern. From this prevailing framework, reparation involves a series of economic, administrative, and symbolic actions through which past harm is acknowledged, responsibility is assumed, and compensation is offered.

Following Derrida (1995) and Foucault (2003), I have argued that two forces govern the productive power of an archive: on one hand, an instituting, creative, innovative, and disruptive force that identifies and enunciates;

on the other, a power of conservation that excludes, repeats, organizes, and safeguards. With these two forces in mind, I have approached the archive as a reaction to destitution and destruction; as an instituting power that rises with a claim to truth; as a place of belonging and affiliation, an active and reactivatable space—a sociomaterial device with enunciative, affective, and affiliative powers.

In the previous pages, I attempted to show that during state terror, the human rights archive mobilizes and inscribes practices of contestation, resistance, and care that engender forms of individual, collective, and public repair we need to consider if we want to fully understand how societies cope with and heal their wounded worlds. Such forms of reparation are sustained by the creation of spaces of trust within which atrocity can be spoken, recognized, and inscribed in the voices of those affected by repression as well as their families and comrades. Reparation is also identifiable in the willingness to give testimony on behalf of those who have been silenced and in the detachment of the individuals subjected to violence from the field of the bare life (Agamben 1998) and dictatorial impunity. I also see reparation in the formation of interwoven ways of caring, in mundane and repetitive practices, and in extraordinary occasions: listening, offering company, bearing witness, being there to envelop the dead in a shroud and bury them when their relatives could not. These ways of caring are sustained by the construction of collective subjects—mothers, witnesses, survivors, activists—working through the present, protecting lives, reducing risks, and mitigating harm.

Rather than presenting agreed-upon, complete, and closed histories, the archive that emerges "from below"—as part of the efforts to provide assistance and denounce state violence—constructs and sustains a political, affective, and cognitive fabric that is insurgent, fragmented, and open. Following the defeat of the dictatorial regime, this archive forges connections between the stories it preserves and contemporary acts of memory, contestation, and belonging. Consequently, the *appeared reality* instantiated by the archive remains latent, waiting to lend itself to the appropriations of future generations in the hope of new connections between artifacts and words. It is a haunting presence, waiting for affiliations from "vicarious audiences" (Sosa 2014) that may sustain the space of appearance and, with it, the archive's disruptive power to help imagine other ways of living based on the remembrance of who and what was lost.

Echoing the complex systems through which precious objects circulate, we can trace how new forms of political belonging emerge around civil society's archives—through the power of their artifacts to circulate, the routes they travel, and the people and places they connect across time and space. As suggested earlier, this capacity is not reduced to discursive or written elements; it also emerges out of different forms of matter the archive instantiates, out of ways of speaking and hearing, of being present, of being together, and of reclaiming the rule of law and respect for human rights.

Notes

1 Over time, reparation projects have expanded to deal with other forms of dispossession, exploitation, and harm that may include a different time framework, such as in the case of colonial occupation, enslavement, colonial restorative projects, or environmental damage. See Barkan (2000) for the question of whether this ever-spreading trend represents a new moral order in world politics.

2 For a brief characterization of the documentary collections of human rights in the country, including these digital repositories, see Townsend and López (2017).

3 See Kelly (2013) on the origins of transnational human rights activism and Bernasconi (2019, 229–236) on the role of this particular archive.

4 Managed by a board of directors formed by the Vicaría's former staff members and by three professionals who serve the public, the archive remains the private property of the Catholic Church. In 2017, it became the first of its kind to be declared a historical monument by the Council of National Monuments. The foundation receives a regular grant from the Ministry for Culture, Arts and Heritage.

5 Human rights archives also include bureaucratic records created during the abuse itself, which are recovered or disclosed to fulfill human rights functions (Ketelaar 2001, 138). "They consist, for the most part, of records and files on individuals under surveillance, duty logs, registers and witness statements at times extracted under torture, but they also contain records seized by the authorities during raids on suspect organizations and political opponents" (Boel, Canavaggio, and González 2021, 29). In Latin America, a paradigmatic case of subverting the purposes of a repression archive is the Intelligence Service of the Police of Buenos Aires Province (Dirección de Inteligencia de la Policía de la provincia de Buenos Aires, DIPBA), removed from the domain of the perpetrator to make it available to the victims and the general public through the work of the Comisión Provincial por la Memoria, an autonomous and public body created in 2000, after the 1988 police reform that exposed the archive (Raggio et al. 2024). Paraguay, Brazil, and Guatemala have also recovered archives of police and armed forces security services and have put them to the service of human rights promotion (see Da Silva and Jelin 2002; Weld 2014).

6 Transitional justice itself generated human rights archives through truth commissions, victims' programs, and judicial processes. In previous works, we have shown how in Chile, not only case folders, judicial processes, press clippings, international organizations reports, lists, and statistics but also narrative structures, a whole vocabulary, and a number of experts have been drawn from the human rights archives to substantiate the work of truth commissions (Bernasconi, Lira, and Ruiz 2018; Bernasconi, Mansilla, and Suárez 2019), judicial processes (Accatino, Bernasconi, and Collins 2022; Hau, Lessa, and Rojas 2019), reparation programs (Lira 2006), and memorialization practices (Accatino and Suárez 2021).

7 Since 2015, I've been involved in five research projects that have explored the role that human rights archives and documentary artifacts and practices play in a society's capacity to confront state violence and its enduring impacts. These projects are Political Technologies of Memory: A Genealogy of the Artifacts of Registration of Human Rights Violations Under the Chilean Dictatorship; Political Technologies of Memory: Contemporary Uses and Appropriation of Past Human Rights Violations Registry Devices in Chile; Political Violence and Human Rights Violations Accountability: Circumstances, Uses and Effects of Forced Disappearance Registration: Lessons from a Comparative Perspective in the Americas; and Beyond the Victim's Paradigm: Genealogy of Performative

Devices of the Subject of State Terrorism (Chile, 1973–1990). More at https://www
.memoriayderechoshumanosuah.org/.

References

Accatino, Daniela, and Rodrigo Suárez. 2021. "Dispositivos de visibilidad situados: Un marco
conceptual para la composición museográfica en ex centros de detención recuperados como
Sitios de Memoria." *Revista Austral de Ciencias Sociales*, no. 41, 175–196.

Accatino, Sandra, Oriana Bernasconi, and Cath Collins. 2022. "Permanence et transposition
des actes écrits qui ont dénoncé par la voie judiciaire les atrocités de la dictature chilienne."
Langage et société 181 (1): 17–45.

Agamben, Giorgio. 1998. *Homo Sacer: Sovereign Power and Bare Life*. Stanford, Calif.: Stanford University Press.

Agamben, Giorgio. 1999. *Remnants of Auschwitz: The Witness and the Archive*. New York:
Zone Books.

Arendt, Hannah. 2015. *La condición humana*. Buenos Aires: Paidós.

Arfuch, Leonor. 2008. "Archivos y derechos humanos: Usos actuales, posibilidades y limitaciones." In *II Encuentro Regional Archivos y Derechos Humanos: Archivos y derechos humanos:
Usos actuales, posibilidades y limitaciones*. Buenos Aires: Memoria Abierta.

Barkan, Elazar. 2000. *The Guilt of Nations: Restitution and Negotiating Historical Injustices*.
New York: Norton.

Bell, Vikki, Oriana Bernasconi, Jaime Hernández-García, and Cecilia Sosa. 2021. *Archives of
Violence: Case Studies from South America*. London: Goldsmiths, University of London.

Bernasconi, Oriana. 2018. "Del archivo como tecnología de control al acto documental como
tecnología de resistencia." *Cuadernos de Teoría Social* 4 (7): 68–92.

Bernasconi, Oriana, ed. 2019. *Resistance to Political Violence in Latin America: Documenting
Atrocity*. London: Palgrave Macmillan.

Bernasconi, Oriana, Manuel Gárate, Daniela Mansilla, and Rodrigo Suárez. 2019. "How to
Sustain a Human Rights Organisation Under State Violence." In *Resistance to Political
Violence in Latin America: Documenting Atrocity*, edited by Oriana Bernasconi, 41–78.
London: Palgrave Macmillan.

Bernasconi, Oriana, Elizabeth Lira, and Marcela Ruiz. 2019. "Political Technologies of
Memory: Uses and Appropriations of Artifacts of Registration and Denunciation of State
Violence." *International Journal of Transitional Justice* 13 (1): 7–29.

Bernasconi, Oriana, Daniela Mansilla, and Rodrigo Suárez. 2019. "Las Comisiones de la Verdad en la Batalla de la Memoria: Usos y efectos disputados de la verdad extrajudicial en
Chile." *Colombia Internacional* 97:27–55.

Boel, Jens, Perrine Canavaggio, and Antonio González. 2021. *Archives and Human Rights*.
Abingdon: Routledge.

Butler, Judith. 2007. *El género en disputa*. Barcelona: Paidós.

Butler, Judith. 2017. *Cuerpos aliados y lucha política*. Barcelona: Paidós.

Buur, Lars. 1999. "Monumental History: Visibility and Invisibility in the Work of the South
African Truth and Reconciliation Commission." Presentation at Wits History Workshop:
The TRC; Commissioning the Past. University of the Witwatersrand.

Calveiro, Pilar. 2012. *Violencias de Estado: La guerra antiterrorista y la guerra contra el crimen
como medios de control global*. Buenos Aires: Siglo XXI.

Caswell, Michelle. 2014. *Archiving the Unspeakable: Silence, Memory and the Photographic
Record in Cambodia*. Madison: University of Wisconsin Press.

Collins, Cath. 2010. *Post-Transitional Justice: Human Rights Trials in Chile and El Salvador*.
University Park: Pennsylvania State University Press.

Comaroff, John, and Jean Comaroff. 1992. *Ethnography and the Historical Imagination*. Boulder, Colo.: Westview Press.

Das, Veena. 2007. *Life and Words: Violence and the Descent into the Ordinary*. Berkeley: University of California Press.

Das, Veena. 2008. *Sujetos del dolor, agentes de dignidad*. Bogotá: Ediciones Universidad Nacional de Colombia.

Das, Veena. 2015. *Wording the World: Veena Das and Scenes of Inheritance*. Edited by Roma Chatterji. New York: Fordham University Press.

Da Silva Catela, Ludmila, and Elizabeth Jelin, eds. 2002. *Los archivos de la represión: Documentos, memoria y verdad*. Madrid: Siglo XXI.

Del Villar, María Soledad, Boris Hau, María Teresa Johansson, and Manuel Guerrero. 2019. "Professions and Profiles: Epistemic Communities and the Registration of Human Rights Violations." In *Resistance to Political Violence in Latin America: Documenting Atrocity*, edited by Oriana Bernasconi, 79–115. London: Palgrave Macmillan.

Derrida, Jacques. 1995. *Archive Fever: A Freudian Impression*. Chicago: University of Chicago Press.

Eng, David. 2010. *The Feeling of Kinship*. Durham, N.C.: Duke University Press.

Fanon, Frantz. 1970. *Black Skin, White Masks*. London: Paladin.

Foucault, Michel. (1979) 1992. *Microfísica del poder*. Madrid: Ediciones de la Piqueta.

Foucault, Michel. 2003. *La arqueología del saber*. Buenos Aires: Siglo XXI.

Gatti, Gabriel. 2015. "Duelos felices, teorías ágiles." *Papeles del CEIC* 3 (135).

Geiger, Till, Niamh Moore, and Mike Savage. 2010. "The Archive in Question." CRESC Working Paper Series, WP 81.

González, Alejandro. 1981. "El Departamento Jurídico de la Vicaría de la Solidaridad del Arzobispado de Santiago: Una experiencia de Defensa Legal de los Derechos Humanos Fundamentales." Report presented in the Primera Conferencia sobre Organización y Prestación de Servicios Legales el Latinoamérica y el Caribe, San José de Costa Rica. Available at FUNVISOL archive.

Hau, Boris, Francesca Lessa, and Hugo Rojas. 2019. "Registration of State Violence as Judicial Evidence in Human Rights Trials." In *Resistance to Political Violence in Latin America: Documenting Atrocity*, edited by Oriana Bernasconi, 197–227. London: Palgrave Macmillan.

Hertz Cádiz, Carmen. 2017. *La historia fue otra: Memorias*. Santiago: Penguin Random House.

Kelly, Patrick. 2013. "The 1973 Chilean Coup and the Origins of Transnational Human Rights Activism." *Journal of Global History* 8:165–186.

Ketelaar, Eric. 2002. "Archival Temples, Archival Prisons: Modes of Power and Protection." *Archival Science* 2 (3): 221–238.

Lara Ali, Liu, Colin Ashley Wen, Akemi Nishida, Rachel Liebert, and Michelle Billies. 2017. "Affect and Subjectivity." *Subjectivity* 10:30–43.

Lazar, Sian. 2004. "Citizens Despite the State: Everyday Corruption and Local Politics in El Alto, Bolivia." In *Corruption: Anthropological Perspectives*, edited by D. Haller and C. Shore, 212–228. London: Pluto.

Lira, Elizabeth. 2006. "The Reparations Policy for Human Rights Violations in Chile." In *The Handbook of Reparations*, edited by P. de Greiff, 55–101. New York: Oxford University Press.

López, Loreto, and Ana Guglielmucci. 2019. "La experiencia de Chile y Argentina en la transformación de ex centros clandestinos de detención, tortura y exterminio en lugares de memoria." *Hispanic Issues On Line* 22:57–81.

Mbembe, Aquille. 2011. *Necropolítica*. Madrid: Melusina.

McKemmish, Sue, Livia Iacovino, Eric Ketelaar, Melissa Castan, and Lynette Russell. 2011. "Resetting Relationships: Archives and Indigenous Human Rights in Australia." *Archives and Manuscripts* 39 (1): 107–144.

Moon, Claire. 2012. "What One Sees and How One Files Seeing: Human Rights Reporting, Representation and Action." *Sociology* 46 (5): 876–890.

Pittaluga, Roberto. 2006. "Prefacio." In *Historia, Memoria y Fuentes Orales*, edited by V. Carnavole, F. Lorenz, and R. Pittaluga, 16–18. Buenos Aires: Ediciones CeDInCI.

Posel, Deborah, and Graeme Simpson, eds. 2002. *Commissioning the Past: Understanding South Africa's Truth and Reconciliation Commission*. Johannesburg: Witwatersrand University Press.

Precht, Cristian. 1998. *En la Huella del Buen Samaritano: Breve Historia de la Vicaría de la Solidaridad*. Santiago: Tiberíades.

Raggio, S., A. L. Bustamante, J. C. Agüero, and M. L. Ortiz. 2024. "L'utilisation pédagogique des archives des atrocités." *Langage et société* 181 (1): 69a–98a.

Rancière, Jacques. 2006. *Política, policía, democracia*. Santiago: LOM Ediciones.

Richards, Nelly. 2019. *Eruptions of Memory*. Cambridge: Polity.

Rousso, Henry. 2018. *La última catástrofe*. Santiago: Editorial Universitaria.

Ruiz, Marcela, and Oriana Bernasconi. 2019. "Human Rights Reports: Categorization, Classification and Denunciation of Human Rights Violations." *Discourse & Society* 30 (1): 44–63.

Ruiz, Marcela, and Antonia Torres. 2021. "Archival Operations in Post-Dictatorship Novels: Memory and Chilean Human Rights Records." *Archives and Records* 43 (1): 56–74.

Seigworth, Gregory, and Melissa Gregg. 2010. *The Affect Theory Reader*. Durham, N.C.: Duke University Press.

Skaar, Elin, Jemima García-Godos, and Cath Collins. 2017. *Transitional Justice in Latin America*. New York: Routledge.

Sosa, Cecilia. 2015. "Affect, Memory and the Blue Jumper: Queer Languages of Loss in Argentina's Aftermath of Violence." *Subjectivity* 8:358–381.

Stoler, Ann Laura. 2009. *Along the Archival Grain: Epistemic Anxieties and Colonial Common Sense*. Princeton, N.J.: Princeton University Press.

Suárez, Rodrigo. 2021. "Filiaciones postsanguíneas: Experiencias de afectación en la Agrupación por la Memoria Histórica Providencia de Antofagasta, Chile." *Iberoforum: Revista de Ciencias Sociales* 1 (1): 1–30.

Taylor, Diana. 2020. *¡Presente! The Politics of Presence*. Durham, N.C.: Duke University Press.

Townsend, Brandi, and Loreto López. 2017. *Guía de archivos de memoria y derechos humanos en Chile*. Santiago, Chile: Universidad Alberto Hurtado.

Trouillot, Michel-Rolph. 2015. *Silencing the Past: Power and the Production of History*. Boston: Beacon.

Vanthuyne, Karine. 2021. "'I Want to Move Forward. You Can Move Forward Too': Articulating Indigenous Self-Determination at the Truth and Reconciliation Commission of Canada." *Human Rights Quarterly* 43 (2): 355–377.

Vezzetti, Hugo. 2001. *Historia y Memorias del Terrorismo de Estado en la Argentina*. College Park: Latin American Studies Center, University of Maryland.

Vicaría de la Solidaridad. 1977. *Un Año de Labor*. Santiago: Arzobispado de Santiago.

Vicente, Camilo. 2019. *[Tiempo Suspendido] Una Historia de la Desaparición Forzada en México, 1940–1980*. London: Perlego.

Walker, Margaret. 2006. *Moral Repair: Reconstructing Moral Relations After Wrongdoing*. Cambridge: Cambridge University Press.

Weld, Kirsten. 2014. *Paper Cadavers: The Archives of Dictatorship in Guatemala*. Durham, N.C.: Duke University Press.

Wilson, Richard. 2001. *The Politics of Truth and Reconciliation in South Africa: Legitimizing the Post-Apartheid State*. Cambridge: Cambridge University Press.

Zeitlyn, David. 2012. "Anthropology in and of the Archive: Possible Futures and Contingent Pasts: Archives as Anthropological Surrogates." *Annual Review of Anthropology* 41:461–480.

2

Memory Caught in
the Everyday

• •

A Case of a Salvadoran
Reparation Ethnography

HENRIK RONSBO

One evening in 1996, during fieldwork in the village of Alchuapa,[1] I sat watching the news with twenty-two-year-old Santiago. He was the nephew and driver of the shop owner next door and had therefore become my mechanic. The main story, as was often the case in El Salvador then, was one of violence and murder. Not far away, in a town on the Pacific coast, five members of a family had been murdered with assault rifles by a group of masked assailants. The only survivor was a toddler, found hiding under a bed. As in other similar cases, the neighbors heard the gunfire but were unable to provide a description of the attackers, nor had they any idea about their motives. Despite this lack of information, Santiago immediately asserted, "They are killing families again!"

At this conjuncture of Salvadoran history in the late 1990s, violence was seen to have escalated even beyond that which was experienced during the civil war (Moodie 2002). As we sat there in the midst of images and narratives of "post-war," "neoliberal" violence (Williams 2002), I wondered what Santiago meant by "again." The last time they were "killing families" was in the early 1980s at the beginning of the Salvadoran civil war (1980–1992); he was only six years old then. But none of his immediate kin had been killed, and since his family's compound lies outside the village, he never witnessed any atrocities. That evening, as we sat on the couch in front of the TV, I was taken aback by the seeming excessiveness of Santiago's expression, but I never understood it then.

A few years later, Santiago had "left for the North," while I kept coming and going following life in Alchuapa. Alchuapa is a small rural municipality in western El Salvador dominated by *milpa* agriculture (cornfields) and cattle. The settlement is of pre-Columbian origin (Fowler 1989). It is mentioned in the sixteenth-century tributary list[2] and throughout the colonial period had been referred to as a *común* or *pueblo de Indios*.[3] From the nineteenth century to the present, its Indigenous community has maintained communal land ownership,[4] securing access to clay used for the production of earthenware by the female community members and access for the men to small plots for their *milpas*.

When I began preparing a psychosocial, social memory project with some members of the community in 2011, I could not help but reflect on Santiago's expression. It could not be "killing families again" in any experiential sense, as in the resurfacing of an intrusive memory or the (re)living of a traumatic experience; it was "killing families again" as emergent from the knowledge that everyday family life in a world shaped in the shadows of persistent state and privatized violence was always precarious. I suggest we understand expressions such as Santiago's outburst and exchanges as figures of inordinate knowledge (Das 2020) generated from within lives shaped by militarized (disciplinary, torturous, and genocidal) and racialized state formation processes (Ronsbo 1998).

The project I was reflecting upon had taken shape serendipitously when I met staff from the Committee de Derechos Humanos de El Salvador (CDHES) at a seminar on violence in San Salvador in 2010. CDHES had documented a massacre on an Indigenous cooperative in western El Salvador but were unaware of my work in the region and that another Indigenous community/cooperative in western El Salvador, that of Alchuapa, had endured a similar massacre at the onset of the civil war, when twenty-six men were killed during an army massacre in the village and some seventy more were abducted, tortured, and killed during the following two years (Comisión de Derechos Humanos de El Salvador 2017).

The CDHES staff members were young and had very little experience with psychosocial interventions, such as those developed through nearly two decades of practice in Guatemala, but were eager to learn from them. With funding from my employer, DIGNITY (Danish Institute Against Torture),[5] and leveraging my connections with Guatemalan psychologists I had previously collaborated with (Ronsbo and Paniagua 2014) as well as a Salvadoran anthropologist I already knew, we managed to create a team during 2011 with the capabilities necessary to address experiences of mass violence from both a psychosocial and a social memory perspective. During this period, I paid two shorter visits to the village, working with the group of survivors who came to acknowledge and accept the presence of visiting CDHES staff in preparation for the upcoming project.

Often encounters between communities and psychosocial projects such as this have been understood as encounters between everyday life and therapeutic governmentality (Pupavac 2001; Rose 1996), with therapeutic power shaping a field of desire, practice, and norms. However, I argue that anthropologists can and should work within such encounters, and for want of a better term, I call it *reparation ethnography*, an ethnographic practice that meticulously identifies figures of inordinate knowledge that validate and acknowledge the traditions and histories people strive for and claim from the continuities and ruptures of everyday life. In this ethnographic practice, survivors are recognized as authors of these figures while they simultaneously make them accessible to therapeutic practitioners and thus facilitate their integration in formal reparative processes.

Figures of the Inordinate in Reparation Ethnography

I argue that this lens on everyday life generates a specifically anthropological form of knowledge (Das 2020) that can contribute to the understanding of reparation interventions, particularly when these are framed as community based. I suggest that this kind of anthropological knowledge, inordinate yet coconstructed because of the ways in which it is shaped and generated in the now through coevalness—between remembrance, fear, and hope—enables us to foreground figures of the everyday such as mourning (Das 2007), shame, humiliation, and hope (Sider 1993) in processes of reparation without striving to fix these in forms such as signs, imaginaries, or subjectivities that lie beyond the everyday and mundane. It is in this way that the figures of inordinate knowledge, as illustrated in Santiago's statement, work both with and against the grain of psychosocial reparation projects.

Projects of community-based psychosocial reparation have been and continue to be implemented in a variety of postconflict settings in South and Central America and beyond. When approaching such interventions, I suggest we distinguish between three subtypes. First, psychosocial accompaniment, a strategy developed in Latin America, builds on principles associated with Freire's dialogical conscientization-problematization (Freire 1970) and Martín-Baró's reflection-action (Martín-Baró 1986) paradigms. As a pragmatic methodology, it proceeds by questioning the harm (e.g., disappeared relatives) and desired outcome (e.g., reburial) of a given community, group, or organization while simultaneously supporting the community in the attainment of these goals. A second form of community-based intervention sees communities as therapeutic tools. Here, group dynamics build a climate of support and promote proactive and constructive resources that prompt an emotional catharsis through the sharing of and listening to personal and collective testimonies of suffering, loss, and grief (e.g., torture in prison) and current fears and worries (e.g., lack of livelihood). At the group's initiative, the focus will shift from the therapeutic to psychosocial recovery by devoting efforts to community-based action (e.g., struggle for economic reparation). Finally, there is community-based psychosocial reparation in which an NGO, or nongovernmental organization (the "implementing organization") recruits or mobilizes community members ("beneficiaries"), individually or in groups, to participate in reflections and activities that support individual- and group-based witnessing and acknowledging of loss, communal healing, and truth telling. It is this third type of intervention that I explore in this chapter.

Each of these three models of intervention inevitably unfolds in linear temporality; they open with preliminary encounters where participants (staff/therapists and survivors/beneficiaries) seek to identify and cocreate a meaningful space of work. Next, the therapeutic, learning, or other types of reflexive action are undertaken in either individual or group format, and, finally, as educators, therapists, or memory workers withdraw, the interventions close in a scripted, ritualized way (Asad 1993) with the intention that the spaces—and the emotions, feelings, interpretations, and actions they contain—will continue to be cared for and developed by their new residents the survivors.

The returns of emotions, experiences, memories, and dreams, figures of inordinate knowledge that emerge in the reparative processes, are nested not only in this new space but likewise in the everyday lives of persons and communities, in ways that raise questions not only about the past but also about hopes for the future. I follow a methodology that brings these subjunctive figures to the fore in an emergent space of anthropological knowledge and explores how they are interpellated and produced in the transactional spaces of psychosocial work in ways that involve not only the survivors and therapists but also the anthropologist. This way, I believe we can overcome an "impulse to generate two orders of description in which one is the order of everyday life . . . and the second, the apparatus of law, medicine, social work, police and bureaucracy" (Das 2020, 245). To achieve this, I share both ethnographic descriptions and autobiographic reflections about what, following my interlocutors, I refer to as the "tragedy," as these have emerged during my many times in Alchuapa,[6] and from there engage with some of the key outcomes of the intervention. What I hope to show is that while some everyday figures of war and violence as past events, with specific memory effects, align well with the temporal linearity of a psychosocial intervention, other figures of knowledge and memory that are braided into everyday life in conversations and dreams are far more difficult to situate within the temporal linearity of an intervention of this nature. Nonetheless, it is important not to see this incommensurability as a failure, as a lack of closure. Psychosocial interventions, often small and time bound, cannot be expected to undo centuries of racism and violence. I therefore conclude on a cautionary note for anthropologists and other practitioners, to hope for only what is possible given the linearity laid out by a reparation project. Indeed, undoing the rhythms of everyday life and the knowledge of how to live with and through loss and pain that enables such life to endure is beyond the reach of such projects, the experts of this art being those who live it daily.

Testimony, Therapy, and Temporality in Central America

For people (re)living mass violence, civil warfare, and genocide, memories of these events and the ways in which they manifest in their bodies become the very form in which the "I" returns as a question. To explore these returns is to explore *how* questions that shape people's becomings and their projects emerge: "How do I return to the world when my four sons have been killed?" "How do I return to the world when the child I was carrying in my arms died, because his small body absorbed the shrapnel destined for me?" "And how might my now crippled arm return to the world and right my wrongs?"

Such (re)living is not memory in abstract forms related to time, symptoms, or narrative but memory from the perspective of the subject caught within the everyday (Das 2007). As suggested in the opening of this chapter, such returns come in familiar and recognizable figures, as that of a family being killed in 1996, resonant of the killings that took place in Alchuapa in the early 1980s.[7] This is what I mean by memory caught in the everyday. It is the remembering situated in forms of daily life. Such a view contrasts with much of the work on memory related to Central American mass violence of the twentieth century, which takes narrative memory as its point of departure (Falla 1992; Hale 1997; Sanford 1999; Stoll 1999), framing narratives in relation to issues of representation, politics, and position.

In order to understand the role of narratives in Central America, it is useful to explore the history of the genre of the *testimonio*,[8] which emerged during the late 1960s. With ethnographic roots, the *testimonio* is a narrative, often written in the first person, by an informed outsider on the basis of interviews with a subaltern subject. It produces an autobiographical narrative that unfolds in linear temporality with violence, resistance, suffering, and personal growth marking the progress of time. During the 1970s and 1980s, its use grew not only in Latin America but in North America and Western Europe as well, with Rigoberta Menchú, an Indigenous rights activist who used the *testimonio* style in her writing, receiving the Nobel Peace Prize for her work in 1992.

In her intriguing exegesis of this genre in the context of postconflict Guatemala, McAllister (2013) argues that by exploring the notion of *conciencia* (the transformation of ego) and how this interpellates the audience, we are able to distinguish between what she denotes as the "revolutionary" and the "therapeutic" subgenres of *testimonios*. Revolutionary texts are "romantic," as they move "in the direction of an end already in some sense known in advance" (Scott 2004, 70), while the "therapeutic paradigm" is defined by "secular acts of confession and witnessing [that] liberate [us/ego] from the past's weight on our present, orienting us towards a future in which we can finally 'free the self we truly are'" (Rose 1996, 97, as cited in McAllister 2013, 95). According to McAllister, the "therapeutic genre" becomes "humanitarian" as it is scaled up from individual to collective psyches (Fassin and Rechtman 2009), leaving anthropologists working in these contexts to question, "How can we produce accounts of the violence our interlocutors have suffered without simply becoming a cog in the humanitarian apparatus ourselves?" (McAllister 2013, 95).[9] I recognize in McAllister's question an echo of what Badiou (2002) identified as the split between the "victim-Man" and the "good-Man," but I extract a different lesson about the possibilities and conditions for producing anthropological knowledge from Fassin and Rechtman (2009) than she does.

McAllister argues that the humanitarian ethnographer is an "imperfect witness" of the narrated trauma and, together with the narrator—who, following Badiou, is by implication therefore a victim—is drawn "into the fraught space humanitarianism describes" (McAllister 2013, 101). However, I would argue that this space is fraught irrespective of humanitarianism. As we imperfectly bear witness (Levi 1988) to torturous ruptures of everyday life and the arrivals and returns of death and terror with it, we are allowed to touch figures of enduring mass violence, racism, and poverty that are folded and deposited into the crevasses of the everyday and, in a limited sense, share some of the burden borne by the other.

This chapter argues for generating this kind of anthropological knowledge, from the entangled and confused everyday transactions where figures emerge, return, and circulate within specific forms of life, as Santiago expressed that evening in front of the TV when he exclaimed, "They are killing families again!" Hence I read Fassin and Rechtman's critique of humanitarianism not as a call for disengagement but rather as an argument for critical engagement with humanitarian assemblages and the forms of knowledge through which they are reproduced.

From this follows my proposition that if we begin to bear witness to such figures of the everyday, we can account for the forms of inordinate knowledge that are emergent in the everyday of abandonment, marginalization, and enduring violence (Das 2020), at which point the subject of anthropological knowledge emerges not as a stable point of departure but as dispersed subjunctivities (Whyte 2002). As we explore the return of war and terror in experiences of the everyday, we need to address the incommensurability of psychosocial projects and everyday temporalities. This is not because temporality explains everything that goes on in such meetings but because it highlights the divergence between project rationales and the lived experiences of the people they are aimed at. Thus, by paying attention to the incommensurabilities, we can better understand the ways in which the "tragedies" in countless communities of Central America and beyond are folded into the flow of the everyday and how psychosocial interventions relate to this kind of "fraught" or "poisonous" knowledge when performed in such settings.

Through these encounters, survivor-subjects and practitioner-scholars can come to shared understandings of how the flows of the everyday and violent events overlap, helping ethnographers grasp the pain at their intersection[10] by engaging with the "tragedy" of Alchuapa through the contrasting lenses of the performative and the everyday. In this chapter, I therefore share a series of ethnographic moments that reveal how enduring mass violence continuously shapes what we know about the world and how we know it.

The chapter opens with a brief description of my state of mind, presented as not only personal but also reflective of men in the village from my own generation, as it developed during an intense working relationship with survivors. It then examines the contours of the "tragedy" and its impact on the lives of survivors, with a specific emphasis on those widowed during the war. Following this, the discussion unpacks how this condition continued to resonate within village spaces fifteen and twenty-five years later, manifested both through the repetition of past violence and through acts of protection and resistance. The narrative then shifts to a detailed account of the psychosocial intervention, tracing its progression from inception to closure, along with the subsequent sense of disappointment with its outcomes. The chapter concludes with an exploration of village peers, focusing on a particular person named Pato. I argue that his disjointed and conflicting forms of memory, as he shared them with me over a period of a year, aptly serve as a metaphor for memory in Alchuapa's Indigenous community—a temporal mélange of repetition and difference.

Returning to Alchuapa, October 2012

Naldo is looking at me, his eyes brimming with tears. From the smell of his breath, I know he is struggling with the aftermath of another bout of heavy drinking, but I am also aware of his fragility more than ever. Since our first encounter almost two decades ago, I have sensed this fragility. Despite his physical strength, evidenced by sheer muscle volume, I constantly fear that he will break under the weight he seems to be carrying. His face is now more bruised than it was just a year ago, when I was last here, and I reckon it must have absorbed more falls, more punches, more punishment. A crescent-shaped, dark-blue scar has appeared below his left eye. His nose seems more broken, but its bridge still rises defiantly above his arching cheekbones. I always feel the need to protect him, yet I am aware that the simplicity inherent in the notion of protection belies the complexities of his victimhood (Jensen and Ronsbo 2014). He is also a soldier. He served in the Atlacatl Battalion during the latter part of the Salvadoran civil war, and of this, he is proud.

This time I am back in the village to organize the Historical Memory and Psycho-Social Healing project with the broad aims of "implementing psychosocial healing and support[ing] the creation and dissemination of an inclusive historical memory that may dignify the relatives of the victims of mass violence and forced disappearances," focusing in particular on the massacre perpetrated by the army on February 26, 1980 (DIGNITY 2015).

But Naldo's victimhood and emotional fragility are not all there is. Over the years, I have come to know that there is also rage when he drinks, there is conversational skill when we eat pupusas together, and most of all, there is his ignorance. Not the ignorance of an *indio ignorante*, a derogatory term commonly used by non-Indigenous residents of Alchuapa to refer to members of the Indigenous community, but the ignorance he must claim or fight for in order to make life bearable in the face of chronic poverty, violence, and racism. Ignorance as in his response when I asked him in 2008, "What happened to Conejo?" Conejo was the goalkeeper on our football team. He had an astonishing ability and could leap from standing flat on his feet on the goal line to a vertical position, suspended in the air just below the crossbar. Naldo answered, "One morning they came and told me he had been killed! He was lying in a ditch at the entrance to the village. He was shot, his ears cut off, and all beaten up." "But why?" I probed. "Andaba chingando, siempre andaba bolo, a la gente no le gustaba" (He was always fucking around, always drunk; people did not like him). "But who shot him then?" I asked. "¿A saber . . . a saber?" (Who knows . . . who knows?). Ignorance requires work and effort; it is an active process in which experiences, memories, and narratives are actively selected, worked on, and performed; ignorance and unknowing are crucial attributes of this form of life.

This sense of willed ignorance also surrounded the killing of my old field assistant and friend, Diablo. During a conversation with Diablo's uncle Raul (his mother's brother) regarding his death, from her position behind the *pila* (water container and washing table used widely in Central America), Raul's wife, Celia, subtly remarked, "El se fue temprano" (He left early). Diablo was one of my closest friends, and with his high school degree, he was a skilled field assistant. He was born in 1975 in Santiago de María in Eastern El Salvador. When his mother died in 1982, Diablo's father moved in with a new woman, and Diablo was sent back to Alchuapa, his mother's native village, to live with her kin. There he joined his aunt Ilsa's household, next to Raul and Celia's. Ilsa was an independent and single woman (*soltera*) with only one son at the time, though three more children would later come. At the age of fourteen, following continuous conflicts with his two male cousins, Diablo was expelled from the household. He moved in with another of his mother's sisters, along with her husband, in the village where I met him in 1995. Diablo always claimed he was too smart to join any of the factions in the village, yet like Conejo, he "left early." He was gunned down just after sunset by a group of masked men as he walked home to our compound outside the village, where he had moved in with another one of his uncles after spending almost ten years in Seattle.

As with Conejo, everybody claimed ignorance about why Diablo was killed and who killed him. Silence surrounded both of these killings, alongside references to personality and transgressive behavior: "Hablaba mucho de la verdad" (He spoke the truth too often), his uncle said one day when we talked about Diablo, "pero mucho de mentira tambien" (but also a lot of lies). This was not far off the mark. Diablo had a complicated relationship with many of his family members and neighbors, me included.[11] However, what is notable here is that there were no public stories accompanying the deaths of both Diablo and Conejo. No narratives of male conflict over women or property, as was the case in numerous other instances. There seemed to be only a void. This form of public secrecy is one of the most valuable forms of social knowledge, "sensitive to . . . the sensory impressions of social relations" (Taussig 1986, 464)—it is the knowing of what not to know.

The transience of human life and the willed ignorance that accompanies it struck me a few days earlier. I was sitting on the porch with Raul and Celia, the river rushing by just seventy-five meters away, brown from the silt brought down from the volcanoes. It was hot and humid, and it had not rained for a day and a night. It was time to cut coco, Raul decided, since "the stem is dry so you can crawl on it." I was having my second coco, and it was fresh (*tierno*), with a twist of salt. Celia was humming around on the porch, stoking the fire that had been burning all morning under the corn and beans. Raul was taking down a third large branch of coco, so we now had over thirty of them. Daniel, an eleven-year-old grandchild of Ilsa's, came around after having been down by the river and said, "I heard they murdered a woman yesterday." "Yes," Celia replied, "and just because she saw them killing somebody else." In fact, two women had been killed just one kilometer south of the village, and the day before that, a man had been killed just a few minutes' walk to the east.

I had returned to the village to prepare for the arrival of the project team of two psychologists from Guatemala, two anthropologists from El Salvador, and a coordinator from CDHES. In retrospect, I can see that sitting on that porch, I felt scared like I had never been before. Diablo, whom I knew personally, had been recently killed. And then, in the week prior to my arrival, in a municipality of approximately seven thousand, three others had been killed by unknown assailants.

My anxiety was so high that I thought it was visible to everyone. For several days, I could not sleep, and when a tropical storm hit western El Salvador, bringing such heavy rains that water started to seep through the walls of the house I had rented, I woke from nightmares of being buried beneath earth and rubble coming down the hillside against which the house was leaning. My notes from those days belie my emotional state. I tried to persuade myself that the hillside was stable. "It has been there for centuries," I wrote in my diary to calm myself. Yet I fled and relocated to Celia and Raul's compound, to their porch and the intimate conversations that both kept my mind at ease and simultaneously triggered my fear. Looking back today, I know it was not really a concern about the water seeping through the walls of the house. It was the killings. I was there to start a social memory and psychosocial healing project, and yet the killings were ongoing. In her work with widows in the Guatemalan Highlands, Green (1999) reflects on similar experiences of fear and how she came to "realize that terror's power, its matter-of-factness, is exactly about doubting one's own perception of reality" (60) while, I would add, simultaneously making the unknown return to you as figures of inordinate knowledge in dreams and casual exchanges of gossip and news in everyday life.

Most of the villagers linked, in some general sense, the three killings in the week prior to my arrival to the *maras* and their conflicts with the police. In my field notes, I rhetorically ask myself, "How could I ever become involved and be at risk?" Apart from a rented car, a company laptop, a wristwatch, and a worn silver ring, I possessed nothing of value to them. Yet my response was to leave my home, seeking out the compound of Raul and Celia. These were people I could relate to, a woman at the stove to talk with, a friend with whom to watch football, do some gardening, and go down to the river to take a bath in the late afternoon when the heat subsided. This everyday life on the outskirts of the village aroused an ambivalent feeling of, on the one hand, knowing the intricate relationships and conflicts between Raul's kin in Seattle and Ilsa's daughters but, on the other hand, also knowing not to know who the masked men that killed Diablo were and, by extension, not reflecting on how violence, race, property, and poverty shape lives and futures. I was disoriented, and I stopped visiting the village in the evenings, as so many other neighbors had done.

While setting out to organize the psychosocial, social memory project with its distinctly linear GANT-chart and log-frame organized phases of activities, I began to realize that the heightened sense of unsettledness that followed me during my work was part of the psychic reality of the village as much as it was part of my own and that this psychic reality forms a part of the inordinate knowledge that is crucial to reflect upon in anthropology. In the subsequent pages, I would like to explore this theme in greater depth.

When the "Tragedy" Started, Alchuapa, February 26, 1980

"It was around five o'clock in the morning when the tragedy started . . . and afterward, well around eight, or maybe nine, we collected the dead boys." This is how Gonifasia, her daughter, and her grandson's wife begin their story when they share it with me during our conversation in early 1996 in Alchuapa. Gonifasia lost four sons and her husband on that day. Her daughter continues, "They tortured them, because [my husband] came tortured, all beaten up, or rather when I found him, he was all beaten up, all beaten up, and after they had beaten him up, they shot him, because he had five bullet holes and after those five shots he died."

On February 26, 1980, army units from two military bases, with assistance from the National Police, the National Guard, and the Police of Tax and Revenues, traveled along the Pacific Highway and arrived at the Cerro Partido to the south of the village. From here they fanned out to surround the village, posting infantry units with mortars on the hillcrests surrounding the village to the east and west and then closing the perimeter at the banks of the river by the northern exit toward the volcanic highlands. At sunbreak they moved in from all sides. As they advanced, they were met by a group of men armed with hand-guns. The resistance was easily broken, and army units assisted by members of the local civil patrol then went from house to house, identifying the remaining *subversivos*.

By late morning, twenty-six men had been killed. They were all members of Alchuapa's Indigenous community and had all participated in the local agri-cultural cooperative that farmed the Indigenous community's lands with agricul-tural credit and spiritual support from the Diocese of the Catholic Church in Sonsonate. Many of them most likely also participated in the popular move-ment LP-28 (Ligas Populares 28 de febrero), and some no doubt took part in the clandestine military-political structure (party) ERP (Ejército Revolucion-ario del Pueblo), organizing late-night shooting practices on the outskirts of the village as well as participating in the regional party organization's military buildup.

The "tragedy" took place as El Salvador was shaken by a profound social con-flict that culminated in the killing of Archbishop Romero a month later. On one side was a popular movement made up of organizations of agroindustrial labor-ers, peasants, students, the industrial working class, elements of the catholic clergy, and sectors of the middle class that pushed for a democratic revolution with labor rights and an agrarian reform mimicking the transition underway in Nicaragua. On the other was an agroexport sector in coffee, cotton, and sugar cane and a financial elite, tied together and supported by multiple internal secu-rity agencies, conservative clergy, and a large U.S.-backed army.

As young men from rural settlements such as Alchuapa joined—relatives would later use the term "were conquered by" (*conquistados*)—the revolution-ary organizations, violent forms of political action had begun to emerge. In December 1979, a small group of men from the village launched an attack on a coffee finca in a neighboring municipality where villagers had worked harvest-ing coffee since the early twentieth century. The plan had been to kill a despised labor supervisor (*caporal*), but for reasons unknown, the attack went wrong, and in the ensuing shootout, one of the assailants was wounded and arrested. In the subsequent weeks, several men from the village were taken (*sacados*) by the army, tortured, killed, and left on display on the sides of the dirt roads that crisscross the countryside. Then came the "tragedy" on the 26th of February 1980, and during the following three years, approximately sixty more individu-als were taken and killed by the army, the police, the civil patrol, and the death squad, referred to as the "White Hand" (Mano Blanco), alluding to 1932 and the history of genocidal mass violence in the region. All but one of those taken were male, and around 80 percent were members of the Indigenous community living in the upper barrio. By the end of the war, the majority of the men from Alchuapa's Indigenous community born before the mid-1960s had been killed, had disappeared, or had fled the region.

The "tragedy" and the targeted killings that followed sparked a wider change in the relationships within the village. The women, now without male partners, lost access to important resources for their livelihoods: the milpas the men had controlled through complex transactional tenancy relations; the harvests these generated in corn, beans, and sorghum, key food items in their diets; the small but important amounts of income men generated through day labor; and the clay, sand, and firewood used in the production of earthenware, the primary economic activity among female community members.

One woman from the community said, "We were left with only our kids, struggling, because we were left alone and some laughed at us, because many people at seeing us in this situation laughed at us, content with seeing us in this condition." This "condition" left the widowed women with their children hauling firewood, mining clay, collecting sand in the river, and being targets of ridicule, sexual harassment, and assault from neighbors, soldiers, and patrol members in the village.

Dancing with Devils, Alchuapa, December 26, 1995

Fifteen years later, the "condition" reemerged as young men from the Ladino landowning families in the lower barrio of Alchuapa mockingly reenacted this period. They had organized a procession known as "Las viejas disfrazadas" (The disguised old women), where participants would dress as old Indigenous women to ridicule male authorities. However, this year they were dressed not only as Indigenous women in *cortes* (an Indigenous style skirt) but also as civil patrol members in military fatigues and devils in red costumes. As they moved through the village, accompanied by the booming of techno cumbia from a large sound system on the bed of a pickup truck, followed by the rowdy crowd of men from the lower barrio and the neighboring cantones, these figures cheered, shared drinks, and danced with each other.

As they moved forward from house to house, the crowd and the dancers filled the entire street. Members of households in the lower barrio gathered in their doorways, waiting for the spectacle to arrive. In front of each house, the procession made a stop, and the leader of the procession—the Ladino landholder, cattle rancher, and politician—solicited a contribution of ten *colones* from the male head of the household to buy liquor for the dancers. When the contribution had been made, three dances were performed, during at least one of which the men of the household were grabbed by the crowd and forced to dance with one or more of the performers dressed up as Indigenous women, cheered on by devils and patrol members, while the female relatives laughed, giggled, covered their faces, and pointed fingers at the spectacle. Cane liquor was shared among dancers and the men as the procession moved on to the next house.

An intricate field of knowledge was shared and enacted when male heads of households accepted the invitation to engage with the dancers dressed as Indigenous women. The female members of Ladino households may have laughed at the humiliation of their own men, but even more so, they seemed to laugh at the humiliation of the Indigenous woman, surrounded by, vulnerable to, and unprotected from Ladino men and patrol members following the "tragedy." But they did so while also having to acknowledge that men in their households had engaged in sexual relations with and assaults on these women and, in some cases, had fathered their children. At the same time, male household members knew they had to demonstrate decency and moral standing (most were members of evangelical churches) by pretending to evade the invitations while also knowing that they had to eventually give in, it being expected of them as men. However, each household's particular history had to be considered in order to determine which man would be asked to dance. This required intimate knowledge of the individual household members, their stories, and their wider networks of relations in the village. Thus, the duplicity of decency and denial was enacted in full view of the community through the return of wartime relations between poor Indigenous women and non-Indigenous male property owners.

This poisonous knowledge, sensitive to relations and biographies, was accentuated by the complete covering and hooding of the dancers. Not only did they wear costumes, but underneath they wore long sleeves, gloves, masks, hats, and wigs to hide tattoos, faces, and haircuts—any mark of individuality among these young men. As Gerald Sider (1986) reminds us, in small face-to-face communities, even hands (and necks, I might add) have individuality, as many of the young men had tattoos related to their military service. There is no doubt that the young men did everything they could to remain unidentifiable, even to their neighbors.

Village space, as the setting in which communal relationships are shaped, is in a constant state of emergence and emergency, with fragments of traumatic experiences being continually repeated yet in slightly different ways each time. Relatives and friends of people killed or disappeared were forced to engage in the repetition of the "tragedy" and the "condition" time and again, which led them to suffer *sustos*, unable to leave their houses, "all sad, with no wish to walk and talk." Yet each time such returns of violence emerge in Alchuapa, I am reminded that, though always different, these returns elicit a truth not in the act itself but in its continued repetition. On December 26, as the procession crossed the small creek that marks the boundary between the mostly Ladino lower barrio and the mostly Indigenous upper barrio, the streets of the entire barrio were deserted, and all doors and shutters were closed. The procession passed through the barrio without making a stop, and thus, there was no return of the "condition" but an eerie sense of the return of the "tragedy."

The Diorama Session, Alchuapa, October 19, 2012

The two Guatemalan psychologists who managed the workshop I participated in had worked together for almost a decade. Together they had organized psychosocial projects in numerous Guatemalan communities. I got to know them through a research project on psychosocial interventions in Guatemala (Ronsbo and Paniagua 2014), and I had managed to persuade them to replicate their methodology in Alchuapa. The process of the psychosocial project is fairly simple, as it goes through the following stages: (1) identification and initial briefing of the group of participants, (2) an opening group session where participants create a diorama or 3D model of the site of an event (see figure 2.1.), and (3) subsequent group sessions in which the affects and emotions generated in the diorama session are reflected upon and processed by the group, with some cases being assigned to individual therapy, based on a clinical assessment made on the basis of an individual interview. The diorama session thus seeks to achieve a variety of objectives simultaneously, including exposure to the original event and the immediate shock and pain it releases, taking ownership of one's personal story of loss and pain, sharing it through narration to peers so as to achieve mirroring and mutual acknowledgment, weaving the threads of a communal narrative of suffering, and laying the foundations for collective healing and in some cases legal action.

Phase 1: The male psychologist explains that he wants the participants to re-create the village as it was before the army attacked. Streets are marked with stripes of sand, and small model houses made for the purpose are placed in the diorama, which quickly covers more than ten square meters. Each participant begins to rebuild his or her lifeworld, compounds complete with animals, family members, livestock, utensils, and earthenware. As the older women move about building the village as it looked before the "tragedy," they joke with each other, provide minor corrections, and discuss who lived where and when. "Was it a *casa de paja* [cane house] or *casa de adobe* [clay house]?" The therapists facilitate the work, engaging participants in brief question-and-answer sessions, getting to know each participant better while observing elements of individual and group behaviors and interactions. Slowly the village in which these women lived more than thirty years ago emerges from the floor, complete with streets, homes, people, earthenware, and livestock.

Phase 2: The male psychologist introduces the figures of the soldiers—model soldiers of U.S. Army infantry with uniforms eerily similar to the ones used by the Salvadoran armed forces during the civil war. Participants are asked to place these soldiers where they carried out the attack on the village. The work becomes more serious in this phase and the tone more somber. But still the mode is dialogical, with different voices weaving in and out and decisions being made by the women together. The psychologist continues to question participants, asking them to be specific (in some cases in Guatemala, witnesses to gross

FIG. 2.1 Participant in the diorama session setting up figures. *Source:* Henrik Ronsbo.

human rights violations have been identified through these processes) and to explain how many soldiers there were, what arms they carried, and what units they came from. In the meantime, the female psychologist works the floor, inserting herself in the groups and partaking in the conarration. As a layer of perpetrators is added to the diorama, new details are identified, amplified, or added.

Phase 3: The male psychologist now takes out the box with figures that were used previously as family members and asks the first participant to take a number of figures with attributes that correspond to the family members she lost, hold them in her hand, and tell the group who they are. Voices crack, a woman covers her mouth, and one woman holds her face in her hands as she takes a long break, sobbing. The participant is asked to place the figures in the diorama at the location where their bodies were found and to tell the other participants the story of the search, the conditions of the body, and what happened next. These are deeply emotional stories, with a high level of exposure for each of the participants. The female psychologist moves around handing out Kleenex and bags with *atol* (a sweet corn drink, as sessions such as these consume high levels of carbohydrates) and provides support through affective body contact and soothing vocalization (calm voice) in order to lower the levels of stress hormones while the women in the group comfort each other as they take turns as narrators on the floor. Finally, they are able to sit down in the white plastic chairs that seem to accompany community work globally.

Phase 4: The male psychologist now moves the session toward closure, through a mix of psychoeducational content on trauma and recuperation, by drawing out commonalities in the expressions, narratives, and body language of the participants. Both psychologists then thank each participant individually and embrace them. With that, the day's session is over.

The entire session was recorded by a cameraman and his assistant. The Salvadoran anthropologists and I remained off-stage as the workshop unfolded, unable to contribute and unable to leave. The following week, a second diorama session was conducted with men, at which time I had left Alchuapa.

Following the diorama session, five group sessions were conducted in the two diorama groups. In this period, the two Salvadoran anthropologists (the senior with prior field experience in Alchuapa) collected life stories and other narratives more systematically, which were used in the writing of a booklet on the social history of Alchuapa, distributed among the participants and other villagers. Based on the recordings, a documentary was produced by a team from Universidad Centroamericana José Simeón Cañas (UCA).

Screening of the documentary took place on February 26, 2013, the thirty-third anniversary of the "tragedy." The afternoon was dedicated to a public ceremony in the upper barrio in which the "martyrs" were commemorated, the regional chairman of the Farabundo Martí National Liberation Front (FMLN) and the local FMLN candidate for mayor spoke, and two folkloric presentations were given, one of which was in Nahuat. This was the first time the "tragedy" was officially commemorated in public, and it was only the second time I had ever heard the events referenced as the "tragedy" in public. The podium was framed by two large cardboard trees with leaves carrying the names of all eighty-six people killed, and the bodega of the agricultural cooperative still rooted in the communal property of the Indigenous community was open. Most of the male members used this occasion to receive their receipts for the sale of the year's corn harvest. It was a scene of men celebrating masculine values of combat while their female kin filled the benches in front.

In the evening, when most of the participants had left (around 250 in total), a smaller group composed mostly of the diorama session participants and their family members stayed behind to watch the first screening of the documentary. This took place in the bodega, with around forty people present. We sat on benches and plastic chairs, with the doors and shutters tightly closed and an immense heat inside. When the screening was over, a local male teacher in his forties questioned the neighbors who appeared in the documentary, asking, "Why are you still afraid?" While in the darkness of the room, his own pitch fell to almost inaudible, as silence ensued. The eerie resonance between this scene, the scenes surrounding the procession I witnessed in 1995, and the narratives of the years of the "tragedy" when *patrulleros* roamed the street attests to the ways in which "the theatre . . . [was] multiplied, polyscenic, simultaneous, broken into separate scenes that refer to each other, and where [they] encounter without any trace of representation (copying or imitating), the dance of masks, the cries of bodies and the gesturing of hands and fingers" (Foucault 1977, 171). This is how I suggest we understand the notion of figures of inordinate knowledge.

Later, standing outside after a long and tense day, people chatted in small groups. The full moon was rising above the village, neighbors were saying good-bye to each other, and a small woman in her late sixties came up to me. I know her but did not recall ever having interviewed her, but she held me around my waist and arms and said, "Gracias, Don Henrique!" As I held her to me, feeling her bony shoulders, I saw her two remaining teeth sparkling through her smile.

A year later, the project was evaluated by a Guatemalan psychologist with the key conclusion that while most participants reported that they had benefited from the intervention personally and that they were proud of what they had achieved in preserving the history for the "jovenes de la communidad" (young members of the community), they had also hoped it would attract more atten-tion, generate other forms of assistance, and last longer.

Pato, Alchuapa, February 2012

One evening in 2012, I was having tacos, pupusas, and coffee with Pato; his brother, Naldo; and some other middle-aged men. Most of these men I had met for the first time during the Fiestas Patronales in late August 1995, when we made *globos* (glued paper globes that rise from the heat generated by a can-dle) together in the *casa de cultura* (house of culture and small library). It was a group I came close to after joining their football team, "Las Vegas," in March 1996 (Ronsbo 2003). Men from this generation, born in the second half of the 1960s and the early 1970s, had all been too young to be targeted in the early 1980s and later served as professional soldiers in the combat units of the Salva-doran Army. They were all coerced into service while at the same time realizing that, having lost their fathers, uncles, and older brothers during the "tragedy," their wages, pensions, or compensation if they were killed or wounded would make a substantial contribution to their families' survival. They scared me tremendously back then and at times still do. I know that violence nests in a domain of tacit knowledge they share and that one single mistake can unleash a sudden and brutal response. Both despite and because of the many years we have known each other, I can never put this sensation to rest.

On that evening, they suddenly began sharing stories about nocturnal female bodies, some coming apart, others luring men to transcend the boundaries between the living and the dead, serpents living in caves, and stories of conju-gal betrayal and brothers cheating brothers, stories told in dialogical mode with strong Mesoamerican themes and narrative structure (Campbell 1985; Schultze Jena 1935). Such storytelling is a way of sharing knowledge about the unknow-able. "Show composure [*compostura*]!" Pato warned us, "If you meet a little crea-ture that sounds like a rattling skeleton but cannot be seen . . . then do not throw a stone; it will only multiply." Pato knew this because his father was a "great *brujo*" (sorcerer). But his father was dead, as one of those killed in the "tragedy." For this reason, Pato had joined the diorama project we conducted with the group of men, parallel to the one for women, described previously. Similar in structure but saturated by a tone of fight, struggle, belligerence, assault, bombs, and death. Pato participated, though intermittently and reluctantly.

His body, harnessed by his six years as a soldier and a life of hard physical labor, betrays his smiling brown eyes. He has a loud, coarse voice, with an unmistakable Salvadoran accent, so full of slang and jargon indexing his military background that at times I have to ask him to repeat himself. His voice cuts through the afternoon sounds of the village, teasing and joking with women, enticing me or other men to join whatever pastime venture he is planning: drinking beers, going to the football pitch to place bets on the teams, eating pupusas, going to the beach, or hiking around the caves and waterfalls in the hinterland of the village. He has a restless energy, never stable for long, constantly announcing itself through the motion of his right leg, jerking and jolting whenever he sits down.

Pato is a carpenter, bricklayer, ex-soldier, husband, father, brother, and son. During the project period, from 2012 to 2013, I spent more time with him than I ever had before. To me he is singular; he does not represent others—not Diablo, not Naldo, not even his own brother. He does not even, as I seek to convey, represent himself. He is literally in constant motion, doubling back upon himself and his memories, re-creating difference in every move he makes. He once summarized his account of the "tragedy" with this short statement: "Well, here nothing really happened; well, they killed my four uncles on my mother's side and my father and his two brothers, but nothing really happened."

Earlier, during a group meeting, as Pato talked about the effects the massacre had on his family and the number of deaths they sustained, his eyes switched imperceptibly between slightly twinkling and searching among the group session participants for affirmation and acknowledgment. One corner of his mouth pulled upward, smirking, perhaps only so much as he needed for me and other participants to be skeptical about his presence within and ownership of what he was saying. On other occasions, he lamented the loss of his father yet blamed it on his uncles, who he felt no doubt had participated in the military-political organization—a legitimate reason, he concluded on numerous occasions, for them to be killed: "They wanted to take what was not theirs, but my father was not like that." And continuing in a commonsense tone, with his upper body swaying back and forth, his legs constantly moving, he held back his breath, exhaled strongly, and declared, "My father was cheated."

As we broke up the group work at one point to have soft drinks and cake, the two of us moved to the side, and Pato told me a story about a Black female combatant (*negrita combatiente*) he once shot. His voice was soft as he tried to conjure up for me the image of a young woman who, in her Blackness, looked so different from anyone he had ever seen and who most likely died at his hand. She had a cross on a chain lying across her breast. Was there in his voice a recognition of her bravery? Did his need for reconciliation extend beyond the confines of the village, to the many places he had been on duty, places where "something really happened"? I think the answer lies in the dreams Pato shared with me. In one of these, he is back serving in the military, wearing the uniform, on patrol with his old squad, but the places they are moving through are different from the usual ones. It is eerily quiet; nothing is happening, and people leave the street when he asks them to. But then in another very similar dream he has had several times, people shout at his patrol, a man steps up to challenge him, Pato shoots him in the stomach, and as people are fleeing, he shouts, "Is this how you like it to be? Is this what you want?"

Conclusions

The various ways in which Pato and my other interlocutors describe their lives through violence, war, the "condition," and the "tragedy" have brought into focus the notion of the figure. Short statements, performances, dreams, myth-like narratives, and memories—these figures all bear witness to a form of life shaped by racism, poverty, violence, and warfare. In them, there is an acknowledgment of not only the pain that has passed but also the pain that can be expected; that is, they are prognostic rather than retrospective or diagnostic. If you throw stones at skeletons, they multiply and come after you; if you covet another's property, you will die. These are subjunctive, voicing the need for reparation, as when Pato ruminated over the dead *combatiente* and when he recounts the dream of being listened to and respected when soldiering among civilians. He asks me to bear witness to all these figures.

We also see moments in time captured through expressions, in the twisted returns of the "condition" of the 1980s, in the mocking reenactment carried out in 1995 and the closure of the upper barrio with which the procession was met, and once again in 2013 at the enclosed and secretive screening of the documentary. These figures of inordinate knowledge express how to protect oneself and survive when inhabiting a life shaped by violence, poverty, and racism. And all of this in a reality seized by the everyday terror of neighbors, kin, and friends being killed, in ways and for reasons that we purposely unknow and keep ourselves *ignorante* about, only to see such knowledge return through dreams of disaster and *susto* attacks.

When we insert psychosocial reparations into such social spaces, what closure could we possibly hope for? In the case of Alchuapa, at least on one occasion, the knowledge and histories surrounding the "tragedy" were brought out in the streets of the village and commemorated. Though voiced in the genre McAllister (2013) identified as a humanitarian testimonial, it was, for the participants in the event, a necessary return of the names of their kin and victims of state violence and the Amerindian language of the community to the village space without shame and ridicule.

Psychosocial reparations unfold in a linear temporality. In a world of donors, grants, and postconflict policy frameworks, this will remain a condition for such work in the foreseeable future. The literature on Central American mass violence in large measure reproduces such a template in which memory as an ex post social representation of violence or, as phrased by Diane Nelson, as "the construction of a new narrative that makes sense of past blows" (2009, 102).

What I suggest to add is a "reparation ethnography" that pays attention to lessons of learned ignorance and skepticism not only toward others but, as importantly, toward the self—as a means of exploring repetitions, returns, and polyscenic folds of past and present, in which gestures, masks, and images mimic, reproduce, and multiply without the traces of representation typically found in the linear narrative of the humanitarian assemblage. By paying attention to these figures of inordinate knowledge, we can contribute to reparation processes and outcomes with anthropological knowledge, generated together in autobiographical reflection with people as they work to repair and heal.

Notes

1   All place names and persons appearing in this chapter have been replaced with pseudonyms.
2   See the *tasaciones de tributos* of the Alcaldía Mayor de Sonsonate (Acuña 1982).
3   Information available at the Archivo General de Centro América, A1.24, Exp. 10206, Leg. 1562; A3, Exp. 40806, L. 2814.
4   Archivo Municipal de Alchuapa, Medidas de Ejidos de Alchuapa, 1870, Titulo no. 3, June 29, 1897.
5   DIGNITY is a Danish NGO with a specific mandate to work on the prevention of torture and violence and the rehabilitation of survivors. Founded in 1982 by former Danish members of Amnesty International Medical Group as the Rehabilitation and Research Centre for Torture Victims.
6   My fieldwork in Alchuapa is difficult to account for. Between July 1995 and the end of 2015, I completed sixteen to eighteen months of ethnographic fieldwork in total. It began with twelve months from July 1995 to August 1996. Then in 1998, I did two additional months of fieldwork. In 2003 and the following few years, I passed through on numerous occasions, and then in 2008, I returned for a full month with my family. In the years that followed, I paid several more visits, and then from 2012 to 2014, while undertaking the psychosocial project, I spent approximately two months in the village. From 2012 to 2013, my coresearcher was there on a weekly basis generating interview data and observations on social life in the village. I have not returned since 2015.
7   Based on genealogical data collected from survivors, of the eighty-five people killed, 80 percent belonged to eight extended families, all residing in the upper barrio of the village. Such extended families were and are based on an idiom of patrilineal descent, and the key targets of violence were groups of brothers as well as father-son pairings. This is the notion of family that Santiago referred to. A different sense in which the term *familias* is used is *familias de nombre*, which refers to families defined by their surname, being propertied families of Ladino descent.

8   According to Roque Dalton, the author of *Miguel Mármol* and one of the earliest practitioners of this genre, considerable inspiration was drawn from Oscar Lewis's work *Los hijos de Sánchez*, a basis for developing the genre Roque Dalton referred to as the "truth-novel" (Lindo-Fuentes, Ching, and Lara-Martínez 2007, 144).

9   I have argued that the emergence of this psychosocial assemblage in Guatemala must be understood against the background of rapidly increasing donor funds (input) and the need for assistance in exhumations (output). See figures 11.1 and 11.2 in Ronsbo (2015).

10 At this point it seems fitting to acknowledge the inspiration of and dedication to pursuing this line of reasoning from colleagues at DIGNITY—in particular, Lotte Segal, Nerina Weiss, and Helene Risør, one of the editors of this volume.

11 While I was away from Alchuapa for a two-week period in May 1996, Diablo stole my old Toyota Hilux and completely wrecked it. This type of deliberate harm and aggression toward close kin and friends always marred his life.

References

Acuña, René. 1982. *Relaciones geográficas del siglo XVI: Guatemala.* Mexico City: Universidad Nacional Autónoma de México.

Asad, Tala. 1993. *Genealogies of Religion: Discipline and Reasons of Power in Christianity and Islam.* Baltimore: Johns Hopkins University Press.

Badiou, Alain. 2002. *Ethics: An Essay on the Understanding of Evil.* London: Verso.

Campbell, Lyle. 1985. *The Pipil Language of El Salvador.* Berlin: Mouton.

Comisión de Derechos Humanos de El Salvador. 2017. "Masacre Las Hojas." YouTube. Accessed November 11, 2024. https://www.youtube.com/watch?v=mPW8kKOlGYQ.

Das, Veena. 2007. *Life and Words: Violence and the Descent into the Ordinary.* Berkeley: University of California Press.

Das, Veena. 2020. *Textures of the Ordinary: Doing Anthropology After Wittgenstein.* New York: Fordham University Press.

Falla, Ricardo. 1992. *Masacres de la selva: Ixcan, Guatemala 1975–1982.* Vol. 1. San Carlos: Editorial Universitaria.

Fassin, Didier, and Richard Rechtman. 2009. *The Empire of Trauma: An Inquiry into the Condition of Victimhood.* Princeton, N.J.: Princeton University Press.

Foucault, Michel. 1977. *Language, Counter-Memory, Practice: Selected Essays and Interviews.* Ithaca: Cornell University Press.

Fowler, William R. 1989. *The Cultural Evolution of Ancient Nahua Civilizations: The Pipil-Nicarao of Central America.* Norman: University of Oklahoma Press.

Freire, Paulo. 1970. *Pedagogy of the Oppressed.* New York: Herder and Herder.

Green, Linda. 1999. *Fear as a Way of Life: Mayan Widows in Rural Guatemala.* New York: Columbia University Press.

Hale, Charles R. 1997. "Consciousness, Violence, and the Politics of Memory in Guatemala." *Current Anthropology* 38 (5): 817–838.

Jensen, Steffen, and Henrik Ronsbo, eds. 2014. *Histories of Victimhood.* 1st ed. Philadelphia: University of Pennsylvania Press.

Levi, Primo. 1988. *The Drowned and the Saved.* New York: Summit Books.

Lindo-Fuentes, Héctor, Erik Ching, and Rafael Lara-Martínez. 2007. *Remembering a Massacre in El Salvador: The Insurrection of 1932, Roque Dalton, and the Politics of Historical Memory.* Albuquerque: University of New Mexico Press.

Martín-Baró, Ignacio. 1986. "Hacia una psicología de la liberación." *Boletín de Psicología* 22:219–231.

McAllister, Carlota. 2013. "Testimonial Truths and Revolutionary Mysteries." In *War by Other Means: Aftermath in Post-Genocide Guatemala*, edited by Diane M. Nelson, 153–177. Durham, N.C.: Duke University Press.

Moodie, Ellen. 2002. "'It's Worse Than the War': Telling Everyday Danger in Postwar El Salvador." PhD diss., University of Michigan.

Nelson, Diane M. 2009. *Reckoning: The Ends of War in Guatemala*. Durham, N.C.: Duke University Press.

Pupavac, Vanessa. 2001. "Therapeutic Governance: Psycho-Social Intervention and Trauma Risk Management." *Disasters* 25 (4): 358–372.

Ronsbo, Henrik. 1998. "State Formation and Property—Reflections on the Political Technologies of Space in Central America." *Journal of Historical Sociology* 10 (1): 56–73.

Ronsbo, Henrik. 2003. "The Embodiment of Male Identities: Alliances and Cleavages in Salvadorean Football." In *Sport, Dance and Embodied Identities*, edited by N. Dyck and E. P. Archetti, 173–194. Oxford, U.K.: Berg.

Ronsbo, Henrik. 2015. "A Republic of Remedies: Psychosocial Interventions in Post-Conflict Guatemala." In *The Clinic and the Court: Law, Medicine and Anthropology*, edited by Ian Tobias Kelly and Akshay Khanna, 265–295. Cambridge: Cambridge University Press.

Ronsbo, Henrik, and Walter Paniagua. 2014. "Between Recognition and Care: Victims, NGOs and the State in the Guatemalan Post-Conflict Victimhood Assemblage." In *Histories of Victimhood*, edited by H. Ronsbo and W. Paniagua, 124–143. Philadelphia: University of Pennsylvania Press.

Rose, Nikolas. S. 1996. *Inventing Our Selves: Psychology, Power, and Personhood*. Cambridge: Cambridge University Press.

Sanford, Victoria. 1999. "Between Rigoberta Menchú and La Violencia: Deconstructing David Stoll's History of Guatemala." *Latin American Perspectives* 26 (6): 38–46.

Schultze Jena, L. 1935. *Indiana II: Mythen in der Muttersprache der Pipil von Izalco in El Salvador*. Jena: Verlag von Gustav Fischer.

Scott, David. 2004. *Conscripts of Modernity: The Tragedy of Colonial Enlightenment*. Durham, N.C.: Duke University Press.

Sider, Gerald M. 1986. *Culture and Class in Anthropology and History: A Newfoundland Illustration*. Cambridge: Cambridge University Press.

Sider, Gerald M. 1993. *Lumbee Indian Histories: Race, Ethnicity, and Indian Identity in the Southern United States*. Cambridge: Cambridge University Press.

Stoll, David. 1999. *Rigoberta Menchú and the Story of All Poor Guatemalans*. Boulder, Colo.: Westview Press.

Taussig, Michael T. 1986. *Shamanism, Colonialism, and the Wild Man: A Study in Terror and Healing*. Chicago: University of Chicago Press.

Whyte, Susan R. 2002. "Subjectivities and Subjunctivities: Hoping for Health in Eastern Uganda." In *Post-Colonial African Subjectivities*, edited by R. Werbner, 171–190. London: Zed Press.

Williams, Gareth. 2002. *The Other Side of the Popular: Neoliberalism and Subalternity in Latin America*. Durham, N.C.: Duke University Press.

3

Being Repaired

• •

Reparations and
Remediations in Peru

MARÍA EUGENIA ULFE

I open this chapter with two case studies, one related to the lived experience of a relative of a disappeared student seeking reparations and the other surrounding remediation for a devastating oil spill that caused extensive environmental damage in several Indigenous communities.[1] These case studies serve as examples that demonstrate how the incommensurability of damages plays out in reparation and remediation processes. These are two cases about reparation processes: one relates to human rights and occurred during the period of the armed conflict, between 1980 and 2000, in Peru; the second one occurs in the Amazon in the context of the climate crisis. The two cases show the state's (inevitable) failure in providing basic rights. In the process, we will discuss how political subjectivities emerge. The two cases show different approximations and definitions of what is commensurable, what is repaired, and how imagination plays in portraying some ideas about reparation processes.

   On September 16, 2020, in the midst of the pandemic, Gisela Ortiz, whose brother was disappeared during the armed conflict in Peru, wrote on her Facebook fan page, "Open grief, ongoing for more than 30 years for the disappearance of a loved one, should not be a pending issue of the state's obligations, year after year." Ortiz then shared a lengthy tale of the years she spent searching for her brother Quique, who was then a young student at the Enrique Guzmán Valle National University of Education, better known as La Cantuta. On the night of July 18, 1992, he was forcibly taken from his student residence, tortured, murdered, and disappeared by members of the so-called Colina Group, a death squad with a direct line to former president Alberto Fujimori, who was eventually convicted for crimes against humanity for this, among other cases. Later investigations showed that the young man, several of his peers, and his professor were murdered, their bodies buried near the central highway and then unearthed and transferred to another location in Cieneguilla, near Lima. According to the final report of the Comisión de la Verdad y Reconciliación (Truth and Reconciliation Commission, CVR), in August 1993, several keys found near the bodies were used to identify the victims: "With one of the keys, the prosecutor opened a lock on student Juan Gabriel Mariños Figueroa's closet door. With another key, the prosecutor opened the closet belonging to student Armando Amaro Cóndor. Another key was found to open the door to the Federated Center of Electromechanics, where José Mariños had been a student leader. Finally, a key opened the door to the house where Mrs. Rayda Cóndor, the mother of the student Armando Amaro Cóndor, lived" (Comisión de la Verdad y Reconciliación 2003, 240). The Dirección General de Búsqueda de Personas Desaparecidas (General Directorate for the Search for Disappeared Persons, DGBPD), part of the Ministry of Justice in Peru, came into existence in 2018 with responsibility for investigating and reporting the forced disappearances that occurred between 1980 and 2000 in Peru (a period that includes the internal armed conflict and the years of the authoritarian Fujimori regime). To this end, the Registro Nacional de Búsqueda de Personas Desaparecidas (National Search Registry for Disappeared Persons, RENADE) presented them with a list of 21,334 disappeared persons.[2] However, Gisela Ortiz's testimony reveals how family members of the disappeared seek to know more about what happened to their relatives and demand that the state facilitate searches and the restitution of bodies and provide reparations for the loss of loved ones.

In a January 2021 summary of weekly achievements,[3] the Constitutional Court of Peru, the supreme court in the country, reported a ruling in favor of four Indigenous communities from the Urarinas District in Loreto. The lawsuit was presented against the state petroleum company Petroperú[4] and concerned damages caused by oil spills—the largest of which occurred in June 2014, where it is estimated that more than 2,500 barrels of oil contaminated the waters of the Cuninico Stream, a tributary of the Marañón River, primarily affecting the communities of Cuninico, Nueva Santa Rosa, San Francisco, and Nueva Esperanza. The Constitutional Court ordered Petroperú to comply with the Supreme Decree,[5] ordering them to compensate these Indigenous communities for the oil spill. However, to do so, an "inventory" of the damage to people, property, and the environment had to be carried out. The lawsuit went largely unnoticed both within Peru and internationally.

Slowness is typical of the state's processes. Making people wait is a way in which the state exerts its power and domination (Auyero 2013) and enacts its political and disciplinary culture. In this case, it took five years of the Federation of United Cocamas Peoples of the Marañón (FEDEPCUM) petitioning the lawsuit before the Constitutional Court responded, agreeing to their demands. Further, despite the outcome, in an interview via Zoom, lawyer Juan Carlos Ruiz from the Legal Defense Institute, who worked on the case, expressed his ongoing concern, stating, "It is not enough to win the case; the execution of the sentence must be followed up."[6] Ruiz's words echo similar restitution and reparation demands made by Ortiz and others in the movement to address missing and disappeared persons and seek human rights, truth, and justice in Peru following the political violence that took place between 1980 and 2000.[7]

But how are victims of forced disappearances truly repaired? Similarly, how are communities, nature, and rivers compensated for oil spills? As Diana Nelson (2015) asks, "Who counts?" And how do we count? Under a dominant neoliberal rationale, the need to draw exact and concrete equivalences is problematic. That is to say, how is it possible to adequately measure and compensate for loss, death, rape, or a contaminated environment?

I have been conducting studies on conviviality and care systems in Cuninico, a community in the Urarinas District of the Amazon region of Loreto, since 2019. The 2014 oil spill previously described occurred here, in the Cuninico Creek, where spills have been ongoing since the construction of the Northern Peruvian Pipeline in the mid-1970s. I am also involved in the remediation process there, led by the Legal Defense Institute, with the support of the Vicariate of Iquitos and other civil society organizations. Further, I have worked on human rights reparations programs in Peru, including the Programa Integral de Reparaciones (Comprehensive Reparations Program). Drawing on this work, in this chapter, I am interested in highlighting the intersections that involve knowing the truth of an act of violence (claims of memory, justice, and truth) and the duty to repair (remedy) and to compensate (to whom, for what), which are framed under different epistemologies, placing together in relation to the state and its representatives, the people who suffer the consequences, the events that mark the damage caused, and the names with which they are newly assigned. In these processes, there are translations and equivalences being made, the measurement of pain and pollution in economic terms. However, amid this, there is also the political subject that, with pain, sorrow, and uncertainty, approaches the state for reparations and remediations. Here, the question of translation relates to the constitution of political subjectivities and the question of cultural and historical belonging.

In order to show the difficulties in measuring damage (the questions of who/ what is being repaired), I will begin the chapter by historicizing the reparations process in Peru before considering the two specific examples that narrate or describe—*evidenciar*, as Viveiros de Castro (2013) calls it—what occurs in such cases. An investigation of reparations, transitional justice, and the PIR (the Comprehensive Reparations Program in Peru) specifically will help contextualize the creation and work of the DGBPD in addressing the disappearances that occurred during the period of political violence. Finally, I will explore the Cuninico case and the idea of remediation, which extends the framework of human rights to consider damage to nature and the need for an "inventory" to proceed. In this way I will show how categorization occurs, how the state will inevitably fail to adequately repair harms, and how new political subjects emerge from the intersecting relations that occur in these processes.

Reparation Politics in Peru and Beyond

The final report of the CVR suggests that one of the greatest causes of political violence in Peru has been the fracture between state and society. In an attempt to reestablish this relationship, reparations have been assumed as part of a wider program aimed at the restitution of citizenship among victims of violence and the imagining of Peru as a pacified community. To this end, the Comprehensive Reparations Program emerged as one of the recommendations provided by the CVR to help dignify victims and restore what was broken by violence. It encompasses several initiatives, including economic reparations (both individual and collective), symbolic reparations, and reparations in housing, education, and mental health.[8]

However, in order to proceed with reparations, the state requires the distinct categorization of victims, when in reality, the line between victims and perpetrators is sometimes gray and porous. According to Povinelli (2002), these strategies of categorization become self-serving state projects and, in this case, also create well-disciplined state subjects. Not only can these be seen as opportunities for the state to legitimize its power, but they also make calls on who is being asked to participate and how in the new nation-state. Povinelli (2002, 165) sees, for instance, the Australian court's invitation to Aboriginal Australians in their quest for recognition more as rhetoric than as a genuine opportunity to address the state's role in creating historical subjects and citizens, merely reinforcing the power relationship under the guise of reparations.

Reparation policies in Peru go even before the period of the transitional democratic government of Valentin Paniagua (2000–2001), with two antecedents to the Comprehensive Reparations Program (PIR): first, the Comprehensive Non-Economic Reparation Program, which reviewed 159 cases that were prosecuted in the International Court on Human Rights Court (Magarrell and Guillerot

2006, 22); and next, the Programa de Apoyo al Repoblamiento (Support for Resettlement Program, PAR), which included a set of policies that mainly benefited mayors and local authorities, as evidenced in the wake of the 1983 massacre in the village of Lucanamarca (Ulfe 2013).

There have also been notable reparations programs internationally, such as those designed at the end of World War II, when countries deemed responsible for starting the war had to pay for damages caused to other countries (García-Godos 2008; Mani 2005; Torpey 2005). In this period, reparations were considered synonymous with compensation. In the decades that followed, antiracist struggles of African Americans in the United States and Indigenous peoples in Canada also called for reparations for offenses suffered by these groups (Torpey 2005).

Then in the 1990s, as many countries transitioned to democracy, different mechanisms for transitional justice were consolidated, including truth commissions, reparations, and restorative justice processes (Torpey 2005), while at the same time the global peace and security agenda was developed by the United Nations (De Grieff 2006). Reparations are framed in international law as the recovery of a condition prior to damage endured, the right to the nonrepetition of harms, and the restitution of citizenship. In the institutional logic of the United Nations or of countries themselves, where they undertake compensation and reparations programs, reparations begin by defining subjects. Within the human rights framework, the reparations subject is defined as a "victim," usually in dichotomic opposition to the "perpetrator." While truth commissions work on the exclusive victim-perpetrator dichotomy, when cases are studied in detail, gray areas emerge, and these strict boundaries become problematic, as we will see in the next section. For instance, the daughter of a Shining Path leader in Lucanamarca in Ayacucho lost her parents at an early age (six years old) and cannot register for the program of reparations because of her parental tie to a *subversivo* (Ulfe and Málaga Sabogal 2022). In the Peruvian Code of Criminal Procedure, a victim is defined by the offense they suffered. That is, it focuses on the past to define the aggrieved by considering the damage that provoked the condition of victimhood and who did the damage. Furthermore, in Peru, reparations are often articulated within the complex contexts of poverty and neoliberalism. As mentioned in the introduction to the book, mestizaje appears as a discourse that evades more profound discussions about discrimination, race, and social class. Though marginalization is historically and culturally constructed in Peru, its colonial roots operate constantly but in manifold ways.

As I have written about before, the neoliberal reforms that took place in the mid-1990s directly impacted the way in which the Comprehensive Reparations Program was framed as a tool for those struggling against poverty (Ulfe 2016). Women tend to be poorer than men, and Indigenous women appear at the bottom of the racial and class hierarchy. And it is worse when we speak of the Amazon, a territory usually perceived as marginal and on the outskirts of the state.

Following our work with Ximena Málaga Sabogal (2021) on the history of the development of reparations, subjects are coconstituted in the relationships they establish with each other—as those who declare themselves beneficiaries of the programs (victims) and, on the other hand, those who have inflicted harm (perpetrators)—but also in relation to the damage itself (the affectation) and the state. However, de Greiff (2006) points out that there are no reparations or postconflict programs that have managed to repair people in proportion to the damage they have suffered. The very idea of quantifying the damage is problematic and ensures expectations that probably won't be met due to budgetary constraints, the targeting methodology often used in social programs that prioritizes some things over others, and the inability to create fair equivalences. Indeed, how can pain be monetized?

The Comprehensive Reparations Program in Peru

The demands for limited state intervention and free markets in Peru date back to the government of Fernando Belaunde Terry (1980–1985), while they began to play out in practice during the government of Alberto Fujimori (1990–2000), which coincided with the postwar period. The populist Fujimori government dissolved Congress on April 5, 1992, naming a new Democratic Constitutional Congress, under which a new constitution was formed in 1993. In September of 1992, Abimael Guzmán, the leader of the Communist Party of Peru (Shining Path), was captured. The political context, including Fujimori's drive to stay in power, is important here. That is, the constitution, the postwar period, and Fujimori's populism must be understood as some of the conditions that shaped neoliberal reforms in Peru. The government's push for such reforms was backed by claims of success by highlighting outcomes of social programs—indeed, it was mainly social programs that were (and still are) used as concrete evidence to justify neoliberalism (Ulfe and Málaga Sabogal 2021).

The case for having a comprehensive plan for reparations took shape during the period of the CVR and became one of the measures recommended to repair social bonds and financially compensate victims of violence during the postconflict period. As two sides of a coin, reparations and compensation are important to recognize and restore dignity to victims of violence as well as enable them to recover their damaged ties to society as citizens. However, dignity and citizenship are particularly complex issues in a country such as Peru, with its complicated history of inequality and discrimination.

The conclusions made in the CVR's final report were devastating for Peru. Even though it recognized the Shining Path as the main instigator of the conflict, responsible for most deaths, it also identified the armed forces and other armed groups, such as civil patrols and paramilitary groups, as perpetrators. The report estimated that there were 69,280 people killed during the conflict, and in 2004, one year after the publication of the CVR final report, the Toledo administration signed a presidential decree to create the Comprehensive Reparations Program.

For this purpose, the Comisión Multisectorial de Alto Nivel (High Level Multisectoral Commission) was created to coordinate with the Consejo de Reparaciones (Council for Reparations) and different state ministries and offices to implement the Comprehensive Reparations Program. These two offices, the Council for Reparations and the High Level Multisectoral Commission, were later unified under the Viceministry of Justice and Human Rights.[9] The High Level Multisectoral Commission was created as a means for delivering reparations, charged with developing various programs surrounding citizens' rights, education, health, housing, community development, and symbolic and economic reparations, at both individual and collective levels. However, for the High Level Multisectoral Commission to work effectively, it was necessary to define the victims of violence and the acts that would be considered. Thus, the Council for Reparations was created and given responsibility for the Registro Único de Víctimas (National Registry of Victims), a registry to identify the victims of violence who would be the subjects of reparations.

However, the category of "victim" is not clear cut but is rather a social category that is disputed, appropriated, and used by different groups of people (Ulfe and Málaga Sabogal 2015, 2021, 2022). Thus, although the CVR's final report recognized all 69,280 casualties as victims, the National Registry of Victims did not consider members of armed groups (*subversivos*) to be victims per se. Article 4 in the Comprehensive Reparations Program instead adopts the position that there is a clear dichotomy between victim and perpetrator. For them, a new victim profile was created, defined primarily as Indigenous, poor, and male. Adopting article 4 was a major discrepancy and concession made by human rights movements to carry out the Comprehensive Reparations Program.

To be registered in the National Registry of Victims, a person must prove that an act of violence was perpetrated against him or her because of the armed conflict—that is, between the years 1980 and 2000—and under specific circumstances. The National Registry of Victims established a victim typology based on the action perpetrated and created the categories: dead people; disappeared persons; members of the police; members of the civil patrols; civil authorities that were tortured, seriously injured, or suffered sexual abuses; and finally, the relatives of the dead and disappeared. On this basis, we see that the boundaries between being or not being a victim are certainly permeable (Ulfe and Málaga Sabogal 2021).

In some cases, particularly where there is a lack of information or suspicion that the person was related to an armed group, the National Registry of Victims requests more information. Often, people are asked to include an oral testimony from a witness, such as a village or community leader, who can confirm their victimhood. Where possible, cases are accompanied by news clippings or visual materials (photographs or videos). Nonetheless, for each individual application, there are different requirements and processes. Although the cases are individual in nature, there is recognition at the community level of the collective condition of victimhood.

As a result of the National Registry of Victims protocol, one of the problems we encountered in our fieldwork in Ayacucho was that the testimonies gathered by the CVR and those then given by the same people years later often did not coincide. For instance, some of those whose sympathies leaned toward an armed group had to "clean" their testimonies and adjust them to the rules imposed by the National Registry of Victims. Further, because the type of documentation and evidence required to register as a victim varies from case to case, a significant number of cases remain "under observation," meaning that the information provided is not complete, that the name appears in a previously registered case, or that someone denounced the person as a sympathizer, collaborator, or member of an armed group. Certainly, discrepancies have arisen, highlighting that the labeling of victims is not straightforward.

Nonetheless, as soon as the Comprehensive Reparations Program became public policy, a focus on the categorization of citizens as victims emerged. As Gupta (2012) shows, such focalization is required as part of the neoliberal mandate for evidence, efficacy, and efficiency by pinpointing certain citizens. Through the use of this methodology, some are necessarily prioritized over others, creating both intracommunity and intrafamily conflicts.

The General Directorate for the Search for Disappeared Persons (DGBPD) was the result of many years of political lobbying and social mobilization by different associations of victims, organized civil society groups, and the International Red Cross Committee, among other actors. These groups had been seeking answers to questions about the disappeared, such as their exact numbers and identities, since prior to the research undertaken by the CVR, little was known. On June 22, 2016, a law[10] creating the DGBPD was passed, following a year of debate to confirm that it should become a directorate (Dirección) rather than a program, such as the reparations one, in the Ministry of Justice and Human Rights. On October 27, 2017, the protocol for the creation of a registry of the disappeared was published. As with the program of reparations, this required describing the features that characterize a person as disappeared, although in a less bureaucratic manner than the RUV.

In 2018, the newly formed directorate presented their initial list of people who had disappeared between the years of 1980 and 2000—a list containing information from a variety of databases but primarily compiled by relatives of victims who emerged from the CVR and the list provided by the PIR with the names and burial locations of more than 8,000 victims. The registry listed 20,329 disappeared persons, of whom there was no information for 13,764 of them and very little information for 5,700. Most were likely buried somewhere, but uncertainty remained, as merely 865 people had been found and had their remains returned to their relatives. These numbers were presented as a point of departure for the registry, and indeed, by December 2020, the number of disappeared had grown by more than 1,000.

By naming the victims and providing some details about the tragic events they suffered, the DGBPD aims to recuperate the dignity of the disappeared. It seeks not to name perpetrators but to create a path forward in the search for truth; it has also recommended the creation of a DNA bank for identification purposes (November 22, 2017). Thus, whereas the PIR is victim centered, with compensation going to relatives or to the victim, if possible, the DGBPD works with the families of the disappeared using what they refer to as a humanitarian approach that seeks to recuperate a name and identity for each victim. There is no insistence on exhumation, and the DGBPD tries to respect the family decision as to how they wish to proceed in this regard. Following this humanitarian approach, Jairo Rivas, director of the Dirección de Registro e Investigación Forense (Directorate of Registration and Forensic Investigation), explains that for many, "knowing what happened is more important than exhumation."[11] However, authors like Fassin (2008, 2011) and Agier (2010) discuss the problematic nature of the "humanitarian" approach to reparations programs. Fassin (2008) focuses on the use of the victim category, what constitutes it, who identifies with it, and how transitional justice entrepreneurs tend to mediate between the one who gives testimony (victim) and the public sphere, validating the presence of transitional justice actors with phrases like "being there" as if they were the victims-testifiers. Agier (2010), on the other hand, shows the effects of such politics in terms of power and geopolitics, explaining how places become part of global police exercises of control over "the vulnerable." For Agier (2010), "The humanitarian world is based upon the fiction of humanity as an identity and conflates universalism and globalization. . . . It operates on the basis of a universalistic type of thinking: it deals with humanity as unique, and in particular with its extreme embodiment in the problem raised by the unmediated, nameless victim, who is not an 'other' recognized through her own voice but the very same humanity who is abused and whose human qualities are diminished, incomplete, or unexpressed" (32).

What we get then is a hierarchical classification of victims based primarily on the damages suffered in such programs of compensation. What is critical is to consider what constitutes "vulnerability" and how it is seen for these programs. These programs are also part of a global apparatus; as Agier (2010) argues, "The humanitarian world is also a globalized apparatus: a set of organizations, networks, agents, and financial means distributed across different countries and crisscrossing the world as they herald a universal cause" (32). Yet still, actors involved in political violence seek out these programs in order to discover what happened; memory is a disputed battlefield, and these programs are an important aspect of settling these disputes as well as locating the remains of loved ones. Nonetheless, considering the concerns raised by Fassin and Agier, we must also assess reparations programs critically in terms of how they have been implemented, how the state acts upon them, and how people are being classified further, beyond the category of citizen.

Very few of the dead disappear without a trace. The traces are often invisible to our eyes, but they remain out there, hidden but susceptible to opening doors. In an interesting early reflection on the current COVID-19 pandemic, Judith Butler (2020) analyzes the invisible traces on objects, on things; the mark that those who have handled an object leave behind; how contagion remains on surfaces and viruses can reach a home through these objects; how we attempt to wash away these traces of contagion through sanitation with bleach and soap, for instance. The objects that arrive in our homes are not only a visible part of specific production, distribution, and consumption processes, containing traces of the people and places through which they have passed, but, as the author points out, they also embody these same processes, which in turn reach even to the state itself. As Butler (2020) explains, to ask about the trace of an object is to question the conditions of life and death inherent to the organization of work in our societies.

Thus, just as the body of the worker never sheds the traces of the objects it puts into circulation, traces from the bodies of the owners of the keys found in the Cieneguilla area were not erased; rather, they became evidence of a crime. Not only were they evidence in a judicial process, but they also introduced us to the horrors perpetrated by the state, opening Pandora's box. What happens to the state when it discriminates by selecting its citizens and determining who lives and who dies? What happens when a state tries to repair that damage? What mechanisms are available?

This necropolitical approach taken by the state accounts for a long history of exploitation and domination. The keys in the Cantuta case opened wounds for the families of the tortured and disappeared students. They also left evidence of the difficult path to justice, uncovering an unequal system and the possibility of going beyond merely counting the dead. Surely, each of the students and the professor represent a universe of relationships. As the extensive work of Nelson (2015) shows, numbers tend to dehumanize subjects and ignore their stories and life histories. Victims of violence mostly wish to remain remembered. The PIR provides statistics such as the number of disappeared, financial compensation provided, and development program outcomes that prove their efficiency. But how can pain, loss, broken social ties, and destroyed systems be monetized? Indeed, none of those interviewed for our research said that monetary compensation repaired the loss suffered from the disappearance of their relatives (Ulfe and Málaga Sabogal 2021).

In his already classic *Seeing like a State*, James Scott (1998) shows how legibility and administrative order are imposed by certain states to prostrate civil society and even Indigenous populations. Reparations, including those that take a humanitarian approach, such as the DGBPD, appear as technologies for categorizing people's suffering and their rights to justice and truth. Gisela

Ortiz deplores how bureaucratic these decisions and compensations have become, shifting, for instance, the burden to the victims to prove they fit within the required categorization. But can we say that the humanitarian approach of the DGBPD is any better? Is seeking truth and giving the disappeared a name and a story a true form of repair? Since it is a move toward dignity rather than economic compensation, it becomes a form of recuperation of the almost lost humanity of the disappeared. It does not contradict Fassin's arguments about humanitarianism; rather, it looks at the way the state considers such programs and how citizens are classified and sometimes even instrumentalized.

Oil Spills in Cuninico

Oil is a materiality, a thing that exists in many senses at the same time. Oil appears contained in words, thoughts, actions, the pipeline that carries it, the roads, the highways, the well-being, the light, and the energy that comes out from under the ground to the surface—"it composes the bonds that tie people together and force them apart" (Cepek 2018, 234).[12] Certainly, oil appeared in nearly every conversation we had in Cuninico.

Oil exploration in Loreto dates back to the 1950s and 1960s, and construction of the oil pipeline began there in the 1970s. The North Peruvian Pipeline crosses Cuninico when it enters the district of Urarinas in Loreto. From San José de Saramuro in Urarinas, the pipeline takes crude oil to Bayóvar in Piura, crossing the jungle and a mountain range to reach the coast where it is exported. The state-owned company Petroperú oversees the maintenance of the pipeline. Mr. Diómedes, a member of one of the founding families of Cuninico, explains how it is home to a majority who identify themselves as Kukama Kukamiria and a territory of varzea, lands that flood with the rising rivers and rains. He still remembers when the oil first gushed: "It was green," he tells us, so it still could not be exploited. Back then, Mr. Diómedes explains, Cuninico was not in the place it is today.

He sadly relays that his community has been dealing with contamination related to the pipeline since 1975, one year after its construction began. He says it was a Friday when "several of us [had] gone to see what [the drilling, the exploration of oil] was going to shoot out. Three boats entered, and when they fired the drill, black oil came spewing out. Two gringos got dirty. They were very *negritos* [black]" (interview, Mr. Diómedes, October 2019). The construction of the pipeline has also caused the deaths of many fish, boas, and lizards. The 2014 spill was the last "le ha yapeado" (in the sequence of a series of previous spills).

Flor de María, the Madre Indígena (Indigenous Mother, a leading political actor in the community) in Cuninico, says that the spill came as a black tide of dead fish. They did not understand what was happening. Radio Ucamara (a local radio station), the priests of the Vicariate of Iquitos, a North American journalist living in the jungle, and lawyers were among the first to come to their aid. They took photographs as evidence and began to circulate them in the national media and foreign press. The lawsuits against the state and Petroperú began immediately. Several juridical cases have been raised against the state in response to the spill. The Federación de Pueblos Cocamas Unidos del Marañón (Federation of United Cocama Peoples of the Marañón, FEDEPCUM) filed an environmental complaint with the Organismo de Evaluación y Fiscalización Ambiental (Agency for Environmental Assessment and Enforcement, OEFA) for the oil spill in Cuninico that affected the Indigenous communities of Cuninico, Nueva Esperanza, Santa Rosa, and San Francisco. Later, and with the help of IDL (Instituto de Defensa Legal), they presented a constitutional lawsuit before OEFA to request the remediation of rivers and water sources and administrative sanctions against Petroperú for failure to maintain the pipeline. In 2015, OEFA issued a directorial resolution that, for the first time, recognized Petroperú's administrative responsibility for the lack of maintenance of the pipeline, responsibility for the damages caused to flora and fauna, and responsibility for potential harms to life and health.[13]

When the oil spills happened, Petroperú paid for the remediation and cleaning of the contaminated section, providing employment for local men as well as women, who cooked for the engineers who came to repair the pipeline. The state created health services, a service to process rainwater, and cash transfer programs and even hired a telecommunications company to install an antenna when requested. Nonetheless, permanent changes to the ecosystem had occurred. As Marlita,[14] vice president of the Asociación de Mujeres Indígenas de Cuninico (Association of Indigenous Women of Cuninico, ADMIC), explained in one of our many conversations, to fish and hunt today, residents must travel much farther, as the fish and animals have left the creek. As a result, local food habits have changed.

Then in December 2020, the Constitutional Court issued a ruling ordering Petroperú to compensate the Indigenous communities of Cuninico, San Francisco, Nueva Esperanza, and Santa Rosa affected by the 2014 oil spill that occurred in their territories. However, to do so, the Constitutional Court and Petroperú required an inventory of damages for which to compensate. But how are contaminated water, fish, animals, and bodies monetized or accounted for? How can an inventory of relationships be traced? Paraphrasing Nelson, who decides what it means to go back to something relatively similar to the previous state?

In an interview with the economist responsible for conducting this inventory, she explained that there is a difference between assessment and valorization. Soil, land, concrete materials, and culture can be assessed in economic terms. However, she explained, valorization requires an explanation that considers the cultural significance of these elements, necessarily involving emotional and subjective aspects, relationships, and identification processes that consider well-being, culture, and politics. Thus, valorization implies different things for each of the four communities that suffered from the oil spills, making it difficult to think in exact equivalences. The soil in one community was being eroded by the river, and they were looking to move to a better place. Another community, such as Cuninico, was looking for a satellite antenna to be installed for better communication. Something in common was to ask for a "tópico de salud" (health topic) with basic medicine, which was useful when the pandemic started.

The inventory for the lawsuit requires that these two approaches, assessment and valorization, be combined. Although the economist did not have experience in qualitative research, she understood that only qualitative valorizations could help them fully understand the true magnitude of harms and how these could be translated into economic terms.[15]

Numbers, Statistics, Inventories

In *The Order of Things*, Michel Foucault begins with a quote from the Argentinian writer and poet Jorge Luis Borges about a particular classification given in an ancient Chinese encyclopedia highlighting how taxonomies, classifications, typologies, and even representations emerge arbitrarily: "In the wonderment of this taxonomy, the thing we apprehend in one great leap, the thing that, by means of the fable, is demonstrated as the exotic charm of another system of thought, is the limitation of our own, the stark impossibility of thinking *that*" (Foucault 1994, xv). Despite the seemingly odd classification system, each of the categories has meaning. Resemblance is the operation at work in building a taxonomy. The work of resemblances is also the work of relationships.

An inventory is yet another form of classification. But "who counts?" Nelson (2015) reminds us to ask. The work of the DGBPD is to count the disappeared, to unearth bones, to return bones and bodies to families, and to sometimes replace a number with a name—that is, to go beyond the statistics of death. In late capitalism, statistics and numbers are always at work. As Povinelli (2011) writes, "Liberalism, late liberalism, neoliberalism do not exist as things in the ordinary sense of the term but rather as actions like a sighting or a citing. They exist insofar as they are evoked to conjure, shape, aggregate, and evaluate a variety of social worlds" (16). She conceptualizes neoliberalism as "a series of struggles across an uneven social terrain" that allows us to see "the conditions for new forms of sociality and new kinds of markets and market instruments (or 'products')" (17). Certainly, numbers and statistics can be used by the state as evidence of the success of social programs in order to further its own neoliberal agenda. In Peru, both reparations through the PIR and remediations in the case of the Cuninico oil spill could be seen as examples of such state programs, where the tidy counting and categorization of harms is employed and used as a measure of achievement.

Reparations are framed within a human rights paradigm, and remediations also emerge in contexts of violations of different human rights, such as the right to water, the rivers, and the environment. In environmental law, remediation refers to carrying out operations to restore the quality of contaminated soil, subsoil, or bodies of water. However, going back to the previous state is not possible in these cases. Juan Carlos Ruiz, the lawyer from IDL who worked on the case, believes that "it is very difficult to *remediar*; it is very complicated because there are no ways to repair the damage already done—in this case, the contamination" (interview, Zoom, June 8, 2020). *Remediar* comes from the Spanish term *remedio*—to remedy, as with medical treatment—but is there such a thing that can adequately heal the community and the environment and restore the relations between these communities and the state? Further, as Juan Carlos Ruiz insists, it is not merely enough to win a judicial process surrounding environmental remediations. Rather, it is critical that the rulings are followed through on. Gisela Ortiz made similar demands on the reparations process for families of the disappeared.

Nevertheless, the biggest problem is the contradiction of rationales. Equivocation happens precisely in these mistranslations or almost-intended literal translations, which are impossible. However, it is not only a matter of equivocations, since in the case of Cuninico, the state and the law itself are in a process of construction and interpretation of concepts that are also new to them. The only antecedent is the PIR. The state, as in the case of reparations, requires that damages be identified and is particularly concerned with identifying those affected and specific harms done to the environment. But how can the state understand that fish, animals, and rivers are part of a complex cosmology in which humans and nonhumans interact? What is a fair price for the contaminated water, the dead fish, or the change in eating habits that have resulted from the spills? There is also a challenge of materialities, which are impossible to measure in exact quantities and to equate with other things.

In conclusion, in remediations, the state proceeds in similar ways as with reparations: It enumerates, catalogs, characterizes, draws equivalences, and gets confused. The reparations mandate is expanding to consider environmental liabilities—that is, damage caused to the environment—in this case, by the state oil company. Oil is as much a part of the lives in Cuninico as the river, the fish, and the animals. But oil is also part of what is damaged and lost. As Viveiros de Castro (2013) writes, differences (cultural, cosmological, political) have become measurable; these coexist in the same space, as at a glance we can see how reparations and remediations seem to share the same principles and actions of the state. However, "the truth is that they have increased their potential for differentiating" (19).[16] As these different worldviews and cosmologies enter into contact and cohabit the same space, the differences become noteworthy. In both cases, in reparations for the disappeared and remediations for the oil spill, the inability to measure loss of persons and ecosystems makes the problem of governmentality more visible. Finally, the ability to define only partial or "controlled" equivalences makes reparation and remediation in exact terms more difficult, impossible even.

As mentioned in the introduction to this book, imagination is grounded in memory and past conceptions, and it is important for grasping the future. Reparations and remediations are ways of imagining futures, recuperating past conditions, and embracing new beginnings and belongings. The relatives of the disappeared have made claims for truth, justice, and the return of the bodies of the disappeared while also identifying with other victims and emerging as new political subjects. When the black tide of dead fish came down the river in Cuninico, people were afraid and did not understand what was happening—that they were experiencing the impacts of oil extraction and devastation. But out of this devastation, people made changes to their diets and recuperated medical knowledge to harvest plants to alleviate conditions and illnesses caused by the oil spills and even to address COVID-19 symptoms. Thus, periodical forms of violence can also create new conditions of citizenship and agency and new forms of political subjectivities, where resistance becomes a form of political struggle and reparations and remediations turn into mechanisms with which to relate to the state and each other.

Notes

1 For their support, I would like to thank the Fondo de Apoyo a la Investigación of the Dirección General de Investigación (DGI), 2020, and Vicerrectorado de Investigación, Pontifícia Universidad Católica del Perú. Most of the information for this paper is possible thanks to the research project Desde los márgenes del Estado peruano: Corporalidades, contaminación e identidades étnicas en pobladores Kukama del Bajo Marañón, supported by Vicerrectorado de Investigación, CAP 2019, Pontificia Universidad Católica del Perú. Special thanks to Roxana Vergara, Lisette Gamboa, and Fernando Bracho.
2 By November 2023, the number of disappeared increased to 22,551 persons (Dirección General de Búsqueda de Personas Desaparecidas 2021).
3 The Constitutional Court of Peru's video appears on its Facebook page: https://www .facebook.com/tribunalconstitucionalperu/videos/sentencia-del-tc/174037334505266/.
4 See https://tc.gob.pe/jurisprudencia/2020/03799-2018-AC.pdf.
5 Decreto Supremo N° 081-2007-EM (Reglamento de Trasportes de Hidrocarburos por Ductos), art. 4.
6 The session was via Zoom and took place on January 12, 2021. Juan Carlos Ruiz is a lawyer from the IDL and is the adviser to FEDEPCUM on this and other legal proceedings.
7 It is beyond the scope of this chapter to describe the struggles that the pandemic provoked in Peru; however, during the pandemic, the country and Cuninico had thousands of disappeared after a series of tropical epidemics and a disastrous oil spill.
8 There are several studies about reparations in Peru; see Jave and Ayala (2017), Ramírez and Scott (2019), Guillerot (2019), Ulfe (2013), Ulfe and Málaga Sabogal (2021), among others.

9   The Toledo administration (2001–2006) assigned CMAN (Comisión Multisectorial de Alto Nivel) the role to facilitate access, service, and dialogue with other state institutions and ministries. This strategy was designed to bring legitimacy to CMAN by enabling it to coordinate directly with local and regional governments to establish a Comprehensive National Reparations Program—a program that includes different dimensions like education, mental health, roofing, and economic compensation. As a protocol, potential victims had to register in the Registro Único de Víctimas. In 2011 CMAN was reassigned to the Ministry of Justice and Human Rights. This move restricted the coordinating power of CMAN and its multisector approach.

10 Law no. 30470, Ley de búsqueda de personas desaparecidas durante el periodo de violencia (1980–2000).

11 DGBPD is organized into two directorates: Dirección de Registro e Investigación Forense (Directorate of Registration and Forensic Investigation) and Dirección de Atención y Acompañamiento (Directorate of Attention and Accompaniment). The conversation with Jairo Rivas took place on June 19, 2020, via Zoom.

12 Working among the Secoya people in Ecuador, Stine Krojer explores relationality in the context of oil spills but in different ways than Cepek. For more information, see Krojer (2019).

13 The judicial process in the Cuninico case was reduced to a series of trials, each taking a different approach. The first process was the environmental remediation that Cuninico won before OEFA. The second one was the case presented for health and compensation as part of the remediation requested before the judiciary. There was another process through which OEFA ordered Petroperú to maintain the pipeline, made in front of the Constitutional Court. And finally, a fourth process sought payment for land use easements to Indigenous peoples.

14 The field research in Cuninico happened between 2019 (in situ) and by telephone interviews and WhatsApp conversations during the pandemic in 2020.

15 This conversation took place via Zoom on March 11, 2021.

16 The complete quote is "Las diferencias, no se terminaron, lo que sucede ahora es que se volvieron mensurables, porque cohabitan en un mismo espacio: la verdad es que aumentaron su potencial diferenciante" (Viveiros de Castro 2013, 19).

References

Agier, Michel. 2010. "Humanity as an Identity and Political Effects (a Note on Camps and Humanitarian Government)." *Humanity: An International Journal of Human Rights, Humanitarianism, and Development* 1 (1): 29–45.

Auyero, Javier. 2013. *Pacientes del Estado*. Buenos Aires: EUDEBA.

Butler, Judith. 2020. "Human Traces in the Surfaces of the World." ConTactos. Accessed June 10, 2021. https://contactos.tome.press/human-traces-on-the-surfaces-of-the-world.

Cepek, Michael. 2018. *Life in Oil: Cofán Survival in the Petroleum Fields of Amazonia*. Austin: University of Texas Press.

Comisión de la Verdad y Reconciliación. 2003. "Informe final: Tomo VII" Accessed June 10, 2021. https://www.cverdad.org.pe.

De Grieff, Pablo. 2006. "Repairing the Past: Compensation for Victims of Human Rights Violations." In *The Handbook of Reparations*, edited by Pablo de Grieff, 275–284. New York: Oxford University Press.

Dirección General de Búsqueda de Personas Desaparecidas. 2021. *Reporte Estadístico N° 2: Registro Nacional de Personas Desaparecidas y de Sitios de Entierro al 31 de julio de 2021*. Lima: Ministerio de Justicia y Derechos Humanos.

Fassin, Didier. 2008. "The Humanitarian Politics of Testimony: Subjectification Through Trauma in the Israeli-Palestinian Conflict." *Cultural Anthropology* 23 (3): 531–558.

Fassin, Didier. 2011. *Humanitarian Reason: A Moral History of the Present*. Berkeley: University of California Press.

Foucault, Michel. 1994. *The Order of Things*. New York: Vintage Books Edition.

García-Godos, Jemima. 2008. "Victim Reparations in Transitional Justice: What Is at Stake and Why." *Nordisk Tidsskrift for Menneskerettigheter* 26 (2): 111–130.

Guillerot, Julie. 2019. "Reparaciones en Perú. 15 años de reparación." *Reparations, Responsibility & Victimhood in Transitional Societies*. Accessed June 10, 2021. https://reparations.qub.ac.uk/assets/uploads/Peru-Report-ESP-LR.pdf.

Gupta, Akhil. 2012. *Red Tape: Bureaucracy, Structural Violence, and Poverty in India*. Durham, N.C.: Duke University Press.

Jave, Iris, and Henry Ayala. 2017. *La beca Repared: Oportunidad y derecho en el Programa de Reparaciones en Educación*. Lima: IDEHPUCP.

Krøijer, Stine. 2019. "In the Spirit of Oil: Unintended Flows and Leaky Lives in Northeastern Ecuador." In *Indigenous Life Projects and Extractivism: Approaches to Social Inequality and Difference*, edited by C. Vindal Odeegard and J. J. Rivera Andía. Cham: Palgrave Macmillan.

Magarrell, Lisa, and Julie Guillerot. 2006. *Reparaciones en la transición peruana: Memorias de un proceso inacabado*. Lima: APRODEH e ICTJ.

Mani, Rama. 2005. "Reparation as a Component of Transitional Justice: Pursuing 'Reparative Justice' in the Aftermath of Violent Conflict." In *Out of Ashes: The Reparation for Victims of Gross and Systematic Human Rights Violations*, edited by Koen Feyter, Stephan Parmentier, Marc Bossuyt, and Paul Lemmens, 53–81. Antwerpen: Intersentia.

Nelson, Diane. 2015. *Who Counts? The Mathematics of Death and Life After Genocide*. Durham, N.C.: Duke University Press.

Povinelli, Elizabeth. 2002. *The Cunning of Recognition: Indigenous Alterities and the Making of Australian Multiculturalism*. Durham, N.C.: Duke University Press.

Povinelli, Elizabeth. 2011. *Economies of Abandonment: Social Belonging and Endurance in Late Liberalism*. Durham, N.C.: Duke University Press.

Ramírez, Iván, and Rogelio Scott. 2019. "From Victims to Beneficiaries: Shaping Postconflict Subjects Through State Reparations in Peru." *Latin American Perspectives* 46 (5): 158–173. https://doi.org/10.1177/0094582X19861097.

Scott, James. 1998. *Seeing like a State: How Certain Schemes to Improve the Human Condition Have Failed*. New Haven: Yale University Press.

Torpey, John. 2005. "Victims and Citizens: The Discourse of Reparations at the Dawn of the New Millennium." In *Out of Ashes: The Reparation for Victims of Gross and Systematic Human Rights Violations*, edited by Koen Feyter et al. Antwerpen: Intersentia.

Ulfe, María Eugenia. 2013. *¿Y después de la violencia qué queda? Víctimas, ciudadanos y reparaciones en el contexto post-CVR en el Perú*. Buenos Aires: CLACSO. http://biblioteca.clacso.edu.ar/clacso/becas/20130628122643/Ydespuesdelaviolencia.pdf.

Ulfe, María Eugenia. 2016. "Neoliberal Reforms, Reparations, and Transitional Justice Measures in Torn-Apart Peru, 1980–2015." In *Building Sustainable Peace: Timing and Sequencing of Post-Conflict Reconstruction and Peacebuilding*, edited by A. Langer and G. K. Brown. Oxford: Oxford University Press.

Ulfe, María Eugenia, and Ximena Málaga Sabogal. 2015. "Los nuevos suplicantes del Estado peruano: Las víctimas y el Programa Integral de Reparaciones." In *Políticas en Justicia Transicional: Miradas comparativas sobre el legado de la CVR*, edited by L. Huber and P. del Pino. Lima: IEP.

Ulfe, María Eugenia, and Ximena Málaga Sabogal. 2021. *Reparando mundos: Víctimas y Estado en los Andes peruanos*. Lima: Fondo Editorial PUCP.

Ulfe, María Eugenia, and Ximena Málaga Sabogal. 2022. "Incommensurable Worlds, Irreparable Wounds: Transitional Justice Politics and Personal Violent Pasts in Postconflict Peru." *Memory Studies* 15 (6): 1484–1496. https://doi.org/10.1177/17506980221133519.

Viveiros de Castro, Eduardo. 2013. *La mirada del Jaguar: Introducción al perspectivismo amerindio*. Buenos Aires: Tinta Limón.

4

"Here? Justice?"

• •

Enacting Repair on the
Boundaries of Justice
in Argentina

NATASHA ZARETSKY

"Here? Justice?"

Tita looked at me skeptically from across the small table at which we sat in the Café Banchero in downtown Buenos Aires. Tita, whose official name was Rebeca Sakolsky, stared intently with her bright eyes, questioning the idea that justice was possible in Argentina after so much time had passed. On that winter day in 2013, it had been decades since she first had become involved in protests advocating for victims of state violence and impunity. This started after her own detention and torture during the 1976–1983 dictatorship and continued after the 1994 bombing of the Asociación Mutual Israelita Argentina (Argentine Jewish Mutual Aid Society, AMIA), one of the worst terrorist attacks in Argentina's history that killed eighty-five people, wounded hundreds, and has since remained in a state of impunity.

Since the 1980s, she had attended countless protests. She would go to the Plaza de Mayo (the main public square in Buenos Aires, in front of the presidential palace) every Thursday for the weekly protests organized by the Mothers of the Plaza de Mayo (Madres de Plaza de Mayo), whose children had been disappeared during the dictatorship. And she would also go every Monday morning to the Plaza Lavalle, facing the high courts, to demand justice for the victims of the AMIA bombing. Week after week, she would go to these *actos* (protests), despite the complicated terrain of justice in which she stood.

Indeed, since Argentina returned to democracy in 1983, the experience of justice has been uneven on the ground. Rather than thinking about the path toward justice as a linear process, citizens and family members of victims of political violence in Argentina have been living through periods of varying ebbs and flows of impunity and accountability. The brutal 1976–1983 dictatorship resulted in up to thirty thousand people being disappeared, a number that includes students, teachers, psychologists, Jews, priests, and others who were considered "subversive" to the national order through a framing of "us" and "them" deriving from the anti-Communist national security doctrine (see Zaretsky 2018). The powerful social movements that arose in response demanded justice for those disappeared and that they be returned alive, their losses recuperated, their lives restored.

These demands from the 1970s and 1980s continued through the activism of the Madres de Plaza de Mayo, the Abuelas de Plaza de Mayo (Grandmothers of the Plaza de Mayo), the HIJOS (Children for Identity and Justice Against Forgetting and Silence), and a number of other human rights organizations (such as Centro de Estudios Legales y Sociales [CELS], Liga por los Derechos Humanos, and others). They sustained the memory in the consciousness of the nation during the era of impunity in the 1990s. Such memory practices rely on an embodied presence in the streets, a presence that remains vital to activism throughout the Americas, as described by Diana Taylor in her recent book, *¡Presente!* (2020). In Argentina, it began during the dictatorship when human rights groups demanded the return of those disappeared by the state, also raising awareness of the violence the state sought to erase and silence in those years.[1] Not long after the dictatorship ended in 1983, amnesty laws heralded an era of impunity, precluding juridical prosecution while also allowing for truth and memory to emerge as social forms of collectively holding perpetrators to account through memory practices such as the *escraches* (street protests directed at perpetrators), with truth serving as a mechanism for recovery and sustaining the nation without a return to violence. Even after amnesty laws were overturned in 2005, during the era of human rights trials, embodied practices of collective remembering remained a vital way of confronting and challenging the state and offered citizens spaces for recovery and the performance of their citizenship. These strategies also demonstrate the sustained power of the culture of memory for Argentine civil society, even decades after the return to democracy.

Yet despite these advances, political violence and impunity continue to plague Argentina, revealing an uneven terrain of justice. This has been evident with the impunity surrounding the 1994 AMIA bombing as well as in new cases of political disappearance and deaths, such as the 2017 cases of

Santiago Maldonado and Rafael Nahuel in relation to Indigenous land claims. The ongoing impunity marks fissures, raising questions about the rule of law as well as spaces for civil society to cultivate citizenship as they demand justice and memory. In response, activists have turned to protests that invoke the embodied practices of the Madres, seeking to render visible that which the state may wish to silence or disappear. Indeed, memory practices continue to be a form of translating the demands of civil society to the state, representing a desire for repair. Such repair can take the form of juridical accountability, societal acknowledgment, memory-based initiatives, and other forms of reparations. Yet what does such repair and recovery mean if the terrain of justice remains uneven? What is the value of such acts of repair when the possibility of justice might remain hovering perpetually on the horizon, perpetually out of reach?

In this chapter, I explore these questions by first examining the history of the politics of memory and efforts for justice in Argentina within the context of a human rights framework. I proceed by exploring several cases of impunity in Argentina that have served as flashpoints for justice and citizenship, including the 2017 disappearances of Santiago Maldonado and Rafael Nahuel as well as the case of the 1994 AMIA bombing. Despite the lack of justice and the profound liminality in which these cases reside, the response of social movements in civil society underscores the important way in which citizens have cultivated spaces of agency and belonging. While their struggles for justice may be ongoing, I conclude with reflections on the significance of such agency for the creation of political subjectivity and communities. Even if justice remains perpetually hovering out of reach, these practices offer possibilities for sustaining civil society that can serve as a form of social and symbolic repair.

Memory and Justice: Constitutive Tensions

In many ways, contemporary Argentine political subjectivity was shaped through memory-based struggles in the aftermath of political violence. During the years of repressive state violence and dictatorship (1976–1983), Argentines turned to memory as a space for protest and dissent. Groups like the Madres, whose children were disappeared, took to the central plaza of Buenos Aires to protest the repression of the state, marching every week. Some wore white headscarves stitched with their children's names and the dates of their disappearances, while others also held images of their children. By marching around the plaza, demanding to know what happened to their children, their bodies disrupted the flow of collective time and space, reorganizing it every Thursday afternoon. Through such embodied memory practices, these mothers resisted the idea that their children had simply "disappeared," inspiring a modality of protest formative for the civil society that would take shape after the dictatorship ended in 1983.[2]

In Argentina, truth and memory became especially important in response to the overwhelming silence of the dictatorship. The detentions, tortures, and disappearances were waged in a clandestine way, with the military in power attempting to disappear not just human beings but also the truth of that time. Indeed, in many ways, the power of the state's repressive apparatus depended on the terror and fear of the populace—a silence disrupted by the protests of the Madres and the work of other human rights organizations, like the Asamblea Permanente de Derechos Humanos (Permanent Assembly for Human Rights). These social movements actively resisted the official narratives denying ongoing human rights abuses and crimes against humanity. Through their protests and advocacy, these groups also inscribed memory into public spaces and the political ethos of democratic Argentina.

Some form of accounting, however, became critical to the transition from violence to democracy. One of the first acts of newly elected President Alfonsín was to create the National Commission on the Disappeared (CONADEP) in 1983 in order to investigate and document the systematic abuses committed by the state from 1976 to 1983.[3] As one of the first truth commissions, the CONADEP served as an important model for transitional justice, seeking to address the patterns of human rights abuses without rendering Argentina vulnerable to another military coup. The report produced, *Nunca más* (*Never Again*), became a bestseller and allowed for the collective witnessing of the violence and state terror that took place. Although this 1984 commission did not explicitly mention reconciliation or healing, in contrast to the 1991 South Africa Truth and Reconciliation Commission, the CONADEP process and the *Nunca más* report nonetheless served as a form of reckoning for society—a reckoning that did not seek reconciliation between perpetrators and victims but instead held space for healing and accountability and the possibility of a latent justice on the horizon. Through truth commissions, reparations, and other judicial and nonjudicial mechanisms, many nations have sought ways to provide collective structures and frameworks of social accounting, even where juridical prosecution may not be attainable (Hayner 2001). The CONADEP in Argentina, then, offered a possible model for national repair and sustainable transition into democracy.

Yet for many of the human rights groups involved, actively remembering their children and the victims of the dictatorship remained imperative, as did the possibility for justice and greater accountability, particularly given the institution of amnesty laws that heralded an era of impunity in the 1990s. Without justice, memory took on an even more prominent role in Argentine politics. In addition to the Madres, other human rights groups were also active in those years, such as the Abuelas de Plaza de Mayo, whose mission was to search for their grandchildren who had been kidnapped by the state or born while their parents were detained. Many of these children were adopted by military families, and some have since been reunited with their biological families through DNA matches (Gandsman 2012). HIJOS, representing the children of the disappeared, was formed in 1995 to demand justice for crimes against their parents. They chose another modality of protest, still occupying public spaces, but rather than marching in the central plaza of Buenos Aires, they relied on *escraches* (see figure 4.1), noisily marching down the streets where perpetrators lived to call them out for their crimes and render visible that which would otherwise vanish under the surface of everyday life.[4] Beyond this, as noted by Noa Vaisman, the HIJOS designed these protests both to "produce justice and to rebuild the 'social fabric'" (Vaisman 2015, 368). While using performance (following Taylor 2002) to disrupt the public sphere, these practices also underscore the way the political and social are intertwined—that these disruptions are also reframing and reconstituting civil society.

Memory thus came to shape civil society in powerful ways that would later lead to political changes, especially under the leadership of Néstor Kirchner (2003–2007) and Cristina Fernández de Kirchner (2007–2015), as the state incorporated the memory of repression into its human rights platform. In 2002, for instance, March 24 became a national holiday, named the National Day of Memory for Truth and Justice. Additionally, those terms—*memory*, *truth*, and *justice*—were engraved on pillars adorning important sites like the ESMA (the Navy School of the Mechanics), where thousands of victims had been kidnapped and tortured, in a space located within the periphery of Buenos Aires. That same site became known officially as the "ex-ESMA," also referred to as the Space of Memory, and came to house the offices of the human rights groups noted earlier as well as the archive Memoria Abierta (Open Memory), which includes a substantial collection of testimonies related to the state violence.[5] This attempt to reinforce memory in the social landscape developed throughout Argentina, with various official sites of memory being installed, signaling the ongoing salience of memory to Argentine politics and citizenship.

Yet while memory and truth became significant parts of civil society after the end of the dictatorship, they continued to exist in a state of constitutive tension with justice—or the lack of justice—in the decades that immediately followed state violence. In 1985, the "Trial of the Juntas" prosecuted just nine high-ranking military officers, with five ultimately sentenced and four acquitted. However, even those trials lost their meaning shortly after with the passing of two amnesty laws: the Full Stop Law in 1986 (limiting prosecution to lawsuits indicted within sixty days of the law's enactment, effectively silencing the six hundred pending charges) and the Due Obedience Law in 1987 (essentially giving blanket amnesty to everyone involved). Then in 1989–1990, the newly elected President Menem pardoned those officers who had been sentenced or court-martialed.[6]

In the period of impunity that followed, memory and truth became even more significant in the absence of justice. In 2003, the Argentine government

FIG. 4.1 Image of March 2018 Escrache. *Source:* Natasha Zaretsky.

overturned the amnesty laws that were instituted in the late 1980s.[7] That year the Supreme Court also began permitting extraditions for crimes against humanity, which then opened the door to the prosecution of those perpetrators who had been living without accountability for decades. The first such trial took place in 2006, focusing on Miguel Etchecolatz, with an estimated six hundred defendants. There have now been over two hundred such trials and over five hundred convictions, with trials taking place throughout the nation, including in Tucumán, Córdoba, and Buenos Aires (Human Rights Watch 2019).

Perhaps one of the most significant trials that emerged investigated the crimes that took place at the notorious ESMA, where an estimated five thousand people were tortured, disappeared, and repressed. This clandestine torture center and concentration camp operated within the boundaries of the city of Buenos Aires and became a site of extensive repression. After decades of advocacy, the ESMA megatrial began in 2012, with sixty-eight former officials facing eight hundred charges, including kidnapping, torture, and murder. Some of the most notable accused and tried there included high-ranking naval officer Alfredo Astiz, as well as eight death flight pilots. On November 29, 2017, the ESMA megatrial came to a close, with twenty-nine perpetrators sentenced to life in prison and nineteen sentenced to eight to twenty-five years for their roles in the brutal repression during the 1976–1983 military dictatorship.

In this way, justice arrived in the land where memory predominated, along with a strong affirmation of what is known as the "right to truth"—a precedent developed in response to the phenomenon of forced disappearances and one that is supported by the American Convention for Human Rights and further reaffirmed through transitional justice mechanisms (such as CONADEP) and now the juridical sphere through these trials.[8] These trials certainly represent a significant step forward in the path toward retributive justice and accountability, representing both a juridical and a symbolic form of repair.

Yet while this kind of justice can be seen as a form of juridical and symbolic reparation from the state for its past violence against its citizens, there were additional forms of reparations as well. Economic reparations have also been a part of the landscape, although as studies have shown, such material reparations have not resulted in "healing" for many survivors and family members of victims of Argentine state violence (Sveaass and Sønneland 2015). As noted in the introduction of this volume, reparation politics concerns ways of anticipating and imagining the future and the definition of who are considered worthy citizens of the nation-state.

In this way, the politics surrounding the repair of past injustice addresses precisely the way in which Argentines are "anticipating and imagining the future"—and how to define whose histories and whose possibilities are included in that imagining. The dynamics of reparation, however, expose the limits of such processes in response to the needs for healing and recovery, also revealing the critical fault lines related to memory and repair that have been exacerbated by a terrain of justice that is uneven. Indeed, with more recent shifts toward denialism in society (notable under the presidency of Javier Milei, who was elected in 2023), the memory of this violence continues to play an important role in the way society is negotiating what it means to be Argentine.[9]

In what follows, I turn to the dynamics of this uneven terrain of justice, first by examining the response to the 2017 deaths of Santiago Maldonado and Rafael Nahuel, both related to confrontations with the state over Indigenous land claims. Specifically, I explore the discursive framings that emerged from civil society and the state and what they reveal about processes of repair. I then turn to another case of ongoing impunity, the 1994 AMIA bombing, one of the most significant terrorist attacks in Argentina's history, which still remains unsolved despite numerous investigatory efforts. This leads me to question how subjects engage with memory and activism in the face of pervasive impunity. That is, given these uneven terrains of justice, what are the futures that can be imagined? What can we learn by looking at the process of demanding justice and seeking accountability as a form of embodied practice, even if the desired goals of justice or truth may never materialize? And what social and political value might embodying such repair have for these subjects?

State Violence and the National Imaginary: The Maldonado and Nahuel Cases

The disappearance of citizens during the 1976–1983 dictatorship was one of the most pervasive mechanisms for state terror in those years. Any forced disappearances postdictatorship, therefore, naturally raise profound distress in civil society, including in the case of disappearances related to conflicts over Indigenous land claims, which led citizens to draw parallels to the past.

In August 2017, at the age of twenty-eight, Santiago Maldonado went missing in the province of Río Negro.[10] Maldonado had been living in the town of El Bolsón for several months when he traveled about seventy kilometers to the province of Chubut. He had been participating in a protest organized by Mapuches over Indigenous land claims on territory that had been seized from the Benetton family. Maldonado was there in solidarity with the Mapuche people, and after a confrontation with the National Gendarmerie, some of the protesters tried to flee. Santiago was among them. And that was the last time anyone saw him. He had gone missing. Disappeared.[11]

Quickly, a viral campaign started, with Argentines wondering, "¿Donde está Santiago?" Where is Santiago? The idea of someone simply disappearing, potentially at the hands of the state, had a powerful resonance for Argentines because of their particular history with state violence. A recognition of that history was also evident in the attempt by the Argentine state to shift the discourse from looking at Santiago's case as one of "forced disappearance" to instead one of "missing person."

In the weeks following his disappearance, false information circulated about Maldonado, including the idea that he hadn't really disappeared but was simply traveling. This denial of his disappearance was met by demands for an investigation, with thousands protesting, calling for his reappearance and demanding the truth. These demands also spread to human rights organizations, both local and international, including Amnesty International, Human Rights Watch, the Inter-American Commission for Human Rights, and the U.N. Commission on Enforced Disappearance. The Argentine people also continued to ask, "Where is Santiago?" flooding Facebook pages and Twitter with their questions—questions that inevitably hinged on a collective memory of past violence.

In September 2017, a month after Santiago was last seen, a march was organized around his disappearance. In Buenos Aires, an estimated 250,000 attended, while other cities, including some outside of Argentina, drew thousands of supporters (90,000 in Córdoba and 40,000 in Rosario). The people held posters demanding that Santiago be returned alive and well. Indeed, it seemed to be about more than just Santiago, as people marched in the same spaces in the Plaza de Mayo where the Madres first started marching forty years prior, demanding that their own children be returned "con vida" (alive), inscribing their images on posters, their names stitched into headscarves, as a way to resist the notion of absence—the idea that they had simply disappeared. What was palpable was the desire for truth that animated these struggles for justice, especially during the 1990s, when amnesty laws effectively protected perpetrators and the state from any official accountability for the past.

What Santiago's disappearance revealed was a kind of fissure—a disruption in the neat passage of time—that connected to other moments of political violence for Argentines, linking this particular life to the thousands of other continued absences and disappearances that shape Argentina. Bodies that are missing and that were killed compelled other bodies to gather in public spaces, calling for justice and seeking some kind of truth, closure, and accountability.

Civil society situated Santiago Maldonado's disappearance within the discursive framework of the dictatorship and the human rights movement through the use of phrases such as "Aparición la vida" (Appearance with life) and through the wide circulation of his image throughout the protests, creating opportunities for engagement for everyone in civil society. As Verónica Capasso and Ana Bugnone (2019) argue, using photos of Santiago Maldonado's face was a representational tactic from the dictatorship-era activism, linking those disappeared during the dictatorship with this disappearance during the democracy (also see Gresham 2017).

This focus on circulating images was a means of resisting the state's erasure of bodies. As Capasso and Bugnone (2019) note, Maldonado's portrait was circulated through stencils, flyers, and posters and was also etched onto the very walls of city streets through murals. In this way, they argue, "this image took on an increasing value as a claim against the state, in the same way as it developed in the visualization of the disappeared by the Mothers of the Plaza de Mayo" (29). This served to situate Maldonado's disappearance within the collective memories of state violence and also offered citizens an opportunity to engage in a form of response through embodied practice, making the image their own and thereby inscribing themselves onto the body of a civil society demanding justice. They thus implicated themselves as mutually responsible for one another (following Michael Rothberg's notion of the "implicated subject" [2019]), also sustaining the principles of civil society and democracy so vital to the resistance of state terror. This highlights the significance of public spaces in rendering visible that which the state might seek to erase or disappear.

Although the use of violence by the state in this case was different, of course, from the scope of violence and repression during the 1976–1983 dictatorship, it is notable that the role of the Argentine National Gendarmerie (under the auspices of the Security Ministry) in the Maldonado case in some ways broke the social contract postdictatorship. As Valeria Weis (2019) suggests, this was an instance of the military being involved in "ordinary policing" again, just as they were during the dictatorship.

On October 20, 2017, Maldonado's family confirmed that his body had been found in the Chubut River, drowned and left in the water for more than seventy days. In November, after burying his body, his family continued to search for answers, pleading for the investigation to remain open and demanding that his case be considered a "forced disappearance" rather than simply that of a missing person. The desire for truth—in this case, for the family members of the victim and other activists—involves advocating for accountability and justice. What is important to note is that part of the battle for this is discursive—to situate Santiago's case within the context of "forced disappearance" (and, potentially, state violence) so that a secondary violence does not take hold through a lack of justice and accountability.

Such state violence in response to Indigenous land claims has a broader scope and context, of course. This was made manifest not long after Maldonado's body was found, when in November 2017, Rafael Nahuel, a twenty-one-year-old Mapuche man from the Lafken Winkul Mapu community in the Río Negro Province near Bariloche, was killed. In a confrontation with security forces, Nahuel was shot in the back by the Albatross group of the Naval Prefecture. The clash arose in response to attempts to evict his community from land they claim is historically theirs. Although the state at first alleged that Nahuel was armed, no weapons were found, and it was eventually established that the security forces had used unnecessary force. According to Amnesty International, this is part of a pattern of criminalization of and discrimination against Indigenous peoples in Argentina, which has developed alongside conflicts over land, which now number over two hundred (Amnesty International 2017). It is estimated that sixteen million hectares of rural land in Argentina are owned by foreign investors, aligning with an increase in mining and oil industry activity over the last twenty years, which has resulted in more struggles between Indigenous communities and corporations (Weis 2019).

The state is clearly using violence in its attempt to forcibly evict Indigenous communities from these lands. Yet symbolic violence is also operating through language, with the state discursively excising Indigenous communities from the national imaginary in order to legitimize its use of force. The state's narratives have created a different kind of rupture and exclusion by labeling Indigenous communities as terrorists, delinquents, and foreigners for their struggles to reclaim land. For instance, the state has associated them with groups accused of terrorist activities, such as the RAM (Mapuche Ancestral Resistance), the FARC (Revolutionary Armed Forces of Colombia), and the Spanish ETA (Weis 2019). This builds on the ways in which the state has used these land claims to create a perception of danger and threat from Indigenous peoples, especially under the 2015–2019 Macri administration. Indeed, the state has cast Indigenous communities as "violent, secessionist, foreign groups" (Caggiano and Mombello 2020, 139).

This, of course, echoes the way the civic-military dictatorship used language in their attempts to frame anyone challenging their vision of national order as being outside the nation—the subversive "other." During the 1976–1983 dictatorship, the state framed its terror as part of what it called a "dirty war" against terrorism and "subversion" of the Western and Christian order. They called this time the *proceso*, or Process of National Reorganization. For the outside world, Argentina's military junta framed this as a war against radical left-wing terrorism, denying any gross human rights violations and affirming that they had to do what was necessary to restore order and combat subversion. Yet it was in this very category of "subversive" that the entire *proceso* was rooted—a category with an entrenched history in the U.S. anti-Communist National Security Doctrine for the Western Hemisphere (see Zaretsky 2018).

As a result, the military pursued anyone deemed to be subversive or potentially subversive to the national order and to what those in power viewed as Argentine civilization. For the military junta in power, preserving their vision of national order required annihilating anyone they deemed subversive, who they felt could be a threat. This included left-wing guerrilla groups, such as the ERP (People's Revolutionary Army) and the Montoneros, along with a large cross section of society that included students, psychologists, Jews, priests working with the poor, and others. To accomplish their goal of order, the state under the leadership of the military junta employed clandestine, extralegal tactics for the disappearance, torture, and murder of an estimated thirty thousand people who were systematically tortured, disappeared, and killed under the leadership of the military junta. Indeed, as anthropologist Antonius Robben (2018) argues, the fundamental betrayal and disruption of trust have left lasting legacies in Argentina.

Framing certain groups as threats, as "subversive" to a notion of order, or as foreigners or terrorists therefore taps into a deeper history in Argentina that imagines certain groups as outside the boundaries of belonging and thereby seeks to justify the use of violence against them. In this way, memories of violence continue to be important sites of contestation between civil society and the state (see Jelin 2003, 2017). And in response to this violence, groups in civil society, ordinary citizens, and institutions like the Asamblea Permanente de Derechos Humanos (Permanent Assembly for Human Rights) continue to demand justice in these cases, reflecting the sustained need for such activism during democracy.

The demands for justice in response to the disappearance and death of Santiago Maldonado and the abuse of force in the death of Rafael Nahuel underscore the fault lines that continue to shape the landscape of justice in relation to the state. They also suggest the importance of imagination (following Di Giminiani et al. 2021) in response to the discursive framing of violence in creating possibilities for citizens to perhaps "anticipate and imagine" futures that turn to memories of past violence as ways to carve out spaces of belonging in the nation. Indeed, Di Giminiani has indicated the ways in which *esperar* in Spanish can translate into hoping and waiting.[12] While hoping for justice and imagining more democratic futures certainly becomes a way to carve out belonging, it also reframes hope itself as a way of knowing—as a way to epistemically position oneself in relation to the world. Such practices of hope, then, may be inevitably liminal and somewhat precarious, and yet through that very precarity, they are open to change and possibilities for transformative imaginings.

On the Boundaries of Justice: The AMIA Case

The 2017 deaths of Maldonado and Nahuel expose the ongoing concerns related to state violence and accountability and how violence exposes fissures in society related to justice and belonging for Indigenous peoples and other minority groups. Indeed, in some cases, there have been years and even decades of impunity. When facing such profound injustice, what compels activists to return, to continue demanding justice, over and over, even if it may never materialize? Such ongoing impunity has plagued the AMIA case since the 1994 attack. The 1994 bombing is considered one of the worst terrorist attacks in Argentina's history, killing eighty-five people and wounding hundreds more, also prompting a crisis of belonging for Jewish Argentines because of the lack of justice. To understand the context for belonging, it is useful to consider where Jews figured in the national imaginary of Argentina and how their very presence in Argentina was predicated on visions of a national order that sought white, northern Europeans to "civilize and populate" the land.[13]

Although Jews arrived in the first major waves of European immigration in the late nineteenth century, along with mostly southern Europeans such as Italians and Spaniards, they were not the European immigrants initially desired. Indeed, this whitening and Europeanizing of Argentina included genocidal policies that targeted Indigenous populations and eventually even excluded and silenced the presence of Indigenous communities in how the nation was imagined (Indigenous communities were not even counted in the official census until 2001; Weis 2019). Within this context, in the 1800s, the state believed that the purpose of immigrants was to "civilize"—populating lands in an effort to conquer and dominate them (Shumway 1991). The first major period of European Jewish migration was a response to pogroms and violence in Eastern Europe and Russia; future migrations took place during the rise of Nazism and in the wake of the Holocaust (Avni 1991). However, over time, while Italian and Spanish immigrants became an accepted foundation for the new nation, the role of Jews remained ambivalent.

Certainly, the national imaginary was developing in ways that generated a tenuous sense of belonging for Jewish Argentines. Although they were able to build community groups, cultural institutions, schools, and places of worship, they also experienced waves of antisemitism. This included the violence of the 1919 Semana Trágica (an urban riot in Buenos Aires targeting Jews) and, later, state policies against Jewish immigration. For instance, many European Jews seeking refuge after World War II were forced to enter Argentina using false names and papers, unable to enter legally as Jews, given Perón's affinity for the ideologies of fascism and Nazism in Europe. While Perón facilitated the entry of Nazis into Argentina (including Adolf Eichmann), most Jews attempting to migrate were instead denied legal entry during the immediate postwar years.[14] Further, during the dictatorship, approximately 12 percent of the disappeared were Jewish, despite that they represented an estimated 1 percent of the population. While there may have been other reasons for their overrepresentation among the disappeared (see Kahan 2019), the institutional antisemitism of the dictatorship has also been well documented in the CONADEP report, *Nunca más*.[15]

While such institutionalized antisemitism forced Jews to question their place in Argentina, they rejoiced with the return to democracy in 1983 and continued to advocate for human rights as members of the Madres and other human rights groups, including the Movimiento Judío por Derechos Humanos (Jewish Movement for Human Rights). This brings us to the early 1990s, which, as already noted, was a time of heightened impunity in Argentina, given the amnesty laws that protected perpetrators from being held accountable. During this period, two terrorist attacks targeted Jewish institutions in Buenos Aires—the 1992 bombing of the Israeli embassy and the 1994 attack on the AMIA.

Carlos Menem, president at the time, sent his condolences to the state of Israel in the wake of the AMIA bombing, which caused Jewish Argentines to question why their president reached out to Israel for an attack that targeted a Jewish community center in Argentina. Did this suggest he did not consider them to be fully Argentine citizens in the way non-Jews were? Many of the Jewish Argentines I interviewed were also struck by the way in which the mainstream news media chronicled the bombing, with newscasters making distinctions between the number of Jewish victims and the number of innocent victims. This discursive framing of Jews as outside the nation only further amplified the sense that they may not fully belong.

The ongoing impunity plaguing this case for over twenty-five years has also exposed important questions about the rule of law in Argentina. There is a pervasive uncertainty that hovers when no one takes responsibility for an act of terror. In 2005, the Inter-American Commission on Human Rights deemed that Argentina failed to provide justice in the AMIA case and that the investigation and process of justice had been marred by significant irregularities and corruption, including the 2015 death of the investigating prosecutor, Alberto Nisman. Despite two trials (2001–2004 and 2015–2019), Argentina is no closer to holding those responsible to account. In 2024, the Inter-American Commission on Human Rights declared that Argentina is responsible for "denying historical truth and justice to the victims and society at large," recommending measures that include access to the right to truth and reparations (CELS 2024). While this official acknowledgment of Argentina's state responsibility for the violation of human rights is meaningful, the question remains of how citizens on the ground grapple with this uneven terrain. What do you do with this lack of justice? How do you find a way forward amid years of impunity and a state that fails to provide justice while simultaneously (and relatedly) suggesting you may not have a place in the national imaginary?

In response, what is interesting to note is how the social movements that formed to demand justice and memory in the AMIA case also invoked the embodied forms of protest initiated by the Madres during the dictatorship and in the many years that followed. Like them, these groups used the images of the victims on posters and other forms of visual representation to render visible those who were killed in the attack and had yet to receive any kind of justice. In this way, they sought to disrupt the flow of ordinary time and challenge the idea that their family members and friends were gone, bringing them back into the here and now through their protests.

This disruption of time also took place through the group Memoria Activa's (Active Memory) weekly actos every Monday morning, the day and time the bombing took place, in the Plaza Lavalle, facing the High Courts of Argentina, where they invited speakers to offer testimonies of how the bombing had impacted their lives. What is notable is the way they inscribed the impunity surrounding this case within a history of impunity in Argentina and how the victims of this AMIA bombing were remembered along with calls to remember the thirty thousand disappeared and other victims of injustice and state violence from the period of the dictatorship. In this way, they were weaving themselves back into the national imaginary, through practices that also allowed participants to build a sense of citizenship and agency even as they grappled with a pervasive sense of impunity.

Since the 1994 attack, three primary groups of family members of the victims and their supporters formed in this case, with a range of positionings in relation to the organized Jewish community, the Argentine state, and the pursuit of justice: Familiares y Amigos de las Víctimas (Family Members and Friends of the Victims of the AMIA), which organized actos directly in front of the AMIA building every 18th of the month (commemorating the date of the bombing; see figure 4.2); APEMIA (Asociación para la Esclarecimiento de la Masacre Impune de la AMIA), a group advocating for clarification and truth, with one of its primary calls to action focusing on the trials against the state and the opening of SIDE (Secretaría de Inteligencia) archives; and Memoria Activa, which organized weekly actos in front of the high courts at the Plaza Lavalle every Monday morning.

Memoria Activa protested weekly from 1994 to 2004, then continued its advocacy in coordination with CELS and actively pursued a case against Argentina in the Inter-American Commission on Human Rights that concluded in 2024 with the Inter-American Commission on Human Rights (IACHR) determining Argentina's official responsibility for violation of human rights. In addition, a small group of concerned citizens who regularly attended the actos continued going to the plaza every Monday even after Memoria Activa no longer convened there, simply calling themselves Ciudadanos de la Plaza (Citizens of the Plaza), carrying on with their vigils for memory and justice until at least 2018.

FIG. 4.2 July 18, 2013, annual commemoration of AMIA bombing. *Source:* Laura Ponte.

During the years after the bombings, many activists actively engaged the public sphere as they sought memory and justice. This included key figures who were family members of victims of the AMIA bombing, such as Laura Ginsberg, Sofía Guterman, Adriana Reisfeld, Diana Wassner, and others. In addition to family members, concerned citizens also found active engagement in these protests a meaningful way to demand justice for victims and to challenge the ongoing impunity in the case, which they found essential for their own sense of political subjectivity.

Tita (Rebeca Sakolsky) was one such activist. Tita was visibly present in Memoria Activa for many years. She was also a regular participant in the Thursday afternoon protests of the Madres, which she first began attending as a survivor of the dictatorship who had been held in two concentration camps, El Banco and El Olimpo. After the 1994 AMIA bombing, she started going to the Monday morning actos to continue her advocacy against impunity in Argentina.

I learned about her history during the years of the dictatorship, long before I ever sat down with her for an interview, because of a story about her encounter with one of her repressors that was famous among the activists who gathered every week in front of the high courts. As one such activist, Adriana, told me, after every Monday morning acto, those who gathered would go to a nearby café, the Banchero, to "volver a la vida" (return to life), as she called it. As the story goes, one such morning, Tita was sitting in the Banchero along with the other activists, and right there in the same space, having an ordinary cup of coffee, was Tita's repressor, Julián the Turk, who she described as torturing her during the dictatorship. Tita went up to him and said to his face, "Why don't you call me 'judía de mierda' [derogatory term for Jew] now, in front of all of these people?"

This was the 1990s, during the years of impunity, when he and so many other perpetrators of violence walked freely. Yet despite this legal freedom, they were not protected from social accountability. And Tita had the chance to say something directly to the man who had repressed her. His response may not have been satisfying—all he said was, "No te conozco" (I don't know you). But Tita knew him. And what impressed everyone in the many retellings I heard of this story was Tita's ability to stand up to him in the way that she did. In this way, these collective spaces for activists also offered unexpected opportunities for agency to those who had survived violence and loss.

Years after the incident, Tita told me this story herself over coffee in the Banchero as she also reflected on how she understood her own history and activism. This was 2013, a time no longer marked by rampant impunity but rather one that saw many human rights trials taking place in Argentina. Indeed, Julián the Turk (whose real name was Julio Héctor Simón) had been tried and found guilty, sentenced in 2006 to twenty-five years in prison for his crimes in the first conviction of the new post–amnesty era. Yet Tita's activism continued. She told me that in addition to going to the plaza on Mondays, she also went to the marches of the Madres on Thursdays out of solidarity, as a survivor of the torture of the dictatorship.

This ultimately inspired her to come to the Plaza Lavalle from the very first Monday she learned that the actos were taking place. She explained, "Porque un espacio de lucha, no se puede dejar. Porque si no, perdiste la lucha" (Because a space of struggle you can't abandon. If you lose it, you have lost the struggle).

Yet after so many years, when I asked if she had any hope in this case, she was emphatic in her response: "No, no, no. I know that nothing will happen." For her, all of the people who had recently stood trial would not be held accountable. In this way, she predicted in 2013 what would happen years later at the conclusion of the trial in 2019. As I noted at the start of this chapter, she asked me pointedly, "Here, justice?" raising her eyebrows. After a pause, she answered her own question. "No," she told me, vehemently shaking her head.

I then asked, "Why do you still come [to the plaza], given your lack of hope?"

And she replied, "To demand justice. Because the most important thing for a person is the ability to demand justice, and [we need to do whatever we can] so that one day, there might be justice."

In this way, Tita reaffirmed the importance of these public sites not only to create spaces of community and support but also to assert her demands as a citizen seeking justice, seeking some form of repair, even if the possibility of finally achieving justice might not materialize. She, along with many others who continue demanding justice in this case and others, felt it was imperative to hold on to this space as a citizen, noting its significance "even if you are the only one here." Her presence, there in that public space, was what mattered to her, to hold on to the possibility of justice. And so this holding on became her act of repair (see Zaretsky 2021).

Conclusion: Reflecting on Temporality and Repair

The cases of impunity that continue to plague Argentina reveal an uneven terrain of justice. This can be seen with the deaths of Maldonado and Nahuel in relation to Indigenous land claims as well as the 1994 AMIA bombing. In response, activists have turned to protests that invoke the embodied practices of the Madres de Plaza de Mayo, seeking to render visible that which the state may wish to silence or disappear. Such memory-based practices have become, as Elizabeth Jelin notes (2003, 2017), sites of contestation between civil society and the state.[16] And indeed, through discursive framings of who belongs and who does not, the state also demonstrates how violence can hinge on forms of narrative inclusion and exclusion. So in the face of these dynamics, what does holding on to justice mean? How can we read these embodied practices that have emerged in response to a desire for a justice that may always be hovering on the horizon, out of reach?

The concept of transitional justice is predicated on the idea that at some point, there may be a period of retributive justice that redresses the crimes of the past. And yet in these cases, we see a society that remains in a state of what seems a perpetual transition from political repression and violence. The idea of passage into a future state is also embedded in normative assumptions of transitional justice, as argued by Alex Hinton (2010).

And even with the normative ideals suggested by this model, we can also see how it underlies much of the logic of understanding the political value ascribed to memory in Argentina. After Argentina returned to democratic rule in 1983, some form of accounting was viewed as critical to the transition from state violence, including the creation of the CONADEP—an important model for transitional justice, with the intended goal of repairing the nation (out of the fear that full prosecution of perpetrators would challenge the new democracy and lead to another military coup). In line with Hinton's work, the CONADEP can be seen as liminal through this framing as part of a passage for Argentina to some imagined future stage of normative order—a way to hold on to the possibility of the rule of law and a future justice as the final stage.

This casts transitional justice as a form of liminality. However, I want to consider here the value of this liminality in other ways in Argentina—as being more than a stage of transition but also holding the possibility of insight and transformation. In this case, these efforts for justice have exposed the way in which the state continues to use violence and force through its actions and through discourse, framing certain groups as outside the national imaginary in order to legitimize impunity and violence. In response, the acts of citizens turning to embodied practices can serve as social forms of repair in sustaining a civil society as a force to question and challenge the state while also offering insights into what citizenship means.

Such insights resonate with what Victor Turner (1967) notes about the liminal state rites of passage. He describes liminality "as a realm of pure possibility whence novel configurations of ideas and relations may arise" (47). Further, he suggests a certain potential to that space as such, beyond its role in the passage to something else, describing the liminal stage as involving an "undoing, dissolution, decomposition . . . accompanied by powers of growth, transformation, and the reformulation of old elements in new patterns" (49).

Perhaps then the liminality sustained here not only has to be about the possibility for a future justice or a transition or passage somewhere else but can also tell us something about the possibilities of repair necessary in a present that is focused on imagining a future. I would like to suggest that these embodied practices offer a version of sustained liminality that might have value in its own right, given its possibilities for "transformation" and insight suggested by Turner. In other words, liminality itself can play an important role in repair, even if it isn't a transition to something else. Further, in those moments when liminality is a shared struggle, creating spaces in the public sphere for demanding justice together, new opportunities for developing political agency and cultivating belonging arise, offering a different form of repair when retributive justice may not be immediately accessible.

For many of these activists, while they continue to demand justice, even if it never arrives, their practices may be doing something else. They have carved out spaces of connection and possibilities for agency that allow them to see their society in a new light and inscribe themselves into the national imaginary. And through this, perhaps they can envision new possibilities for survival and transformation, imagining and building a more inclusive future for their democracy and in so doing enacting new forms of symbolic repair.

Notes

1 For the definitive review of the significance of memory to democracy and human rights in Argentina, see Elizabeth Jelin (2017, 2003, 2002). For more specific analyses, see also Crenzel (2020), Da Silva Catela (2001), and Kahan (2019).
2 For an analysis of their work in the context of performance studies and theory, see Diana Taylor's important study, *Disappearing Acts* (1997). Additionally, for a discussion of the intersection of personal loss and political activism, see Navarro (1989).
3 See Crenzel (2009) for a comprehensive analysis of the CONADEP.
4 See Taylor (2006) for an analysis of HIJOS's representational practices.
5 Although this work focuses largely on memory-based social movements, there were also other NGOs, like the Centro de Estudios Legales y Sociales (CELS), which served an important role in advocating for and documenting human rights abuses.
6 For a detailed account of the history of human rights during that time, see Brysk (1994).
7 The Supreme Court found the amnesty laws to be unconstitutional in 2005, which opened the door for prosecutions of those responsible for the repression during

the "dirty war." Importantly, they also found that statutes of limitations did not apply to these crimes, as they were crimes against humanity. See the Supreme Court of Argentina's 2010 report, *Delitos de lesa humanidad* (Corte Suprema de Justicia de la NaciónSupreme).

8 For an overview of the significance of the "right to truth" to the rule of law in Latin America more broadly, see the Inter-American Commission on Human Rights 2014 report, *The Right to Truth in the Americas*.

9 For more on Milei and the rise of denialism in relation to the dictatorship, see Rajevic and Elgueta (2024); see also Anderson (2024); Iglesia (2024).

10 See Human Rights Watch World Report 2018 for additional analysis of the significance of Maldonado's case.

11 For more on the Maldonado case, see Amnesty International (2018).

12 I expand on this idea of liminality as bearing transformative potential in my ethnography, *Acts of Repair* (2021). This also touches on ideas shared during the Wenner-Gren Reparations workshop (March 2021), and I am grateful to Nancy Postero for her comments about ambiguous positions as giving space to reorganize society and to Piergiorgio Di Giminiani for his comments about *esperar*. While hoping for justice and imagining more democratic futures certainly become a way to carve out belonging, as noted earlier, it is also interesting to consider things from an epistemic perspective, in thinking about hope itself as a way of knowing.

13 The history of Jewish immigration and the analysis of the social movements formed in response to the bombing derive from my ethnography, *Acts of Repair* (2021).

14 From 1945 to 1949, it is estimated that up to 1,500 Jews entered Argentina legally. Many more Jews who attempted to enter Argentina as refugees after having survived the Holocaust were blocked through legal channels, even if they were close relatives of Argentines. As a result, they were compelled to enter illegally (through bordering nations) or under assumed names and religious identities. Perón later pardoned any immigrants who entered illegally, and an estimated 3,300 Jews legalized their status by 1949 (Avni 1991, 192–193).

15 Jacobo Timerman famously wrote about his experience as a persecuted Jew during this period in *Prisoner Without a Name, Cell Without a Number* (1981), one of the first such accounts from the perspective of someone tortured during the dictatorship.

16 There is, of course, significant literature related to memory and human rights in Argentina. This includes Allier-Montaño and Crenzel (2015); Crenzel (2009, 2020); Da Silva Catela (2001); Feierstein (2014); Gandsman (2012); Kahan (2019); Robben (2018); Sikkink and Booth Walling (2007); and Vaisman (2015).

References

Allier-Montaño, Eugenia, and Emilio Crenzel, eds. 2015. *The Struggle for Memory in Latin America: Recent History and Political Violence*. New York: Palgrave Macmillan.

Amnesty International. 2017. "Hay mas de 200 conflictos con comunidades aborigenes en el pais." *La Nacion*, September 17. Accessed December 5, 2024. https://www.lanacion.com.ar/politica/hay-mas-de-200-conflictos-con-comunidades-aborigenes-en-el-pais-nid2063713.

Amnesty International. 2018. *The State of the World's Human Rights*. London: Amnesty International.

Anderson, Jon Lee. 2024. "Javier Milei Wages War on Argentina's Government." *The New Yorker*, December 2, 2024. https://www.newyorker.com/magazine/2024/12/09/javier-milei-wages-war-on-argentinas-government.

Avni, Haim. 1991. *Argentina and the Jews: A History of Jewish Immigration*. Translated by Gila Brand. Tuscaloosa: University of Alabama Press.

Brysk, Alison. 1994. *The Politics of Human Rights in Argentina: Protest, Change, and Democratization*. Stanford, Calif.: Stanford University Press.

Bullentini, Allín. 2017. "Abre la puerta a la impunidad de los genocidas." *Página/12*, May 4, 2017. https://www.pagina12.com.ar/35531-abre-la-puerta-a-la-impunidad-de-los-genocidas.

Caggiano, Sergio, and Laura Mombello. 2020. "Inmigrantes e indígenas en las torsiones de la nacionalidad y la ciudadanía. La construcción de amenazas en Argentina (2015–2019)." *Historia y Sociedad* 39 (July): 130–154.

Capasso, Verónica Cecilia, and Ana Liza Bugnone. 2019. "Activismo artístico y memoria: El caso de la desaparición de Santiago Maldonado." *Cuadernos de Música, Artes Visuales y Artes Escénicas* 14 (2): 23–41.

CELS. 2024. "AMIA Bombing: Landmark Ruling by the Inter-American Court of Human Rights Condemns Argentine State." June 14, 2024. https://www.cels.org.ar/web/en/2024/06/amia-bombing-landmark-ruling-by-inter-american-of-human-rights-court-condemns-argentine-state/.

CONADEP. (1984) 2003. *Nunca más: Informe final de la Comisión Nacional sobre la Desaparición de Personas*. Buenos Aires: EUDEBA.

Corte Suprema de Justicia de la Nación. 2010. *Delitos de lesa humanidad: Informe sobre la evolución de las causas*. Buenos Aires: Corte Suprema de Justicia de la Nación.

Crenzel, Emilio. 2009. *La Historia Política del Nunca Más: La Memoria de las Desaparaciones en la Argentina*. Buenos Aires: Siglo XXI Editores.

Crenzel, Emilio. 2020. "The Ghostly Presence of the Disappeared in Argentina." *Memory Studies* 13 (3): 253–266.

Da Silva Catela, Ludmila. 2001. *No habrá flores en la tumba del pasado: La experiencia de reconstrucción del mundo de los familiares de desaparecidos*. La Plata: Ediciones Al Margen.

Feierstein, Daniel. 2014. *Genocide as Social Practice: Reorganizing Society Under the Nazis and Argentina's Military Juntas*. Translated by Douglas Andrew Town. New Brunswick, N.J.: Rutgers University Press.

Feitlowitz, Marguerite. 1998. *A Lexicon of Terror: Argentina and the Legacies of Torture*. Oxford: Oxford University Press.

Gandsman, Ariel. 2012. "Retributive Justice, Public Intimacies and the Micropolitics of the Restitution of Kidnapped Children of the Disappeared in Argentina." *International Journal of Transitional Justice* 6 (3): 423–443.

Garzón, Baltasar. 2017. "Una amenaza a conquistas históricas." *Página/12*, May 7, 2017. https://www.pagina12.com.ar/36231-una-amenaza-a-conquistas-historicas.

Goñi, Uki. 2016. "Blaming the Victims: Dictatorship Denialism Is on the Rise in Argentina." *The Guardian*, August 29, 2016. https://www.theguardian.com/world/2016/aug/29/argentina-denial-dirty-war-genocide-mauricio-macri?CMP=share_btn_tw.

Goñi, Uki. 2017. "Fury in Argentina over Ruling That Could See Human Rights Abusers Walk Free." *The Guardian*, May 4, 2017. https://www.theguardian.com/world/2017/may/04/argentina-supreme-court-human-rights.

Gresham Beamer, Emily. 2017. "¿Dónde está Santiago Maldonado? El uso del retrato y el activismo artístico para exigir la 'aparición con vida' de las desapariciones forzadas en Argentina." Independent Study Project Collection. https://digitalcollections.sit.edu/isp_collection/2658/.

Hayner, Priscilla B. 2001. *Unspeakable Truths: Facing the Challenge of Truth Commissions*. London: Routledge.

Hinton, Alexander. 2010. "Introduction: Toward an Anthropology of Transitional Justice." In *Transitional Justice: Global Mechanisms and Local Realities After Genocide and*

Mass Violence, edited by A. L. Hinton, 1–22. New Brunswick, N.J.: Rutgers University Press.

Human Rights Watch. 2018. *Human Rights Watch World Report*. New York: Human Rights Watch.

Human Rights Watch. 2019. *Human Rights Watch World Report*. New York: Human Rights Watch.

Iglesia, Facundo. 2024. "'Justification of Dictatorship': Outcry as Milei Rewrites Argentina's History." *The Guardian*, March 23, 2024. https://www.theguardian.com/world/2024/mar/23/javier-milei-argentina-dictatorship-remembrance.

Inter-American Commission on Human Rights. 2014. *The Right to Truth in the Americas*. http://www.oas.org/en/iachr/reports/pdfs/right-to-truth-en.pdf.

Jelin, Elizabeth. 2003. *State Repression and the Labors of Memory*. Translated by Judy Rein and Marcial Godoy-Anativia. Minneapolis: University of Minnesota Press.

Jelin, Elizabeth. 2017. *La Lucha por el Pasado: Cómo Construimos la Memoria Social*. Buenos Aires: Siglo Veintiuno Editores.

Kahan, Emmanuel Nicolás. 2019. *Memories That Lie a Little: Jewish Experiences During the Argentine Dictatorship*. Translated by David Foster. Leiden: Brill.

Minow, Martha. 1998. *Between Vengeance and Forgiveness: Facing History After Genocide and Mass Violence*. Boston: Beacon.

Navarro, Marysa. 1989. "The Personal Is Political: Las Madres de Plaza de Mayo." In *Power and Popular Protest*, edited by Susan Eckstein, 241–258. Berkeley: University of California Press.

Payne, Leigh. 2008. *Unsettling Accounts: Neither Truth nor Reconciliation in Confessions of State Violence*. Durham, N.C.: Duke University Press.

Rajevic, Manuela Badilla, and Elisa Muñoz Elgueta. 2024. "Memory Sites Under Attack." *NACLA Report on the Americas* 56 (4): 364–369.

Robben, Antonius C. G. M. 2018. *Argentina Betrayed: Memory, Mourning, and Accountability*. Philadelphia: University of Pennsylvania Press.

Robben, Antonius C. G. M., and Marcelo M. Suárez-Orozco, eds. 2000. *Cultures Under Siege: Collective Violence and Trauma*. Cambridge: Cambridge University Press.

Roht-Arriaza, Naomi, and Javier Mariezcurrena, eds. 2006. *Transitional Justice in the Twenty-First Century: Beyond Truth Versus Justice*. Cambridge: Cambridge University Press.

Rothberg, Michael. 2019. *The Implicated Subject: Beyond Victims and Perpetrators*. Stanford, Calif.: Stanford University Press.

Shumway, Nicolas. 1991. *The Invention of Argentina*. Berkeley: University of California Press.

Sikkink, Kathryn, and Carrie Booth Walling. 2007. "The Impact of Human Rights Trials in Latin America." *Journal of Peace Research* 44 (4): 427–445.

Soria, Sofía. 2017. "¿Dónde está Santiago Maldonado? Tres imágenes." *Cuadernos de Coyuntura* 1:51–55. https://revistas.unc.edu.ar/index.php/CuadernosConyuntura/article/view/18755.

Sveaass, Nora, and Anne Margrethe Sønneland. 2015. "Dealing with the Past: Survivors' Perspectives on Economic Reparations in Argentina." *International Perspectives in Psychology: Research, Practice, Consultation* 4:223–238.

Taylor, Diana. 1997. *Disappearing Acts: Spectacles of Gender and Nationalism in Argentina's "Dirty War."* Durham, N.C.: Duke University Press.

Taylor, Diana. 2006. "DNA of Performance." In *Cultural Agency in the Americas*, edited by Doris Sommer, 52–81. Durham, N.C.: Duke University Press.

Taylor, Diana. 2020. *¡Presente! The Politics of Presence*. Durham, N.C.: Duke University Press.

Timerman, Jacobo. 1981. *Prisoner Without a Name, Cell Without a Number*. Translated by Toby Talbot. New York: Vintage Books.

Turner, Victor W. 1967. *The Forest of Symbols: Aspects of Ndembu Ritual*. Ithaca, N.Y.: Cornell University Press.

Vaisman, Noa. 2015. "Variations on Justice: Argentina's Pre- and Post-Transitional Justice and the Justice to Come." *Ethnos* 82 (2): 366–388.

Vargas, Mercedes. 2017. "En la frontera, un refugio para la cultura." *Cuadernos de Coyuntura* 1:57–60. https://revistas.unc.edu.ar/index.php/CuadernosConyuntura/article/view/18755.

Verbitsky, Horacio. 1996. *The Flight: Confessions of an Argentine Dirty Warrior*. Translated by Esther Allen. New York: New Press.

Weis, Valeria Vegh. 2019. "Towards a Critical Green Southern Criminology: An Analysis of Criminal Selectivity, Indigenous Peoples and Green Harms in Argentina." *International Journal for Crime, Justice and Social Democracy* 8 (3): 38–55.

Wieviorka, Annette. 2006. *The Era of the Witness*. Translated by Jared Stark. Ithaca, N.Y.: Cornell University Press.

Zaretsky, Natasha. 2018. "The U.S. Role in Argentina's 'Dirty War.'" In *Dirty Hands and Vicious Deeds: The U.S. Government's Complicity in Crimes Against Humanity and Genocide*, edited by Samuel Totten, 278–342. Toronto: University of Toronto Press.

Zaretsky, Natasha. 2021. *Acts of Repair: Justice, Truth, and the Politics of Memory in Argentina*. New Brunswick, N.J.: Rutgers University Press.

5

Indigenous Belongings as Precarious

• •

An Ethnography of Reparation
Activism for Mine-Caused
Damages in Guatemala

KARINE VANTHUYNE

April 9, 2018. This was my third visit to San Miguel Ixtahuacán (San Marcos, Guatemala) as part of my collaborative ethnographic research with the Frente de Defensa Miguelense (San Miguel Defense Front, FREDEMI), a grassroots antimining coalition that formed in 2009 to coordinate the various oppositional movements to the Marlin Mine arising in the municipality since the late 1990s and that disbanded in 2020 following their struggle for reparation's failure. Owned by Montana Exploradora (Montana),[1] the open-pit and subterranean gold and silver mine operated from 2005 to 2017, engendering widespread community opposition (Urkidi 2011) and intracommunity conflict (Cajax 2014). Through a large repertoire of actions, including road blockades, mine site occupations, street protests, local and international juridical actions, and municipal electoral campaigns as a *comité cívico* (civic committee), FREDEMI has contested the very legality of the mine operations on the grounds of inadequate prior consultation (Imai 2007) and illegitimate land grabbing (van de Sandt 2009). It has also denounced the mine's adverse environmental and health

impacts, as witnessed by members and documented by numerous independent studies (Basu et al. 2010; COPAE 2008, 2009; Kamp and Maest 2010;
Robinson 2007; Van de Wauw, Evens, and Machiels 2010). Garnering support internationally (Urkidi 2011), these accusations and studies prompted
the Inter-American Commission on Human Rights (IACHR) to call upon the
Guatemalan government to suspend Montana's mining operations in 2010.
The government agreed with the decision but took no measures to implement
it, and the suspension was later reduced to a call for more benign "precautionary
measures" by the IACHR in 2011—in part as a result of Canadian diplomatic
pressures (Kamphuis and Connolly 2022), Marlin being Canadian owned at
the time.[2] Meanwhile, other San Miguel residents who had gained employment
at Marlin or who considered the mine's financing of community infrastructure
to be essential denounced FREDEMI's claims of nonconsultation, land grabbing, and mine-caused contamination as "lies." They also coordinated violent
repression of its antimining actions. Hence my surprise when, on my first day
in his municipality, Aniseto Lopez-Diaz, then coordinator of FREDEMI,
invited me to a public meeting in San José Ixcanché, a hamlet of San Miguel
adjacent to the mine. I had traveled to the village during previous visits in 2014
and 2016 but covertly. Until recently, San José's local authorities had been in
favor of the mine, and most of its male residents worked there; thus, the hand-
ful of FREDEMI member residents had asked my research assistants and me to
be discreet when visiting them. But on this day in April 2018, FREDEMI was
planning to meet in the *kiosko* (kiosk) of San José's *plaza* (square), in the light
of day and next to the village's town hall, where the entire community would
be gathered to attend the mayor's inauguration of their new local health center.
How did this normalization of FREDEMI's oppositional politics in San José
Ixcanché happen? Since when did FREDEMI activists feel comfortable discussing their antimine actions openly, in sight of and with the full knowledge of
their (former) opponents?

When I posed these questions to Aniseto over the phone, I learned that
around the beginning of the previous year, the mine workers had been informed
by their employer that Montana would terminate Marlin's operations on
May 31, 2017; worried that the mining company would not address the environmental damages its activities had caused in their villages (such as cracked
houses or dried-up sources of water), the workers that lived around the mine
had turned to San Miguel's mayor to voice their concerns. Unlike previous mayors, the one at that time, Ramiro Soto (2016–2020), had begun to regularly
meet with FREDEMI to hear their complaints about the mine, which led him
to encourage the workers to reach out to FREDEMI. As a result, FREDEMI
and a group of the Marlin Mine workers had ended up coordinating their efforts
with the support of the municipal government between 2017 and 2018 in order
to pressure the mining company and the Guatemalan state authorities to assume
their responsibilities vis-à-vis a diverse array of liabilities, including mine-caused

environmental damage and health problems, breaches of company-community agreements, and unfulfilled state obligations to carefully monitor the mine's impacts and implement the IACHR precautionary measures. This collaboration institutionally took the form of the establishment of the Comité de vigilancia sobre el cierre minero (Mine Closure Oversight Committee, Comité), a municipal task force that, at talks with the company and state authorities that were facilitated by Guatemala's Comisión Presidencial de Diálogo (Presidential Dialogue Commission, CPD), represented the ten villages in San Miguel that were most affected by Montana's activities. The collaboration between FREDEMI and the ex–mine workers also took the shape of direct political actions, such as a blockade of the Pan-American Highway in late March 2017 and a fifty-four-day-long mine site occupation in July and August of that same year.

In this chapter, I draw on an ethnography of FREDEMI activism to bring to light the conflicting imaginations of past, present, and futures as well as the contested forms of belonging that are set in motion by reparation claimants and state actors as they assess harms and assign responsibilities while attempting to mend divided political communities following historical and ongoing state oppression. Through claiming reparations for mine-caused damages, FREDEMI members not only asked the Guatemalan government to force the mining company to repair the damages they believed it was responsible for in their municipality; they were more broadly seeking to be recognized as its citizens and thus pursuing remedy for their historical economic exploitation and political subjugation. Although the post–peace accords state first seemed inclined to recognize them as such, it soon became clear to the activists that "intercultural dialogue," as a new postgenocide device, rather served to reproduce their exclusion from the Guatemalan nation. Hence their focus was to at the very least rebuild their Maya-Mam *polis* through mobilizing with their neighbors who had become their enemies as a result of FREDEMI's opposition to Marlin. Yet in the context of the situation of extreme poverty most of them faced, belonging to this political community, as we will see, remained particularly fragile.

After briefly surveying the state of Indigenous citizenship in Guatemala and what specifically led to the formation of FREDEMI in San Miguel Ixtahuacán, I will examine local stories of involvement in, and disinvolvement from, this grassroots organization. In so doing, I will focus not only on the more recent challenge of joining with past opponents that members of this organization faced but on the more general one of being identified as a *true* comrade of FREDEMI's oppositional struggle—and the resulting need for its members to continuously demonstrate their allegiance to it. An examination of how the state responded to the Comité's demands for reparations will then conclude the chapter to demonstrate the pervasiveness of its oppressive logics. Since the same violent structures that have historically motivated Indigenous peoples in Guatemala to demand social justice remain—economic exploitation and political domination—their political mobilization in this country, I argue, remains highly precarious and thus heroic.

From *Mozos Colonos* to Antimining Activists

Colonial relations between Guatemala's non-Indigenous elite and Indigenous majority have profoundly shaped this country's nation-state construction processes (Casaus Arzú 1992; McCreery 1994). Within a highly segregated socioeconomic and political structure, the Indigenous population occupied the bottom of the ladder (Taracena Arriola 2002a), "often in spaces set apart as 'Indians only'" (Hale 2006, 27). While occasional Indigenous riots challenged this situation of domination (Martínez Peláez 1985), a "colonial compact" generally prevailed between the non-Indigenous *finqueros* (large landowners) and their Indigenous *mozos colonos*[3] (McCreery 1994), both before and after Guatemala's independence in 1821. Guatemala's "Democratic Spring" (1944–1954) did not fundamentally challenge the dominant racist ideology that rationalized Indigenous people's political subjugation and economic exploitation (Taracena Arriola 2002b). The abolition of some of its structural anchors, however—such as forced labor laws and the requirement to be literate and exercise a profession to be granted the right to vote[4]—did spur an increasing number of Indigenous males to join unions and political parties in order to challenge their domination by the non-Indigenous minority (Handy 1994).

The 1954 CIA-backed coup to end "communism" in Guatemala (Gleijeses 1991) was quickly followed, in the highlands where San Miguel is located, by the Catholic Action's (CA) liberation-theology-inspired programs of religious conversion, education, and cooperative development (Hernández Sandoval 2019). CA's consciousness-raising workshops initially aimed to discourage Indigenous involvement in Guatemala's growing popular movements. Yet they eventually led to the emergence of Guatemala's first organizations of Indigenous peasants (Konefal 2010), such as the Movimiento Campesino del Altiplano (Peasant Movement of the Highland, MCA) in the department of San Marcos, where San Miguel is located, as well as the involvement of some of their members in the Marxist-inspired guerrilla group that operated in the region in the mid-1970s (Gutiérrez 2011). In San Miguel, as in the rest of the Guatemalan Highlands (Brett 2007; Manz 2004; McAllister 2003), Indigenous involvement in the insurrection was heterogeneous. While some enthusiastically joined the ranks of the Organización del Pueblo en Armas (People's Organization in Arms, ORPA)—the guerrilla movement that was active in the region (Forster 2012)—others refused to, disagreeing with the rebels' reading of their situation or disapproving of their use of violence to meet political ends (Vanthuyne and Dugal 2022). In the eyes of the military, however, all Indigenous leaders were presumed to be revolutionaries and were either "disappeared" or arbitrarily executed (CEH 1999). The genocidal scorched-earth policy that followed (1981–1983; CEH 1999) spared San Miguel's villages. Nonetheless, the majority of its remaining political leaders fled to Mexico as a result, while those who stayed behind were forcefully enrolled in the army's counterinsurgency operations as civil patrols (Vanthuyne and Dugal 2022). Most members of FREDEMI are therefore either ex-patrollers or their descendants—and not the ex-guerrillas some scholars (Bastos and Camus 2013) have presumed Guatemala's antimining activists to be.

Despite significant limitations, the 1996 peace accords reopened the door for Indigenous political activism by demilitarizing the highlands, allowing refugees to return, authorizing a U.N.-mandated truth commission, legalizing leftist parties and organizations, and recognizing human and Indigenous rights (Jonas 2000). The Agreement on the Identity and Rights of Indigenous Peoples, more specifically, recognized their cultural, civil, economic, political, and social collective rights, including the right of participation at all levels, and the right to exercise Indigenous forms of law within the existing structures of the Guatemalan state and international human rights standards (Sieder 1999). The defeat of the 1999 referendum that would have led to the constitutionalization of these commitments critically weakened them—signaling the decline of Guatemala's Indigenous movement (Bastos and Brett 2010) as well as setting Guatemala apart from Ecuador (Becker 2011) and Bolivia (Postero 2007, 2017) in that regard. Yet an increasing number of Indigenous communities nonetheless began revitalizing and strengthening their "ancestral" governance structures[5] thanks to the support of "proreform sectors within the state, academia, local civic associations, non-governmental organizations, and a plethora of international development cooperation agencies" (Sieder 2020, 336). Along with the decentralization policies introduced as part of the International Monetary Fund–mandated neoliberal package of "structural adjustments," this development contributed to increased Indigenous involvement in local politics.

In San Miguel, the *casa del pueblo* (people's house), which includes all of the Indigenous auxiliary mayors from San Miguel's villages—and which had been dissolved as in most of the rest of the highlands (Smith 1990) following the implementation of the civil patrols in the late 1980s—was revived in 2006 as part of a coordinated effort to organize the local opposition to Marlin (van de Sandt 2009), with Aniseto as its leader. Consejos Comunitarios de Desarrollo (COCODEs), Guatemala's main structures of decentralization in the rural areas, were also organized in San Miguel's villages to access and oversee the allocation of municipal funds. According to interviews with FREDEMI members conducted by me and my research assistants, both the auxiliary mayors and these COCODEs, however, were soon co-opted by San Miguel's mayor. The mayor purchased their support for the mine through promises of prioritizing their communities' requests when apportioning the now much larger municipal budget thanks to Montana's substantial royalty payments.[6] In 2009, a local grassroots development organization, the Asociación para el Desarrollo Integral de San Miguel Ixtahuacán (Association for the Integral Development of San Miguel Ixtahuacán, ADISMI), secured international cooperation funds for popular education related to mining environmental impacts and hired Aniseto to tour San Miguel's villages in order to clarify to its residents "that they were being fooled by being offered a small kitchen or the repair of their villages' roads. . . . 'We do need such things, but we cannot accept them [from Montana], since what they are doing is unjust. They are stealing our wealth. And they are going to leave us contaminated'" (Aniseto Lopez, interview by Marie-Christine Dugal, San Miguel, June 15, 2015). To better coordinate the local opposition to Marlin, FREDEMI was soon after created as a coalition of ADISMI, the local Catholic Church, and San Miguel schoolteachers, who were then mobilized against the mine. Along with other movements in "defense of territory" in Guatemala (Alonso-Fradejas 2015; Copeland 2019), FREDEMI soon became a multiscalar one—that is, a movement "composed of actors in different geographical locations that . . . acts in various political spheres, and that . . . is influenced by a combination of international, regional, national, municipal and communitarian social processes and regulations" (Urkidi 2011, 257). Yet like most movements in this country for the defense of territory (Bastos and Sieder 2014; Urkidi 2011), FREDEMI's political and legal activity remained first and foremost grounded in San Miguel. Its focus, as analyzed elsewhere (Vanthuyne and Dugal 2023), also increasingly centered on rebuilding their political community of critically conscious, honorable Maya-Mam peasants. Let us now examine how this change in focus sustained its members' collaboration with the ex–mine workers in the newly founded Comité and the clashing forms of belonging that ensued.

"Aniseto, te quiero pedir disculpas"

A few days after FREDEMI's public meeting in San José Ixcaniché, as I was helping his wife, Eulalia, and their older daughters prepare and cook tortillas for supper in their home, I asked Aniseto how the ex–mine workers had approached him about joining forces to demand that Montana repair the adversarial environmental and health impacts the mining activities had caused in his municipality. I then remembered the violent attack he had suffered at the hands of some of these ex-workers on February 28, 2011. On that day, he and other FREDEMI members, along with allies from local and national antimining organizations, were blockading an important road intersection, one of the few that connects San Marcos's department to the regional and international road network. They were demanding that the state suspend Marlin's activities as ordered by the IACHR more than nine months earlier, highlighting that water sources had dried up since the mine had begun its operations and that independent studies had demonstrated that the mine's contamination threatened their health. A group of narcotraffickers[7] "that defende[d] the mine's rights," explained a FREDEMI member (interview by Marie-Christine Dugal, La Patria, June 2, 2015), and that benefited from the municipal government's blind eye regarding their illegal activities in exchange for their political support then attacked those they had identified as the organizers of the demonstration, including Aniseto. "There was blood that day," continued the FREDEMI member. "Aniseto, they pulled him by the hair, they pulled him by his ears, and locked him up," hitting him with a plank with nails. "I thought I would die that day," Aniseto shared with me during one of our many informal conversations. I was thus intrigued by the fact that Aniseto, who had on this and other occasions been physically attacked and verbally harassed by the mine workers, was now strategizing with them to get the mining company and the state to assume their liabilities. As I helped his wife and daughters flip tortillas on the family's *comal* (skillet), Aniseto, with the smile of someone telling an unbelievable but true story, recounted how the leader of the narcotrafficking group had pleaded with him the prior year to help force the mining company to repair the environmental damage it had caused:

> I want to apologize. I made a mistake. . . . A serious mistake. I hit you, I hurt you, I threatened to kill you. It is my mistake, I recognize it, but today we are screwed by the mine . . . and we want your support. There is nothing we can do [now that the mine is leaving]. The mine says it is not going to do anything. It says it's going to leave everything here as it is, that it doesn't care, that nobody and nothing is forcing it to do anything nice for the closure. Not even the [cracked] houses, not even the [dried-up] sources of water, are going to be repaired. (interview by Karine Vanthuyne, Subchal, April 14, 2018)

As we began eating soup made with freshly harvested vegetables and a chicken Eulalia slaughtered for the occasion, Aniseto shared his mixed satisfaction, anger, and skepticism that this promining leader had finally, but only recently, agreed with his resistance movement's analysis of the mining company's ethos. Montana's executives were not, as they pretended to be on some signboards, "neighbors for progress, who collaborate for the development of the community" (see figure 5.1, my translation). They only cared about their company's profits and would only "collaborate for the development of the community" if that collaboration seemed essential to their growth. Aniseto recounted, still smiling, his response to the narcotrafficker:

> Today, yes, you understand! Apologies, forgiveness, now that I am alive, I gladly accept them from you, but this situation has had a very important cost for me, for my family, for my wife. . . . Now, if you are serious, if yours is a voice that is really worth listening to, I can give you some ideas. Maybe if you are willing to walk together with us, . . . if you don't turn your back to negotiate again with the mine. But what happens if you go back to negotiate with the mine? And us helping you,

FIG. 5.1 Signboard in San José Ixcaniché: "Montana, S.A. Neighbors for progress collaborating for the development of the community." *Source:* James Rodriguez.

that doesn't make any sense. I won't get involved with you if that's the case.... Because us, we never negotiate with the mine. But you, at any moment, you have negotiated with the mine. (interview, Subchal, April 14, 2018)

As demonstrated by Mayan-Mam scholar Jiménez Sánchez (2008) in his ethnohistorical analysis of his people's political subjectivity and my own and Dugal's work with FREDEMI's activists (Vanthuyne and Dugal 2023), critical knowledge and moral integrity are locally considered as key and inseparable ingredients of this Indigenous people's resistance to their historical economic exploitation and political domination by the non-Indigenous minority. "Being in the know" of government or corporate actors' possible egoistical motives when they present themselves as "collaborative neighbors" and refusing any "bargains" with these so-called neighbors are the two main qualities that FREDEMI has sought to cultivate throughout the years, both among its ranks and among those they believed naturally belonged to their political community as fellow Maya-Mam peasants, despite that they stood on the side of their oppressors, given (promises of) socioeconomic benefits in the form of salaries or community infrastructure (such as churches, schools, health centers, or roads pavement). Through their various political and judicial actions, they not only denounced the violation and demanded the respect of their fundamental rights to consultation, a clean environment, and good health; they also sought to regenerate their people's *conciencia*—which, in this ethnographic context, translates as both "being in the know of what is really going on" (critical consciousness) and "refusing to sell oneself out" to corporate or state actors (moral rectitude).

Hence Aniseto's mixed sentiments of joy, resentment, and distrust toward this former mine supporter when he remorsefully admitted he had been wrong. "Today, yes, you understand!" he exclaimed with deep satisfaction. This mine supporter had finally opened his eyes to Montana's real motives, being first and foremost economic profit, with very limited concern for their well-being. Yet Aniseto was quick to remind the narcotrafficker that his previous and often-times violent refusal to acknowledge that Montana's ill impacts overwhelmingly surpassed their benefits had been very costly for him and his family. While Aniseto momentarily left his house to check on his broccoli field just a few minutes' drive away by motorcycle, Eulalia shared with me not only how she had suffered tremendously from the attacks against her husband but that she herself had been the target of bullying from her female neighbors whose husbands worked at the mine. They had repeatedly shamed her at the local weekly market or on her way to work as a primary school teacher, yelling derogatory names while pointing at her and laughing. While Aniseto, as the previous quote shows, was open to welcoming this former enemy into his oppositional movement ranks in order to "give him ideas," he also remembered his own and his wife's pain and thus remained careful not to assume this man's full redemption. Was he only changing his stand toward Montana out of self-interest? Would he "turn to negotiate" with the mining company if it seemed that he could get a better bargain from such negotiations than from collaborating with FREDEMI in denouncing their peoples' rights violations?

Political solidarity, notes Butler (2015, 152), emerges not so much from "deliberate agreements we enter knowingly" but from acting together; when you take to the street, "the people you find in the street . . . are not precisely the ones you chose." As such, there is an unchosen dimension to our solidarity with others, as "the body is always exposed to people and impressions it does not have a say over" (152). These types of alliances across differences, claims Tsing (2012), can be transformative. Despite contrasting freedom agendas, the wild matsutake mushroom pickers she conducted fieldwork with eventually came together to demand the opening up of property from the American state so that they could enjoy more flexible access to patches scattered throughout the national forest. The outcomes of such transformative actions, however, are uncertain: "[They] can work to the advantage of capital and Empire as well as their refusal" (Tsing 2012, 46). How is not choosing who you'll be challenging the state or corporation with and not knowing if this challenge will be further entrenching or debunking their power impacting one's identification as a true ally of an oppositional struggle? Aniseto's mixed sentiments and questioning of this were shared by all of the FREDEMI activists I had an opportunity to speak with during my 2018 visit to San Miguel. As we will see, these reservations regarding both one's true motives and the end results of one's action with them not only concerned the ex–mine workers but also more broadly applied to all of FREDEMI's constituents, including its longtime leaders, such as Aniseto. While such suspicions had much deeper historical roots (Nelson 2009), they nonetheless constituted great obstacles to the organization's current efforts to rebuild the alternate political community of critically conscious, honorable Maya-Mam peasants it believed Marlin had shattered (Vanthuyne and Dugal 2023).

(Un)Becoming an Antimining Activist

When I arrived in San José Ixcaniché for FREDEMI's public meeting, I was met by Miguel Angel and Francisco Salomón Bámaca, two brothers and founding members of FREDEMI. Miguel Angel, now unfortunately deceased, was at the time presiding over the Comité, and Francisco was its secretary. In contrast with Miguel Angel, however, Francisco had not initially opposed the Marlin Mine's construction and operation. Rather, he was hired by Montana to work as its Community Relations Officer in 2003. At this time, Francisco explained to me in an interview, Montana was in the process of "capturing" (*agarrando*) all of San Miguel's local leaders through offers of employment or financial support for their communities' projects: "I had just graduated from high school, and while I was looking for work, the company came to me saying, 'We're going to support you, we're going to give you a job'" (interview by Karine Vanthuyne, San José Ixcaniché, March 19, 2016). Francisco explained that he accepted the position they offered him because he saw it as a valuable opportunity "to see to it that they fulfill their promises" toward his people. His older brother, Miguel Angel, had likewise just completed high school, with the support of San Miguel's Catholic Church, when Montana initiated the construction of Marlin. The company also offered to hire Miguel Angel. However, thanks to his education, he reflected in an interview, "I did not sell out so fast. Since I already had extensive knowledge in health and environmental issues, it was not as easy for them to pick me up like any other object" (interview, Siete Platos, May 19, 2015).

For a while, Francisco and Miguel Angel continuously argued with one another, with the latter accusing the former of "helping an invasive company . . . to damage human health and all of us who are here" (interview by Marie-Christine Dugal, Siete Platos, May 19, 2015). But Francisco then firmly believed that "the mine [was] good for [them]," as a San Miguel Catholic Church leader recalled him saying in the *catequistas* (catechists) trainings she then led (interview by Marie-Christine Dugal, San Miguel, May 21, 2015). "His job was to . . . convince people to be in favor of the company, . . . so every time we discussed the mine [in those training sessions], . . . he took the floor [to promote it]," this church leader explained.

However, Francisco eventually discovered that his employer "didn't want someone that was ahead [of his people to defend their rights]" (interview by Karine Vanthuyne, San José Ixcaniché, March 19, 2016). In 2006, when he reported to Montana's management team that residents had informed him that twenty-eight birds had died from drinking the water that was leaking from the mine's tailing dam, management asked him to continue reassuring people that the fresh water around the mine *was* safe to drink and bathe in. In response, Francisco recalls saying, "'Excuse me, but I cannot lie; that's the way I am. I can't change.' They all stared at me like this [Francisco mimics a face of disbelief]. Then they told me that I was not capable enough for the company, that I should think of my family and 'wise up'" (interview by Karine Vanthuyne, San José Ixcaniché, March 19, 2016) to keep the hefty paychecks coming into his bank account. A few months later, some residents of San Miguel blockaded the mine's entrance road, demanding that Montana address their compensation requests for cracks in their homes, water contamination, and purchases on the cheap of their lands. Believing him to be on the side of the protesters, Montana dismissed Francisco from his position and accused him of "abandonment of work, threats, coercion, instigation to commit a crime, as well as minor and serious injuries" to Guatemala's Ministerio Publico (Public Prosecutor's Office) after the blockade turned into a violent confrontation between anti- and promining residents. According to Francisco, a few days later, "more than 200 police surrounded my house," and it took years of costly legal proceedings to have the charges lifted.

Since his dismissal from Montana, Francisco had tirelessly dedicated himself to FREDEMI's core struggle: rebuilding the moral fiber and political unity of San Miguel's historical political community of Maya-Mam peasants. When I visited him in his home in 2018, I realized that the fact that he himself had once stood in opposition to the community as an employee of Montana did not make him any less inclined to question his fellow activist's true intentions—rather, it was quite the opposite. Aniseto's hesitation in running for the municipal office as FREDEMI's *comité cívico* mayoral candidate raised doubts in Francisco about Aniseto's allegiance to FREDEMI's struggle. In 2011 and 2015, as a complementary strategy to regain control of their municipal lands and governing structures, FREDEMI formed a *comité cívico* to run for the municipal office, with Aniseto as its mayoral candidate (Vanthuyne and Dugal 2023). Yet on the eve of a new election year, as he explained to me when I visited with him and his family, Aniseto paused his campaign. As a salaried employee of San Miguel's municipality—a job he had only been able to obtain thanks to the new mayor's more friendly stance toward FREDEMI—he was currently well paid. Campaigning would mean having to leave his highly prized job and forgoing paychecks for months at a time when his family was growing and he would have more mouths to feed. However, his hesitation to run again for office was interpreted by Francisco as him deserting FREDEMI's struggle:

> We have a comrade in struggle . . . who wants to pull out, who wants to leave the struggle. . . . People have always put their trust in him, . . . giving him their support, but unfortunately, it is hard for him to get here [to our meetings]. [He says to us:]

"Well, I have needs, I have a lot to do, and how am I going to earn my living?"
And, yes, of course, we all have needs, but we are involved in this struggle without
considering our own needs, and thank God when someone is helping us . . .
because we are always in need, and sometimes we don't have money, so what do we
do? (interview, San José Ixcaniché, April 17, 2018)

Upon hearing this, I attempted to encourage sympathy from Francisco toward
Aniseto's socioeconomic situation but failed. Francisco instead listed all of the
personal sacrifices that his own allegiance to FREDEMI's struggle had cost him:
"I am following up on [FREDEMI's files] without resting. Yesterday we were
there, and today we are here . . . but now he, what is happening to him? Is it that
when there is money, I get involved [in FREDEMI's struggle], and when there
is not, I move on? No, . . . it is not like that. What we want is that our leaders and
members follow up on [FREDEMI's files] through good and bad times. . . . This
is a big fight, and it requires one's full presence." As in the rest of Latin America
(Petras 1997), popular mobilization in Guatemala has been greatly impacted by
international donor agencies' agendas, which moved into the country during its
peace negotiations (Vogt 2015). International donors, Petras explains, tend to
favor professionally organized NGOs associated with specific topics rather than
broader social movements pursuing more general political agendas. As a result,
grassroots organizations like FREDEMI end up not only struggling for the
recognition and due protection of their rights; given the situation of poverty
most of its members face and the prohibitive cost of their legal and political
struggles, they also continuously labor to frame their struggle in the latest
terms required to access much-needed international funding to sustain them.
Sometimes, they are successful and receive enough to cover a coordinator's
salary—like when ADISMI hired Aniseto to do awareness-raising workshops.
More frequently, however, they only receive indirect support from international
or Guatemalan NGOs that will cover the cost of their participation in a
capacity-building workshop, for instance, but not that of actually carrying out
the work that workshop will have trained them to do, hence FREDEMI's members' difficulty in "following up on [FREDEMI's files] through good and bad
times," their families' sustenance needs preventing them from giving "one's full
presence" to their organization "without considering our own needs."

Let us now examine how the fundamentally challenging nature of belonging to a political community of completely selfless, critically aware citizens is
engaged with, day-to-day, by its aspiring members: the ex–mine workers and
their family members. How are they performing their allegiance to FREDEMI's
struggle so as to avoid being seen as capable of later "turning one's back to negotiate with the mine"?

"Nosotros que tenemos toda la información"

After briefly rejoicing to be meeting again, Francisco and Miguel Angel guided me to the *kiosko* of San José Ixcaniché's central plaza, where members of the Comité were gathered. I recognized the few faces of those I met during previous visits at FREDEMI's earlier, more private meetings. The others, I would learn over the next few days, were ex–mine workers, their wives or ex-wives, and/or local village authorities who had signed agreements with the mining company through which they committed to politically support Montana's extractive activities in exchange for its financing of their community's projects. As head of the Comité, Miguel Angel opened the meeting by first asking me to introduce myself to the attendants I had not yet met. Following my brief self-introduction, Miguel Angel announced that they would be discussing the extent to which the reduced precautionary measures ordered by the IACHR had been completed, including the provision of safe drinking and irrigation water to five mine-affected villages in San Miguel, including San José Ixcaniché. Carlos Loarca, the Guatemala City–based lawyer who has tirelessly accompanied FREDEMI in its numerous judicial proceedings—from its case at the IACHR to clearing Francisco's judicial record—then announced that despite statements from the mining company and the Guatemalan government at the most recent talks meeting, the precautionary measures had not been fully implemented in San Miguel. Whereas the state was ordered by IACHR to provide clean water to all residents of the five identified villages for free, San Miguel's municipal government had instead presented these measures as "gifts" from Montana to the municipality, requiring its beneficiaries to pay a fee to access them. Commenting on the six hundred quetzales (a little less than $80) she had to pay to get water, Rosario Bamaca, one of the few female attendants, denounced, "The mayor and his village-based political allies declared that we had to pay a fee or we would become spoiled. This is how they soaped up our people's heads." Part of the Comité's demands discussed at its talks with Montana and Guatemalan state authorities included the reimbursement of those fees, as the water was supposed to have been provided to them without charge, Carlos then explained. He went on to add that additional irregularities in the realization of these precautionary measures included excluding those who opposed the mine as their beneficiaries, such as FREDEMI activists; employing cheaper materials to build the water installations than the ones that had been budgeted for; and requiring the free labor of the heads of each beneficiary household for their construction. "There has been a history of Indigenous forced labor in this country; your racist leaders just consider it normal to require that you work for free," deplored Carlos, who is himself non-Indigenous. As the representatives from the five communities that should have had access to safe drinking and irrigation water confirmed to Carlos and Miguel Angel the extent to which these irregularities concerned them, one clarified that he was not actually an official representative of his village but a worried resident. His village's authorities had refused to participate in the Comité's work and thus to officially complain to state authorities and Montana that the IACHR precautionary measures had not been properly implemented in their community. Rosario interjected, "We, who have all the information now and who know how it should be, are not afraid to denounce the company. On the other hand, these people, these authorities, think that when one speaks out, one is worse. But it is not like that. Now, maybe they are still keeping their little salary with the closure of the mine, and that is why they don't want to talk [with us about the company's damages]." A few days later, when I visited Rosario at her house in San José Ixcaniché, I learned that she is actually Miguel Angel's daughter. She had never been to one of FREDEMI's meetings before the Comité began its work, she explained, not only because her husband at the time worked at Marlin but also as a result of her parents' separation. She was closer to her mother, so when her father left, she stopped seeing him. For her, then, joining the struggle itself constituted an "act of repair" (Zaretsky 2021); it allowed her to reincorporate the political community she had grown into, a community that has "all the information now," that knows "how it should be," and that "is not afraid to denounce the company." In contrast to most women from her generation, Rosario was from an early age encouraged by her father to attend school, and it was thanks to being one of the very few in her village with a postsecondary degree that she had been named to represent her village in the Comité.

Being recognized as a member of a political community of completely selfless, critically aware citizens, as we have previously seen, was nonetheless tenuous. I therefore suggest that aspiring members like Rosario sought to perform (Austin 1962; Butler 1990) their belonging in order to realize it. She demonstrated the desired reality of being tied again to that polis by making clear, through discourse, that she adhered to its core values. In the previous quotes from Rosario, we see how she made a point of publicly stating that she now understood and condemned what had *really* been going on in San Miguel. Her people, herself included, had been "soaped up" into believing that the clean drinking and irrigation water project was a "gift" from Montana that they, as residents, should pay a fee to benefit from. If some community authorities were now refusing to denounce their previous mayor's lies and corruption, she suggested, it was out of ignorance, fear of reprisal, or pure self-interest. But how has the state engaged these honorable, critically conscious Maya-Mam citizens? Has intercultural dialogue, which is, as we will see, the CPD's claimed form of intervention, contributed to repairing the historically damaged relationship between Guatemala's non-Indigenous minority and Indigenous majority?

"We, the Civil Servants, Are Not the Cause of Projects Not Being Completed"

The next day, I joined the Comité in the town hall of San Miguel's urban center. We were soon welcomed by a civil servant working for Guatemala's CPD, the entity that was created by the Guatemalan state in the late 2000s, when land occupations became widespread again following the renewed evictions of Indigenous communities, in the name of "economic development," from lands claimed by large investors for industrial farming and mining (Alonso-Fradejas 2015). According to its website (now defunct), the mandate of the CPD, an institution closed by the Guatemalan government in 2020, was to coordinate, with different government entities, actions for the prevention, management, and transformation of social conflict through an "intercultural dialogue approach." This approach was defined on that same website as Guatemala's Indigenous communities' "long-standing tradition of direct dispute resolution." In San Miguel, the CPD got involved in facilitating talks between the Comité, the Guatemalan state, and Montana in early April 2017. The Comité had repeatedly asked the state and Montana to meet with them, but both had refused to hear their demands. As a result, in late March 2017, the Comité blockaded the Pan-American Highway to force state and company actors to comply. The second direct action, the Comité's fifty-four-day-long mine site occupation a few months after talks had finally begun, was deployed to pressure these same representatives to be more considerate of its members' time and limited financial resources; both the government and the company repeatedly changed the day and location of the talks, moving them from San Miguel to the department's capital, located three to four hours away by bus. This made it increasingly difficult for the Comité's members to attend because of the increased traveling costs and missed work hours.

The civil servant began the meeting by clarifying, in a very gentle and warm manner, that he never attempts to rationalize state neglect. Yet he explained,

> The Guatemalan state, since the peace accords, has gone through a really rough process of neoliberalization, the result being that the state institutions have been reduced to their most minimal expression and that their mandates . . . don't allow them [now] to serve the population adequately. . . . So, most of the time, we, the civil servants, are not the cause of projects not being completed. It's rather a whole structure that has reduced our capabilities. . . . But here we are today, . . . as the Comisión Presidencial de Diálogo. Our job has been to . . . look closely at your thirteen demands of reparations, which we are convinced are fully justified. (field notes, San Miguel Ixtahuacán, April 10, 2018)

After having rationalized the state's very late, and only once under pressure, consideration of the Comité's demands as an unfortunate, involuntary outcome of "neoliberalism" and reassuring its members that, despite all appearances, the state did believe their demands were "fully justified," the civil servant explained that we were now gathered to assess the extent to which the IACHR precautionary measures had been completed in San Miguel. "You're the ones that can give us that information," he asserted. He also emphasized that we were sitting in a circle, which was not how Indigenous peasants' meetings with state officials typically operated; they were usually "very vertical."

By presenting the image of a state that did want to attend to them, that considered them worthy, credible citizens who should be interacted with horizontally, not vertically, this civil servant seemed at first to be attempting to repair the historically authoritarian and fundamentally racist relationship between the Guatemalan state and its Indigenous population. And this employee, in particular, appeared to be exceptionally dedicated to that task. In the one-on-one conversation I had with him a few hours after the meeting, I asked him how he evaluated his work as the go-between for the Comité, the state, and the mining company. He responded that before his monthly visits to the municipality, the only central state institutions that traveled to San Miguel from Guatemala's capital (a full day of travel despite the less than three-hundred-kilometer commute) were the Ministerio de Energía y Minas (Ministry of Energy and Mines, MEM) and the Ministerio de Ambiente y Recursos Naturales (Ministry of Environment and Natural Resources, MARN). "And when they came," he whispered, "they would only knock at the mine's door, and the municipality's residents would never see them. But we, the Comisión, we started backward. We went to talk to the residents first" (field notes, San Miguel Ixtahuacán, April 10, 2018). Since state support for the CPD's work was minimal, this employee was actually paying the transportation and lodging costs of his trips to San Miguel out of his own pocket. During this same conversation with him, however, I also realized that his intervention in San Miguel risked reproducing, rather than repairing, the historically authoritarian and racist relationship between Guatemala's non-Indigenous minority and Indigenous majority. How he imagined the harm done and who was responsible for it was deeply shaped by both the non-Indigenous minority's historical racism toward "Indians" and the ideology of neoliberalism it had more recently adopted. As we sipped *licuados de frutas* (fruit smoothies) in one of the town's very few remaining *comedores* (canteens)—many of them having closed in the wake of Montana's dismissal of most of its employees the prior year—he explained that while he agreed with the Comité's members that the damages they were complaining about ought to be repaired, he disagreed with who was at fault. According to him, it was not the mining company but the previous municipal authorities' racism and mismanagement of Marlin's royalties that were to blame: "The problem is that the mining company . . . came to San Miguel with a vision: to become a partner in the municipality's communities, to invest in the development of its residents. It's Guatemalans, through telling the mine owners that these residents were troublemakers always looking for a fight, who have prevented the company from doing so. . . . San Miguel's previous mayors, in the end, deceived the people. Their obligation was to invest in the people's development, but they did not do that. They only invested [a very small amount of Montana's royalties] in a few gray buildings" (field notes, San Miguel Ixtahuacán, April 10, 2018). Besides, he continued, the miners were themselves to condemn for the situation of dire poverty they were now faced with: "From the point of view of an Indigenous person who has no education, what does development mean? Yes, on the one hand, Indigenous peoples want to protect their natural riches, wealth counted in relationships, but on the other, there was this bundle of money coming in. I feel such anguish in these people. They are much poorer than they were before since the main source of work is now leaving. . . . Their 6,000 quetzals per month [around $800], they did not invest it in the education of their children, but in having another home, another wife" (field notes, San Miguel Ixtahuacán, April 10, 2018).

This analysis of the root causes of the situation of dire poverty that San Miguel's residents were now faced with, despite years of a highly profitable mine operating in their municipality, is evocative of the "racial ambivalence" diagnosed by Charles Hale in his examination of contemporary discourses about race in the Guatemalan Highlands. At first, the civil servant mobilized the discourses of racial equality and political inclusion of Guatemala's postgenocide multicultural democracy while construing the CPD as one of its active proponents. In contrast to how the Guatemalan state had thus far related to its Maya-Mam citizens in San Miguel, his governmental institution had gathered with them in a circle and "talk[ed] to . . . [them] first." Through critiquing the attitude of San Miguel's municipal government toward those citizens, this employee also insinuated that *he*, on the contrary, had esteem for Indigenous peoples and did not want to be party to their ongoing subjugation. When he interpreted the sources of their anguish, however, he quickly reverted to employing the new sanitized version of Guatemala's non-Indigenous minority's historically racist discourse toward "Indians." If they were still poor today, it was not just because San Miguel's municipal government had "deceived their people." Maya-Mam cultural values were also at fault. Driven by their cultural (a.k.a. irrational) conceptualizations of "wealth counted in relationships," they had misspent their mine wages on "having another home, another wife," instead of properly investing it in their children's education.

The civil servant's diagnosis of the sources of Marlin's ex-workers' poverty also echoed the "blame the victim" discourse denounced by numerous critics of neoliberalism, the same ideology this state employee ironically condemned, as we saw earlier, when he attempted to rationalize his employer's neglect of the Comité's concerns. As Butler (2015, 14) reminds us, "Neoliberal rationality demands self-sufficiency as a moral ideal at the same time that neoliberal forms of power work to destroy that very possibility at an economic level." In Guatemala, the emergence of agrarian extractivism alongside mining has profoundly exacerbated the precarity of small farmers from the mid-2000s onward (Alonso-Fradejas 2015). On the one hand, an increasing number of these farmers are becoming landless as a result of state land privatization, market pressures (Alonso-Fradejas 2015), and corporate deceit of the kind documented around Marlin (Dougherty and Olsen 2014; van de Sandt 2009). On the other hand, the labor regime brought about by these extractive forms of development has limited wage work opportunities without accommodating a living wage. Hence an increasing number of Guatemala's Indigenous peasants venture to find work in "los Estados" (the United States) despite an ever more hostile environment to Central American migrants (Taylor 2020). They would rather risk indebtment to a "coyote" (human smuggler) and the life-threatening journey to illegally cross the Mexico–United States border than remain "free to starve" (Alonso-Fradejas 2015, 498) in their home country.

If precarious populations are seen as "hav[ing] produced their own situation, then they are not situated within a regime of power that reproduces precarity in systemic ways. Their own actions, or their own failures, are the cause of their precarious situations," reminds Butler (2015, 144). From the point of view of the civil servant, the ex–mine workers, not the extractivist labor regime, were to blame for their poverty-caused anguish. This logic of individual responsibility, I learned toward the end of our conversation, went even further. According to the civil servant, Montana and the Guatemalan state were right to claim that it was the Indigenous peasants' poor construction techniques, not the explosives the mining company had repeatedly used just a few meters underneath their homes, which had caused them to crack. As he paid for our *licuados*, the state employee shared, "They took actions [to sustain their claims for reparations for cracked houses] that had no justification. Their demand for cracked houses is immoral." In contemporary Guatemala, claims Hale (2006, 45), "Ladinos have become complacent with the high ground of their newfound commitment to cultural equality, inclined to burden Mayas with the responsibility for their own ongoing subordination." I can only agree with this observation.

On November 6, 2018, in a five-star hotel in Guatemala's capital, the CPD celebrated the peaceful conclusion of San Miguel's social conflict. Despite the fact that none of the petitioners' demands had been considered valid, with the exception of the one concerning the noncompletion of the IACHR measures, Sergio Flores, the head of the CPD, declared, "The actors are comfortable and satisfied with this" (Abrego 2018). FREDEMI members anticipated that the Comité's work would bear little fruit, and so some of their longtime members had therefore decided to not get involved in it. For Crisanta Pérez Bamaca, for instance, whose epic story of opposing Marlin had become notorious (Macleod and Pérez Bamaca 2013), the verification commissions that the reparations negotiation had engendered were, in and of themselves, adding insult to injury. These commissions comprised representatives from the governmental agencies in charge of assessing the damages (such as the Ministerio de Salud

[Health Ministry] for the mine-caused illnesses), as well as representatives of Montana and the Comité. These governmental agencies, explained Crisanta when I visited her at home in 2018, "had never shown up" before they began denouncing the mine's ill impacts in 2009. Besides, it was clear to her that they were "dominated by the company" (*sometida a la empresa*). When the Health Ministry came to evaluate what she and the Comité believed were mine-caused illnesses, she stated, "It was clear to me that this ministry was holding hands with the company's manager." It was thus not surprising to her that the latter later declared these illnesses to be "common" and thus not mine induced.

It is important to note that by failing once again to recognize them as citizens entitled to state protection from commercial harm, the government not only reinforced their exclusion from the Guatemalan nation it was elected to serve. It also further weakened the alternate political community of honorable, critically conscious Maya-Mam peasants FREDEMI aspired to rebuild. When I visited her in 2018, Crisanta also rationalized her noninvolvement in the Comité's work as the result of having sacrificed and suffered too much already from her participation in FREDEMI's struggle. In 2008, as a result of direct actions she initiated to defend her proprietary rights from being violated by the mining company, Crisanta was accused of "aggravated usurpation." Threatened with arrest and imprisonment by the police, she lived in hiding for six months while pregnant, only returning home to give birth, where she lived in fear until the warrant was dropped in 2012. Yet it was not this experience of criminalization that deterred her from mobilizing with the Comité's for reparations. Crisanta first played a key role in its initial actions. It's rather what she experienced as the state co-optation of her people's struggle for justice through the CPD's verification commissions that led to her resignation from FREDEMI.

Conclusion

As Seo (2019, 558) demonstrates in her work on populist mobilization in Thailand, ethnography "provides a window into the unfinished aspects of political mobilization from the realm of the ordinary." Through the lens of the "anthropology of becoming" theorized by Biehl and Locke (2017, 83), she shows how, as "assemblages," populist political engagements "are constantly constructed, undone and redone by the desire and becoming of actual peoples who are caught up in the messiness, desperation, and aspirations of life in idiosyncratic milieus." In this chapter, I have more particularly shown how ethnographies of reparation activism give us access to multiple and contrasting imaginings of the past, present, and future and contested belongings, as state and citizens perform or claim repair while reinflicting older or newer forms of injuries.

In Guatemala, as in Latin America more broadly (see also chapter 7, this volume, for instance), the three most common domains of reparations politics—political violence, colonial injustices, and socioenvironmental conflicts—not only coexist but are very tightly entangled. Through claiming reparations for mine-caused damages, San Miguel's Comité challenged Guatemala's historically racist, postgenocide state to rightfully acknowledge them as citizens worthy of these reparations. FREDEMI members, more particularly, were not strictly asking the government to force Montana to fix their houses and the other mine-caused harms they believed it was responsible for. As selfless, critically aware Maya-Mam citizens, they were more broadly seeking remedy for their historical economic exploitation and political subjugation by Guatemala's non-Indigenous oligarchy and their corporate allies. In so doing, however, they did not expect the state to acknowledge them as such. They knew too well that it remained fundamentally racist, authoritarian, and corrupt, despite postwar official commitments to multicultural democracy and "intercultural dialogue." They therefore did not consider the CPD-led talks and verification commissions to be "hope-generating machines" (Nuijten 2003). They rather performed (Austin 1962; Butler 1990) their citizenship in order to make it happen. They became "citizens despite the state"—to paraphrase Lazar's work (2004) on marginalized Bolivians.

"We, the people," Butler claims (2015), is fundamentally performative and therefore precarious. It is never preexisting, as the "We, who have all the information now, and who know how it should be" is always "in the process of being made or making itself—both its inadequacy and its self-division are part of its enacted meaning and promise" (169). While some assembled to assert San Miguel's entitlement to reparations through involvement in the CPD-led talks and verification commissions, others, like Crisanta, refused to do so. This represented, I suggest, as an act of "refusal" (Simpson 2014) of the form of political belonging the Guatemalan state was offering them: docile, subservient *mozos colonos*, only acknowledged as citizens during electoral years by congress candidates for their ballots. In so doing, they also performed their political belonging, not as Guatemalan citizens despite the state but as members of their own *polis*, their own imagined community (Anderson 1991) of Maya-Mam peasants, their *kojb'il*, according to Maya-Mam scholar Jiménez Sánchez (2008).

Besides, as Tsing (2012, 46) put it, "The forms of community produced in . . . transformative alliances are unpredictable." Yet performing one's belonging as a citizen despite the state or as a member of one's *kojb'il* is even more unwarrantable. To be sure, and as Gammeltoft (2018, 77) points out, "belonging [in and of itself] indexes fragile, uncertain, and often highly contingent human efforts to be part of something larger." Nonetheless, the mutual relations of possession, attachment, and dependence or any form of belonging become particularly fragile when one's recognition as a true "comrade in struggle" is continuously challenged by life's necessities, repeated experiences of betrayal, and activist fatigue. In a world wherein "any social investment that does not have a clear end in market value . . . fails economically and morally, . . . whether or not the investment is life enhancing" (Povinelli 2011, 23), Indigenous citizenship, as an alternative social project animated by nonmarketable logic, seems to demand heroic endurance or be inevitably condemned to exhaustion. Striving to live ethically, in accordance with their own sense of obligations and responsibilities, FREDEMI members intensely labored to remain in the know and avoid "selling themselves out." Such commitments require heroic endurance because, as Povinelli found in her work with Indigenous peoples in Australia, they require making do with little support at best or while being repressed for realizing these commitments at worst. "Although many Mayas may have given up on radical transformation, others continue to fight for it both through and against the system," claims Copeland (2014, 316). While FREDEMI is a good example of these "others who continue to fight," it is also illustrative of the precariousness of such fights. The same violent structures that have historically motivated Indigenous Guatemalans to demand social justice—economic exploitation and political domination—are fragilizing the contemporary citizenship articulations of Guatemala's Indigenous majority. Ethnographies of reparations politics involving Indigenous peoples and (post)colonial states like Guatemala are thus revealing of "the morally vicious realm of excess, exhaustion, and endurance" (Povinelli 2011, 128), in which those striving to persist in the being they find proper for the world are necessarily enmeshed. It is therefore our ethical responsibility, as researchers studying such enduring yet fragile struggles, to grasp the magnitude of the obstacles they are faced with. Only then will we be able to appreciate their successes, no matter how small.

Notes

1   Montana Exploradora is a subsidiary of American-based Newmont, following the acquisition of Canadian-based Goldcorp Inc. of Glamis Gold in 2006 and Newmont's acquisition of Goldcorp Inc. in 2018.
2   A lawsuit against the Canadian government has been launched on those grounds by a Canadian NGO, the Justice and Corporate Accountability Project.
3   In the *mozos colonos* system, workers, mostly of Mayan origin, received a combination of cash and a small plot of land for both housing and the cultivation of crops in exchange for their labor on the *finqueros* farms.
4   Guatemalan adult literate women only gained the right to vote in 1956, and all adult Guatemalans, male or female, literate or illiterate, in 1965.
5   These structures, now commonly known in Guatemala as "alcaldías indígenas," stem from the colonial "cabildo de indios," which was created by the Spanish Crown to govern the segregated Indigenous population. See Barrios (1996, 1998) for details about these cabildos from the Spanish conquest to the internal armed conflict and Ekern (2011), Rasch (2011), and Sieder (2020) for ethnographies of their more recent revitalization.
6   According to Zarsky and Stanley (2013, 138), "Royalties and taxes paid to the Guatemalan treasury from the Marlin mine between 2006 and 2009 amounted to US$51.9 million—accounting for 6.3% of mine revenues and 15.9% of total mine earnings. Local communities received just under US$4.5 million, or one half of 1% of mine revenues and 1.3% of mine earnings."

7   In the 1980s, Guatemala became a bridge state for cocaine trafficking between Colombian suppliers and their Mexican connections following increased U.S. pressure on the latter (Brockett 2019). The peace process did not put an end to this development. From the beginning to the end of the 1990s, the share of Colombian cocaine that first passed through Guatemala before reaching the United States rose from 15 percent to 50 percent, with some key drug-trafficking organizations headquartered in San Marcos, the department where the Marlin Mine is located. By employing most of the local population in the above-board enterprises set up to launder drug-trafficking profits, providing them free access to much-needed and otherwise nonexisting services (such as health clinics), and intimidating or corrupting the local authorities with the support of high military or governmental officials, these organizations have become central actors in the country's political economy, to the point of sometimes dominating entire regions. For obvious security reasons, I have not sought to document the extent of their influence in the municipality of San Miguel Ixtahuacán, but based on my conversations with some of its residents, I estimate that they controlled at least one or two of its villages.

References

Abrego, Berta. 2018. "Celebran alcance de diálogo impulsado por Comisión Presidencial en San Miguel Ixtahuacán." *Diario de Centro América*.

Alonso-Fradejas, Alberto. 2015. "Anything but a Story Foretold: Multiple Politics of Resistance to the Agrarian Extractivist Project in Guatemala." *Journal of Peasant Studies* 42 (3–4): 489–515.

Anderson, Benedict. 1991. *Imagined Communities: Reflections on the Origin and Spread of Nationalism*. London: Verso.

Austin, J. L. 1962. *How to Do Things with Words*. The William James Lectures. Oxford: Clarendon Press.

Barrios, Lina E. 1996. *La alcaldía indígena en Guatemala, época colonial (1500–1821)*. 1st ed. Guatemala: Universidad Rafael Landívar and Instituto de Investigaciones Económicas y Sociales.

Barrios, Lina E. 1998. *La alcaldía indígena en Guatemala: De 1944 al presente*. Guatemala: Universidad Rafael Landívar and Instituto de Investigaciones Económicas y Sociales.

Bastos, Santiago, and Roddy Brett, eds. 2010. *El movimiento maya en la década después de la paz (1997–2007)*. Guatemala: F&G Editores.

Bastos, Santiago, and Manuela Camus. 2013. "Difficult Complementarity: Relations Between the Mayan and Revolutionary Movements." In *War by Other Means: Aftermath in Post-Genocide Guatemala*, edited by Carlotta McAllister and Diane M. Nelson, 71–92. Durham, N.C.: Duke University Press.

Bastos, Santiago, and Rachel Sieder. 2014. "Pueblos indígenas en Guatemala: La rearticulación comunitaria y la disputa por la legalidades en la democracia neoliberal." In *Nuevas violencias en América Latina: Los derechos indígenas ante las políticas neoextractivistas y las políticas de seguridad*, edited by Laura Raquel Valladares de la Cruz, 141–183. Mexico: Universidad Autónoma Metropolitana.

Basu, Niladri, Marce Abare, Susan Buchanan, Diana Cryderman, Dong-Ha Nam, Susannah Sirkin, Stefan Schmitt, and Howard Hu. 2010. "A Combined Ecological and Epidemiologic Investigation of Metal Exposures Amongst Indigenous Peoples near the Marlin Mine in Western Guatemala." *Science of the Total Environment* 407 (1):70–77.

Becker, Marc. 2011. *Pachakutik: Indigenous Movements and Electoral Politics in Ecuador*. Critical Currents in Latin American Perspectives. Lanham, Md.: Rowman & Littlefield.

Biehl, João Guilherme, and Peter Andrew Locke. 2017. *Unfinished: The Anthropology of Becoming*. Durham, N.C.: Duke University Press.

Brett, Roddy. 2007. *Una guerra sin batallas: Del odio, la violencia y el miedo en el Ixcán y el Ixil: 1972–1983*. Guatemala: F&G Editores.

Brockett, Charles D. 2019. "The Drug Kingpin Decapitation Strategy in Guatemala: Successes and Shortcomings." *Latin American Politics and Society* 61 (4): 47–71.

Butler, Judith. 1990. *Gender Trouble: Feminism and the Subversion of Identity*. Thinking Gender. New York: Routledge.

Butler, Judith. 2015. *Notes Toward a Performative Theory of Assembly*. Cambridge, Mass.: Harvard University Press.

Cajax, Susana. 2014. "Gold Mining on Mayan-Mam Territory: Social Unravelling, Discord and Distress in the Western Highlands of Guatemala." *Social Science and Medicine* 111:7.

Casaus Arzú, Marta Elena. 1992. *Guatemala: Linaje y racismo*. 1st ed. San José, Costa Rica: FLACSO (Facultad Latinoamericana de Ciencias Sociales).

CEH. 1999. *Guatemala: Memoria del silencio*. Guatemala: Comisión para el Esclarecimiento Histórico.

COPAE. 2008. *Informe Anual del Monitoreo y Analisis de Calidad de las Aguas*. San Marcos: Comisión Pastoral Paz y Ecología (COPAE).

COPAE. 2009. *Segundo Informe Anual del Monitoreo y Análisis de la Calidad del Agua*. San Marcos: Comisión Pastoral Paz y Ecología (COPAE).

Copeland, Nicholas. 2014. "Mayan Imaginaries of Democracy: Interactive Sovereignties and Political Affect in Postrevolutionary Guatemala." *American Ethnologist* 41 (2): 305–319.

Copeland, Nicholas. 2019. "Linking the Defence of Territory to Food Sovereignty: Peasant Environmentalisms and Extractive Neoliberalism in Guatemala." *Journal of Agrarian Change* 19 (1): 21–40.

Dougherty, Michael, and Tricia Olsen. 2014. "Taking Terrain Literally: Grounding Local Adaptation to Corporate Social Responsibility in the Extractive Industries." *Journal of Business Ethics* 119 (3): 423–434.

Ekern, Stener. 2011. "The Production of Autonomy: Leadership and Community in Mayan Guatemala." *Journal of Latin American Studies* 43 (1): 93–119.

Forster, Cindy. 2012. *La revolución indígena y campesina en Guatemala, 1970 a 2000: "Ver un día que nuestra raza maya fuera levantada."* Colección Monografía. Guatemala: Editorial Universitaria, Universidad de San Carlos de Guatemala.

Gammeltoft, Tine M. 2018. "Belonging: Comprehending Subjectivity in Vietnam and Beyond." *Social Analysis* 62 (1): 76–95. https://doi.org/10.3167/sa.2018.620106.

Gleijeses, Piero. 1991. *Shattered Hope: The Guatemalan Revolution and the United States, 1944–1954*. Princeton, N.J.: Princeton University Press.

Gutiérrez, Marta. 2011. "San Marcos, frontera de fuego." In *Guatemala, la infinita historia de las resistencias*, edited by Manolo E. Vela Castaneda, 243–314. Guatemala: Magna Terra Editores.

Hale, Charles R. 2006. *Más Que un Indio (More Than an Indian): Racial Ambivalence and Neoliberal Multiculturalism in Guatemala*. Santa Fe: School of American Research Press.

Handy, Jim. 1994. *Revolution in the Countryside: Rural Conflict and Agrarian Reform in Guatemala*. Chapel Hill: University of North Carolina Press.

Hernández Sandoval, Bonar L. 2019. *Guatemala's Catholic Revolution: A History of Religious and Social Reform, 1920–1968*. Notre Dame, Ind.: University of Notre Dame Press.

Imai, Shin, Laden Mehranvar, and Jennifer Sander. 2007. "Breaching Indigenous Law: Canadian Mining in Guatemala." *Indigenous Law Journal* 6 (1): 101–139.

Jiménez Sánchez, Odilio. 2008. "Los caminos de la resistencia: Comunidad, política e historia maya en Guatemala." PhD diss., Department of Anthropology, University of Texas.

Jonas, Susanne. 2000. *Of Centaurs and Doves: Guatemala's Peace Process*. Boulder, Colo.: Westview Press.

Kamp, Dick, and Ann Maest. 2010. *Evaluation of Predicted and Actual Water Quality Conditions at the Marlin Mine, Guatemala*. Santa Fe: E-Tech International.

Kamphuis, Charis, and Charlotte Connolly. 2022. *The Two Faces of Canadian Diplomacy: Undermining International Institutions to Support Canadian Mining*. Toronto: Justice & Corporate Accountability Project.

Konefal, Betsy. 2010. *For Every Indio Who Falls: A History of Maya Activism in Guatemala, 1960–1990*. Albuquerque: University of New Mexico Press.

Lazar, Sian. 2004. "Citizens Despite the State: Everyday Corruption and Local Politics in El Alto, Bolivia." In *Corruption: Anthropological Perspectives*, edited by Dieter Haller and Chris Shore, 212–228. London: Pluto Press.

Macleod, Morna, and Crisanta Pérez Bamaca. 2013. *En defensa de la Madre Tierra, sentir lo que siente el otro y el Buen Vivir: La lucha de Doña Crisanta contra Goldcorp*. Mexico: Ce-Actal.

Manz, Beatriz. 2004. *Paradise in Ashes: A Guatemalan Journey of Courage, Terror, and Hope*. Berkeley: University of California Press.

Martínez Peláez, Severo. 1985. *Motines de indios: La violencia colonial en Centroamérica y Chiapas*. Cuadernos de la Casa Presno 3. Puebla, Mexico: Centro de Investigaciones Históricas y Sociales, Instituto de Ciencias, Universidad Autónoma de Puebla.

McAllister, Carlota. 2003. "Good People: Revolution, Community and Conciencia in a K'iche' Village in Guatemala." PhD diss., Anthropology Department, Johns Hopkins University.

McCreery, David. 1994. *Rural Guatemala 1760–1940*. Stanford, Calif.: Stanford University Press.

Nuijten, Monique. 2003. *Power, Community and the State: The Political Anthropology of Organisation in Mexico*. London: Pluto Press.

Petras, James. 1997. "Imperialism and NGOs in Latin America." *Monthly Review* 49 (7): 10–27.

Postero, Nancy Grey. 2007. *Now We Are Citizens: Indigenous Politics in Postmulticultural Bolivia*. Stanford, Calif.: Stanford University Press.

Postero, Nancy Grey. 2017. *The Indigenous State: Race, Politics, and Performance in Plurinational Bolivia*. Oakland: University of California Press.

Povinelli, Elizabeth A. 2011. *Economies of Abandonment: Social Belonging and Endurance in Late Liberalism*. Durham, N.C.: Duke University Press.

Rasch, Elisabet Dueholm. 2011. "Representing Mayas: Indigenous Authorities and Citizenship Demands in Guatemala." *Social Analysis* 55 (3): 54–73.

Robinson, R. 2007. *Water Quality Monitoring: Marlin Mine, Sipakapa*. San Marcos, Guatemala: Geoconsultants.

Seo, Bo Kyeong. 2019. "Populist Becoming: The Red Shirt Movement and Political Affliction in Thailand." *Cultural Anthropology* 34 (4): 555–579.

Sieder, Rachel. 1999. "Rethinking Democratisation and Citizenship: Legal Pluralism and Institutional Reform in Guatemala." *Citizenship Studies* 3 (1): 103–118.

Sieder, Rachel. 2020. "To Speak the Law: Contested Jurisdictions, Legal Legibility, and Sovereignty in Guatemala." *PoLAR: Political and Legal Anthropology Review* 43 (2): 334–351.

Simpson, Audra. 2014. *Mohawk Interruptus: Political Life Across the Borders of Settler States*. Durham, N.C.: Duke University Press.

Smith, Carol A. 1990. "The Militarization of Civil Society in Guatemala: Economic Reorganization as a Continuation of War." *Latin American Perspectives* 17 (4): 8–41.

Taracena Arriola, Arturo. 2002a. *Etnicidad, estado y nación en Guatemala, 1808–1944*. Antigua, Guatemala: CIRMA.

Taracena Arriola, Arturo. 2002b. *Etnicidad, estado y nación en Guatemala, 1944–2000*. Colección "Por qué estamos como estamos?" Antigua, Guatemala: CIRMA.

Taylor, Diana. 2020. *¡Presente! The Politics of Presence*. Durham, N.C.: Duke University Press.

Tsing, Anna Lowenhaupt. 2012. "Empire's Salvage Heart: Why Diversity Matters in the Global Political Economy." *Focaal* 64:36–50.

Urkidi, Leire. 2011. "The Defence of Community in the Anti-Mining Movement in Guatemala." *Journal of Agrarian Change* 11 (4): 556–580.

van de Sandt, Joris. 2009. *Mining Conflicts and Indigenous Peoples in Guatemala*. The Hague: CORDAID.

Van de Wauw, Johan, Roel Evens, and Lieven Machiels. 2010. *Are Groundwater Overextraction and Reduced Infiltration Contributing to Arsenic Related Health Problems near the Marlin Mine (Guatemala)?* Ghent: Catapa.

Vanthuyne, Karine, and Marie-Christine Dugal. 2022. "Rehabilitating Guerillas in Neo-Extractivist Guatemala." In *Narratives of Mass Atrocity: Justice and Identity in the Aftermath*, edited by Sarah Federman and Ronald Niezen, 113–139. Cambridge: Cambridge University Press.

Vanthuyne, Karine, and Marie-Christine Dugal. 2023. "Regenerating Maya-Mam Ways of Governing: Indigenous Emancipatory Politics in the Age of the Extractive Imperative." *Journal of Latin American and Caribbean Anthropology* 28 (3): 251–260.

Vogt, Manuel. 2015. "The Disarticulated Movement: Barriers to Maya Mobilization in Post-Conflict Guatemala." *Latin American Politics and Society* 57 (1): 29–50.

Zaretsky, Natasha. 2021. *Acts of Repair: Justice, Truth, and the Politics of Memory in Argentina*. New Brunswick, N.J.: Rutgers University Press.

Zarsky, Lyuba, and Leonardo Stanley. 2013. "Can Extractive Industries Promote Sustainable Development? A Net Benefits Framework and Case Study of the Marlin Mine in Guatemala." *Journal of Environment & Development* 22 (2): 131–154.

6

Indigenous Reparations in Plurinational Bolivia

· ·

Entanglement, Hopefulness,
and Restorative Futures

AMY KENNEMORE AND
MAGALÍ VIENCA COPA PABÓN

Why is this historic, brothers? Because before there
wasn't justice for Indigenous people. We've suffered discrimination and marginalization. Lawyers
have taken the bread out of our children's mouths.
Indigenous justice was always on the horizon, brothers. The constitution clearly states it, but it wasn't
easy to achieve. We were in tears the day the judge
handed over the legal files. Tupak Katari and
Bartolina Sisa sacrificed their lives so we could live
better days. Thanks to this struggle, our brother
[President] Evo has installed through his Chamber
of Deputies and the Senate law that gives us equality.
That's why it's historic, brothers! But we still have
work to do, we still have to fight, brothers.
—Tata Juan Basilio, inauguration of the Mixed
Tribunal of Indigenous Native Peasant Justice

On March 19, 2018, leaders of the Tupak Katari-Bartolina Sisa Peasant Workers' Federation (hereafter the Federation) inaugurated a new Indigenous legal
institution, the Mixed Tribunal of Indigenous Native Peasant Justice (hereafter
the Mixed Tribunal). This institution arose from a long-standing land dispute
between two Aymara communities, Sopocari and Titiamaya, over boundaries
used for livestock and agriculture. The communities, located in Quime, a rural
municipality in Bolivia's highland department of La Paz, represent distinct histories and identities. Sopocari, peasants belonging to an agrarian union formed
after the 1953 Agrarian Reform Law, claimed individual land rights based on
their labor. Meanwhile, Titiamaya, a reconstituted Indigenous ayllu (traditional
Andean governance system), asserted collective land rights as restitution for
colonial dispossession. These contrasting frameworks of belonging and historical redress are central to understanding the conflict and the broader stakes of
reparations.

For decades, both communities pursued legal remedies through state institutions, yet overlapping land tenure policies and systemic corruption created an
impasse. Criminal charges related to grazing disputes intensified tensions, illus-
trating how unresolved colonial legacies could fracture community relations.
The 2009 Bolivian constitution, heralded as a decolonizing framework, granted
Indigenous peoples the right to exercise their own forms of justice. Building on
this constitutional shift, Federation leaders formed the Mixed Tribunal in 2016
and successfully petitioned the Constitutional Court to recognize its jurisdiction in 2017. This legal victory marked a significant step in asserting Indigenous sovereignty within a state system historically shaped by exclusion and
dispossession.

For leaders such as Juan Basilio, cited in the opening vignette, the legal victory was historic because it represented a new horizon of hope for historically
marginalized populations who often have little or no access to justice. Yet this
struggle was articulated not in terms of a radical break from the state and its
apparatuses of domination but rather through participation and inclusion
within them. Even as the laws are now designed and implemented by historically excluded sectors of society (now "installed" in government), insistence
that it is the "law that gives us equality" reveals the general consensus that, in
practice, liberal justice is still necessary to realize this historical project (Postero
2017). Addressing such tensions was the ongoing "work" and "fight" that Tata
Basilio referred to at the end of his inaugural speech.

Thus, before the Mixed Tribunal could be established, the nature of its work
also had to be decided. What kind of "wrongs" or social harms had been committed? Who or what should be made accountable for them? Given that state
corruption and uneven land policies were entangled in local disputes, what role
should the state play in resolving them? And who should make these decisions?

This chapter situates the establishment of the Mixed Tribunal within the
broader framework of reparations, as outlined in this volume. By examining

the Mixed Tribunal's efforts to resolve the Sopocari-Titiamaya dispute, we highlight how reparations are entangled with the imagination of justice, translation of harm, and contested notions of belonging. Indeed, gaining Indigenous jurisdiction over the conflict carried with it the onerous task of first untangling an extremely complicated and historically constructed problem, which was caught within legal claims to the disputed land itself. When entangled forms of violence are translated into wrongs to be addressed by specific reparation programs, they inscribe particular economic and political values onto community members' experiences of suffering. Unable to fully dismantle the colonial legacies of liberal justice, Mixed Tribunal leaders had to rely on the state to strengthen their own project and establish legitimacy. As a result, they were constantly confronted with its multiple contradictions and limits, even as they sought to construct alternatives.

Discussions stemming from early chapters for this volume drew attention to conflicting hopes and expectations that converge around different meanings of the Spanish verb *esperar*, including (1) to wait (in hopes that justice might one day arrive), (2) to hold out (in expectation of a better outcome), and (3) to hope against hope (imagining possible futures against all odds). In these different senses of the word, we see various practices of imagination that shape ideas about the nature of harms to be repaired.[1] Liberal legal frameworks tend to prioritize individual harm over collective, systemic, or cultural harms, undermining the potential for reparations to address broader legacies of colonial dispossession and violence. These efforts illuminate the dual nature of state governance: offering hope for repair while perpetuating impasses that obscure alternative visions of justice.

On the one hand, the insistence of community members on using state justice to seek a resolution to their problems, despite awareness of the entrapment and exploitative nature of the system, speaks to the "hope-generating capacity" (Nuijten 2003) of the otherwise incohesive and seemingly endless bureaucratic procedures of the state justice system. On the other hand, for many Indigenous communities, justice extends beyond inclusion in state mechanisms and toward the restoration of sovereignty, kinship relations, and spiritual connections to land and ancestors. As the editors explain in the introduction to this volume, to treat hope as knowledge means to emphasize how understandings of the present, such as the ongoing effects of past violence and dispossession, can draw attention toward the conditions facilitating ongoing harm.

The following section provides historical context for the Sopocari-Titiamaya conflict, tracing overlapping colonial harms and the uneven reparations policies that have shaped their present-day divisions. Using ethnographic data from Mixed Tribunal hearings and site inspections, alongside archival research and Constitutional Court documents, the chapter demonstrates how locally grounded justice practices serve as a lens for understanding the complexities of reparations. By engaging with uncertainty and emergent moments of hope, this chapter contributes to the broader conversation on Indigenous reparations as a dynamic and contested process of imagining alternative futures.

Entangled Acts of Dispossession

The potential of the Mixed Tribunal rested on the ability of its leaders to find a solution to the boundary dispute between Sopocari and Titiamaya. The sheer weight of the 389 pages of legal records that were handed over by the prior judge highlighted how difficult a task it would be. The documents outlined the demands and counterdemands made by both communities over the years and did not offer a clear picture of who rightfully owned the land in question.

The first major impasse in the land dispute was rooted in uneven and contradictory processes of dispossession. The initial broad land reform in Bolivia that followed independence from Spain was introduced in 1874 with the passage of the law of disentailment, which disavowed Native leaders' authority and aimed to break up communal lands by allocating individual titles to proprietors. Early twentieth-century land surveys, devastating to communal landholdings, were unevenly implemented across the country. Gotkowitz shows how in some cases, local surveyors, unaware of (or disregarding) local systems of crop rotation, for example, declared some land lying fallow available for purchase (2007, 31). They were then able to fragment communal holdings by declaring such land vacant and awarding or selling it to community members (*comunarios*) through individual titles (31). For various reasons, ranging from personal interest to coercion or the need to pay off debts to local judges, many natives sold their titles. In some cases, they also became *colonos*,[2] or peasants obligated to work for hacienda owners in exchange for the same plot of land they had sold (31). These processes made it difficult to identify clear acts of dispossession as well as who had committed them.

The discrepancy between different systems of recognition also made it difficult to define boundaries and establish rightful ownership, as multiple documents sometimes existed that partially granted property rights to the exact same parcel of land to different owners. In a 1923 petition by a native Titamayan resident, for example, the petitioner requested the land surveyor return to the area after boundaries had not been registered correctly.[3] In an effort to fix the notary's "error," he defined the proper land boundary as such:

> The boundaries of the Ayllu Cachua are the beginning of the Tatiwichinca Vara varani, Pulchinta, Cellocelloni Villque, Tarojananta, adjacent to the Potoni estate, Coolampata adjacent to the same estate, Calasombreroni at the foot of Potoni, Panca Cillque with the Concha estate, Paconpata, the easy way to Concha at the foot where it crosses the adjoining Chejot with the hacienda Huailluma, Mojonpampa with it, Yaritani with it, Cupani pampa with it, Copani Chico with it, Tambo loma with it, Tojllavilque with the Czech community, Jancoñirque

crosses the foot of the adjoining ex-community Micaya, where Pachachani Chanoa meets the Rio Grande Putunciri, then borders with Micaya through the Ananta valley, Calaguancani, Churi Mojon, Mesmamisto, Itappallonojoco, Chiar Joco, Querin Javira, Murill Javira, Apilloco Javira, Lahua Chiaña, bordering Chimo, and the river de Millocullco. These are the boundaries that separate us from the other haciendas and communities.[4]

However, the very nature of simplistic state titling procedures, which tend to omit such detailed definitions of demarcation, makes these two systems simply incommensurable.

Petitions from the La Paz archives of the early part of the twentieth century also highlight a consortium of semi-illicit practices by state officials in land encroachment. Historians examining colonial and later republican court archives have shown how Indigenous leaders flooded the courts with complaints against the abuses of local authorities in order to maintain their own authority over communal landholdings (Barragán 2012; Gotkowitz 2007; Mendieta 2010; Platt 1982). In addition to demanding notarized copies of land surveys, the petitions from the community of Titiamaya denounced corruption on the part of state officials for overcharging legal fees "under the pretext of [legal] notifications" and for coercing *comunarios* into paying for livestock without resolving any of their underlying demands to correct survey errors.[5] They go on to denounce insufficient government action for "causing serious detriment, given that spending our money and time to travel to the city to denounce our suffering is not sufficient for officials to take action to resolve our issues."[6] These are early examples of the "pillaging" of Native resources by local judges and state authorities that contemporary Federation leaders such as Juan Basilio saw as their job to fight against.

In terms of reparations for dispossession, there are two critical moments in Bolivia's history. The first followed a 1952 national revolution, when the ruling party, the Nationalist Revolutionary Movement (MNR), abolished forced labor and established a land reform program in 1953 that expropriated hacienda estates for *ex-colonos*. The second major land reform came in 1996, when the 1953 land reform law was modified to allow for collective land rights. The modification formed part of a series of multicultural reforms to extend cultural rights and new forms of political participation to Indigenous peoples. These changes followed a series of marches by lowland Indigenous groups demanding "dignity and territory" that began in the 1990s, coinciding with the international Indigenous rights movement and subsequent international human rights conventions. In the highland region, the "ayllu movement," aiming to recuperate Native institutions, also played an important role in helping communities channel demands to the state through newly formed Indigenous organizations.

Historian Carmen Soliz's (2021) examination of land restitution claims following the 1953 agrarian reform law revealed a surge of petitions from comunarios to President Paz Estenssoro framed within nationalist discourse. Contrary to interpretations of this era as one of assimilation and Indigenous disintegration, Soliz argues that comunarios not only reclaimed lands lost to hacienda landlords in the late nineteenth century but also shaped the broader legacy of the agrarian revolution (2021). This history underscores the uneven enforcement of laws, driven by grassroots struggles over land and rights, often pitting comunarios and colonos against hacienda owners and, at times, against each other.

However, despite sharing a common language, culture, and even kin, the two communities appeared to be at odds over identity politics and overlapping land reform policies. The Sopocareños are the grandchildren of former *colonos* who worked for the neighboring hacienda. Shortly after the 1953 land reform, they established a local agrarian union to organize politically and manage their new property rights. During the Mixed Tribunal hearings, representatives of Sopocari identified as peasants and emphasized the suffering, humiliation, and subordination that their relatives faced in slavery-like conditions imposed by the *patrones* before the revolution. They also presented the individual titles they received through the land reform.

In contrast, the Titamayans struggled to maintain their communal land titles throughout the early twentieth century. Their ancestors likely formed part of the so-called *cacique apoderado* movement, a vast network of Indigenous legal activists in the Bolivian highlands who similarly flooded the courts with petitions for land titles in response to land encroachment following the implementation of the 1874 disentailment law privatizing land (see Gotkowitz 2007; Mendieta 2010). During Mixed Tribunal hearings, the testimonies of elder community members from Titiamaya often centered on narratives of racial discrimination and abuse from local authorities who took advantage of their illiteracy. They also linked discrimination to assimilation policies that targeted community members who wore Native clothing or spoke Aymara in public. Present-day Titiamaya was reconstituted as an Indigenous *ayllu* (traditional Andean governance system) in 2015. In their claims to the disputed land, Titamayans presented colonial and early republican era tax registers that their families had recuperated from petitions to the government against local surveyors. Community leaders also cited international conventions such as the Indigenous and Tribal Peoples Convention, 1989 (No. 169), or simply ILO 169, and the U.N. Declaration on the Rights of Indigenous Peoples as well as a list of constitutional rights recognizing collective land ownership.

The main difference between a peasant agrarian union and an Indigenous *ayllu* in highland communities is related to land use, with Indigenous families having both individual property and access to communal lands. In practice, both share similar organizational structures and governance practices based on rotational leadership and decision-making through consensus. Indeed, this was one of the main arguments made by the court when it ruled in favor of the

Mixed Tribunal as a means to resolve the boundary dispute, since the Federation acts as an umbrella institution that oversees the political organization of local institutions representing both communities.

However, whether rights should be awarded on the basis of separate political and ethnic identities (Indigenous, Native, or peasant) or should be all-encompassing (to include all, whether they self-identify as Indigenous, Native, or peasants) was the subject of heated debates at the constituent assembly where the 2009 constitution was eventually produced (Shavelzon 2012, 93). Yet according to the Decolonization Unit of the Plurinational Constitutional Court's interpretation, in the case of the conflict between Titiamaya and Sopocari, the category represents "an all-encompassing and totalizing instrument of the nations and people that inhabited these lands before the colony and the republic," thus preventing the segregation, differentiation, or discrimination of rights for Indigenous, Natives, and peasants belonging to these separate collectivities (UD 2017, 22). Despite this all-encompassing notion of rights, these differences played out as different forms of "suffering for territory" (Moore 2005) according to criteria for claiming the right to the land, as the cases previously mentioned highlight. As we will discuss later, to prevent parties from taking further legal actions, Mixed Tribunal leaders were pressed to orient community members to focus their attention on a common enemy (as opposed to each other).

Yet perhaps even more divisive in their claims to the land were the different land titles presented to the Mixed Tribunal leaders (see figure 6.1). In her analysis of the implementation of the 1953 land reform as well as modifications to the law in 1996, Barragán found that poor technical knowledge and underfunded bureaucratic procedures resulted in complex local notions of boundary marking and their being wrongly registered or misnamed (2007, 100). A topographical map of Titiamaya presented to the Mixed Tribunal highlights a similar misreading. Elaborated by the National Institute of Land Reform in 1973, the map demarcates Titiamaya's boundaries in relation to the eight haciendas that have surrounded the community since the late nineteenth century. At the top center of the map, "Ch'eje Cala" has been written by hand, the root of which is an Aymara word meaning "pasture." This is what Titamayans claim is the correct name of the area in dispute (which Sopocareños declare is called Chijicalpampa).

The indeterminacy of the documents was also the result of land titles taking several years or even decades to be registered following the reforms. This reflects ongoing practices of trickery that are widespread in Bolivia's legal system and are used to stall cases from moving forward. Commonly referred to as *chicanería*, such practices entail a range of strategies for using formal procedures established by law such as filing incident complaints or annulments, practical tactics such as not attending proceedings (e.g., claiming illness), or even arranging to hold one of the parties captive by, for example, trapping them inside an elevator (see

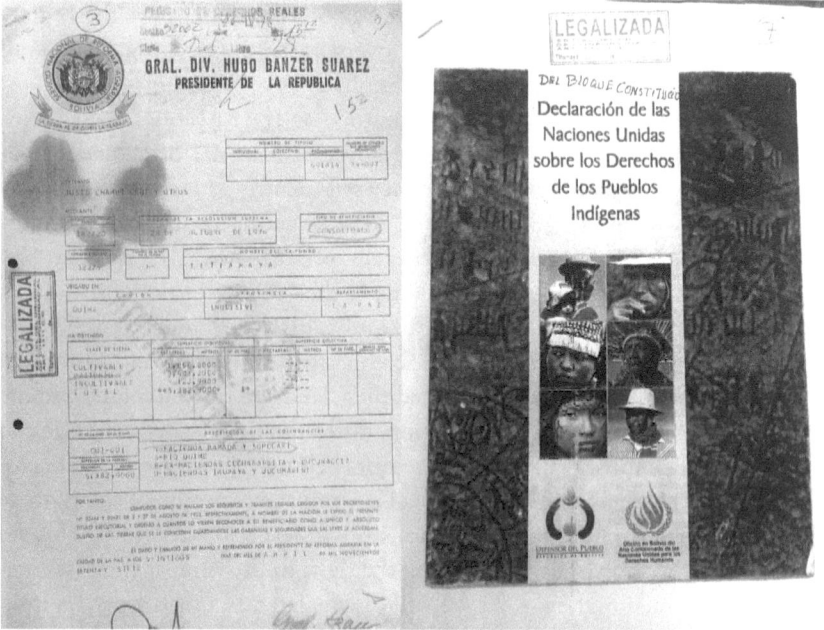

FIG. 6.1 Documents presented to the Mixed Tribunal before the *inspeción ocular* in April 2018. *Left*, a consolidated *proindiviso* title awarded to Sopocari in 1976 by the Military Government of Hugo Banzer; *right*, a notarized photocopy of the U.N. Declaration of the Rights of Indigenous Peoples.

Foronda 2017, 214). In her examination of the expatriation of haciendas to *colonos*, historian Barragán (2007) found legal records showing that *chicanería* was commonly used as a way for both plaintiffs and defendants to seek more favorable outcomes, consider different possible legal arguments, and organize additional forces (influences, resources, or counterlawsuits) that could twist a claim in one's favor.

This is where the strategy of searching for the right broker or intermediary comes into play, either to stall a case or to move it forward. As Monique Nuijten (2003) suggests in her work on the anthropology of power and the state in Mexico, rural peasants should not be seen as victims without agency, exploited by corrupt intermediaries who have access to the secret workings of state power. Instead, both rural peasants and brokers promising to have the right connections engage in the production of an idea of the state that sustains its centrality. What is notable about the Mexican state bureaucracy, Nuijten argues, is the politicizing effect of its capacity to generate hope, drawing people into the bureaucratic machine of the state system for years, even decades on end, in search of justice.

"Actually, I'm outraged by what [lawyers] do to those poor families who have scarce resources, to those whom it costs tears to lose their territories," Juan Basilio said indignantly during an interview when reflecting on the importance of their legal victory. "In ordinary justice, the one who wins is the one who has more money," and "as native authorities, we are the enemies of those who pillage the little that our brothers of Indigenous blood have!" Yet in the case at hand, this hope-generating machine meant that neither side was willing to come to an agreement over the matter without using the state as an intermediary.

Between Impasse and Hope

Uncertainty over the future of the Mixed Tribunal was present from the moment of its inception. The Sopocareños did not attend the inauguration, waiting until the last minute to send a letter explaining that they would not be there. Fermín Huaynoca, an executive of the Federation who sat alongside other Mixed Tribunal leaders during the meetings, read the note aloud shortly after Basilio's inspiring inaugural speech: "For commission reasons, we are unable to attend the hearing convened, for which we request its postponement to another date that, indicated, we will attend without fail." He then listed the names of the five union leaders from Sopocari who had signed it. "Honest brothers, this justice doesn't wait [no tiene espera]," Huaynoca commented. In this way, impasse, as a technology of the "bureaucratic hope-generating machine," was evident from the first meeting.

In many ways, the Sopocareños' disregard of the Mixed Tribunal's authority can be understood as an example of what Moore (2005) calls "situated sovereignties," in that the disgruntled union members strategically used the law to challenge their local union's authority and assert autonomy from it, despite it reinforcing the state's legitimacy. Here, they invited the state into their local land dispute in hopes of it leading to a favorable resolution for them—that is, by "forum shopping" (Pimental 2011) in multiple jurisdictions at the same time. However, the notification excusing their absence also recognized the Mixed Tribunal's authority over the dispute through their commitment to come to the next meeting or face sanctions from their union.

Another leader stepped up to explain the absence of Sopocareños. "Look, as it's been three years, I think they are managing at least two books here," Rene Mamani said while gesturing toward the original copies of the legal records that sat on the desk in front of him. "The brothers have spent so much money, but I think that today they have not spent enough to understand this [no han gastado tanto para entender eso]," adding, "One has to understand that this is what Indigenous justice is for." Here, Mamani extended some sympathy to them as victims of the extortionist practices of state justice. In other words, while critiquing the Sopocareños for not believing in the ability of the Mixed Tribunal to resolve the conflict without the state's assistance, he also acknowledged the challenges in convincing union members to not invest hope in the state justice system.

Assuring the meeting's participants that they would move forward, the executive closed the meeting by reminding them of the Mixed Tribunal's mandate to restore Indigenous justice. "We are not going to waste time, brothers. Not like ordinary justice," Huaynoca said in closing. "We brought the whole province together in the Congress, for what? To mobilize for justice, brothers. We can't suffer anymore, we can't endure. This is *utawijañani* [how we plant it, it will grow], brothers; we work for our justice to move toward what surely many other brothers hope for." In this way, he acknowledged the impasse but with the hope that next time they would find justice.

A few weeks later, a second meeting convened, and this time, the Sopocareños attended. "Indigenous justice is very clear, brothers," Tata Basilio stated. Holding up a copy of the ruling, as he often did throughout the hearings, he added, "We will reach a resolution that ordinary [justice] does not have attribution to revise." Wasting no time, he went on to explain how the hearing would proceed, according to procedures that the Mixed Tribunal leaders had decided upon shortly before the hearing started. In the hearings, each party would have a limited amount of time to present their case. "Simply the six [representatives from each community] will present [their arguments], and the court should listen in silence," Tata Basilio instructed. He then added, "In this way, we would like to weave in how ordinary state justice does it, but we can also veer from the framework a bit."

In Basilio's brief outline of the second hearing, it was clear that there was uncertainty over what role ordinary justice would, or should, play in deciding the case. On the one hand, the Mixed Tribunal's legal mandate to exercise Indigenous Native peasant justice was matched by its members' open acknowledgment of the corrupt and exploitative practices of ordinary justice authorities. Such acknowledgment validated the norms and procedures of their internal organizations as the only legitimate means of administering justice in the case. On the other hand, Mixed Tribunal leaders themselves did not appear to be able to fully exercise authority over their own jurisdiction. This tension was front and center at every meeting—quite literally—in the two hand-sewn oversized books filled with original documents from the court case that always sat alongside the crisp, newly notarized *libro de actas* (institutional registry) during the Mixed Tribunal's proceedings (see figure 6.2).

Following the on-site inspection of the disputed sector of land, Mixed Tribunal leaders decided to hold one final meeting at the Quime union headquarters after carefully reviewing the documents and discussing the testimonies as a group to decide how to make their final decision. "I will listen to whatever you have to say," Mario Conde, then secretary general (head leader) of Sopocari's agrarian union, declared, "but these are final sentences [of the state courts], and I insist that they be upheld." Throughout the hearings, Conde had insisted the issue was already a *caso juzgado* (case closed) by ordinary justice and "reminded" the leaders that the Constitutional Court ruling did not annul the rights their documents gave them. He pointed out that to do otherwise would be to start

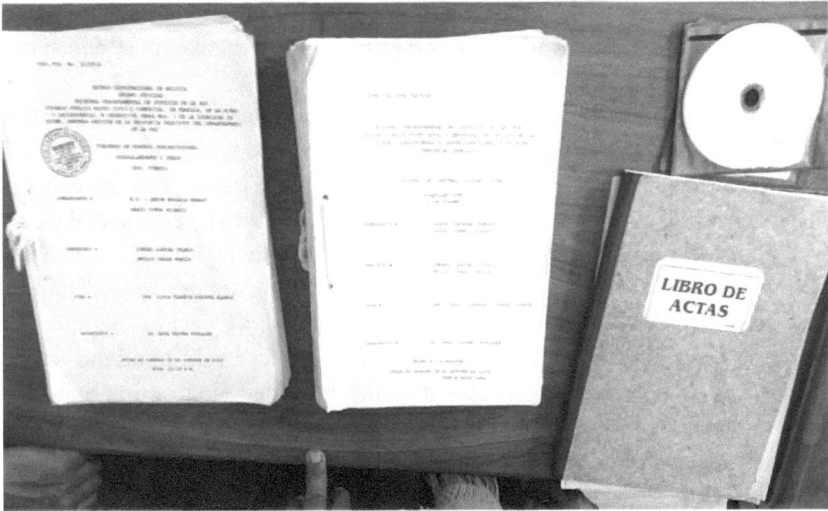

FIG. 6.2 Leaders standing over the legal records from their bench in the Mixed Tribunal courthouse.

from scratch: "If you repeal this, then where am I? Where are we?!" Here we see how the hope-generating capacity of state justice created a barrier to realizing the vision of hope articulated by leaders in the inauguration of the Mixed Tribunal. An unwillingness to invest hope in the Mixed Tribunal to resolve the conflict without mediation of the state meant that all community members would have to continue to wait.

Indigenous Reparations

"Who are we? How have we divided ourselves like this?! Brothers, these damned *q'aras* [whites] have divided us!" Fermín Huaynoca declared at the inauguration of the Mixed Tribunal. Huaynoca sat at a wooden desk at the front of the small brick room, flanked by the other leaders. He'd been quietly flipping through the pages of a medium-sized paperback while listening to Tata Basilio's inaugural speech, and everyone looked down at the floor when he spoke, listening in shame. The book in his hands was a government-issued one on the *Rights of Indigenous Peoples in the Plurinational State of Bolivia*. Opening it to a marked page, he read aloud, "Native Indigenous peasants have the right to define their own denominations in their autonomous territories according to their own norms and procedures." He shut the book and put it back down. "Perhaps we don't know?" he asked, peering over the top of his reading glasses at the room. "We are full of knowledge from our jurisdictions, dear brothers," he added while tapping his finger on the book. Sighing deeply, he asked, "Until when are we going to keep giving money to the *q'aras*? Until when are lawyers going to be managing our affairs, *para sacar plata más, y más* [to take more and more money from us]?"

Going beyond the documents, representatives from both communities offered an alternative criterion. "We don't walk around with flowers," Escarzo, an Aymara man from Sopocari, stated, suggesting the leaders base their judgment on the value of how they used the land. "We show the people real product," pointing out that they work the land and make a living from it, referencing both the 1953 land reform and the discourse of the Morales administration that promoted land distribution for many Aymara and Quechua migrants on this basis. "Social function says just that—the product ought to attend to the people, to the family; that's social function," he added, contrasting Sopocari with Titiamaya, which only used the area for pasture. As a result, the logic went, the Titamayans shouldn't be the rightful owners of the disputed sector of land, "because," as he declared loudly at the end of this presentation, "land is for those who work it!"

In response, the Titamayans argued that their use of the land was also recognized under the terms established in the plurinational constitution and by international law. For instance, in his testimony before the Mixed Tribunal, Emilio Calle, an Indigenous leader from Titiamaya, asserted that if they used the same criteria, they had the right to use the land for rituals and thus not cultivate it, according to their own customs. He cited international conventions such as ILO 169 and the U.N. Declaration on the Rights of Indigenous Peoples, as well as a list of constitutions in favor of collective land rights: "The legal side of this is very clear: territory cannot be divided. This has to be respected, and you all as authorities know this. So, as Indigenous peoples, this ought to be respected."

Calle went on to explain that the "Cochi" in Cochipampa (the specific name of the area in dispute) meant pasture, not farmland: "We've used it for grazing since before time, because you see Cochipampa very clearly, to say 'Cochi,' it's a place of pasture, with water, everything, perhaps it's to say *cochisito* [*bonito*, pretty]." Elaborating this claim on the basis of the value of land use, he added, "Whoever believes them would say the 'land is for whoever farms it.' 'Well,' we'd say, 'how can you think you're the owner? It's for pasture, it has *cochi*, for grazing, it's not for farming.'"

This prompted another rebuttal from an elderly Sopocari man. If they were to go by name, he argued, then that also needed to be cleared up. "As a representative, as a Sopocareño, and as a servant to God, truth be told in my testimony, during my birth until now, I am seventy-two years old, I've always worked in the community," he stated. "I don't go to the city, nor the mine. There [in the community], I have maintained myself [*me mantengo*] all of my life." Then he added, "During this conflict, I have not seen any comunarios talk about or touch on our *achachilas* [ancestral spirits], the foundation of the world, as the Virgin says. Now, they say the limits of Ch'eje Kala, it doesn't have this name, Ch'eje Kala;

it's called Jamphatu Kala. My father always adored this place; it was a toad, it appeared in the form of a toad. It was not Ch'eje Kala, but it is Jamphatu Kala." By accusing Titamayans of not "talking about or touching the *achachilas*," a critical criterion of belonging, he was suggesting that they did not have a rightful place there. Similarly, he was questioning the Titamayans' claim to the land not in terms of legal recognition or on the basis of legal categories of land use but based on their very relationship to the land itself. His logic further demonstrates that identifying as a peasant member of an agrarian union or even as an evangelical did not imply abandoning one's identity as Aymara.

Moreover, by emphasizing the importance of a relationship with the ancestral spirits of the land (the toad), he was rejecting the idea of belonging in terms of language or in terms of making oneself legible for legal recognition. The relational opposition to *q'ara* is being *jaqi*, an Aymara word that refers more generally to the idea of personhood. Canessa argues that for Aymara, being *jaqi* is about not genealogy but rather relatedness; "not what one is but what one does" (2012, 164). However, he also adds, what counts as *jaqi* is always relative and situated for Aymara populations: "People follow different paths, and according to which path one follows one may become *jaqi* or, indeed, *q'ara*, and the path becomes with how one comes into the world" (Canessa 2012, 121). Yet at the same time, he was blending his claim to the right to the land with a logic of inheritance, since it was his father who knew the toad and not he. Moreover, in emphasizing that he belonged because he did not go to the city or the mines, he was excluding a great deal of others present who did, and not necessarily by choice.

Similar to Simpson's account of membership among the Kahnawá:ke (an Indigenous group whose sovereignty is nested with that of the United States and Canada), questions of membership are informed by the deeply entangled forms of colonial violence discussed in the previous section. As Simpson notes, "Seemingly antagonistic processes of 'tradition,' 'modernity,' and 'settlement' are what made forming an agreed-upon membership code in Kahnawá:ke deeply challenging" (2014, 10). In the case of Titiamaya and Sopocari, the difficulty in defining criteria for belonging stems from fluid notions of Indigeneity that are always marked by power relations and tied to different imaginations and fears around national identity (see Postero 2013). Simpson draws our attention to "membership talk" (2014, 15) among Mohawk as a signpost for articulating different knowledges and ethical codes at stake as community members grapple with how to decide what form membership will take and who such criteria will include or exclude, both present and future. She explains, "'Who should be here? How should we do this?' 'Is this fair?' are questions that instill an ongoing preoccupation, a set of normative questions that find no easy juridical answers" (15).

As a project of reparations, the criteria for belonging on the basis of a relationship to land reach an impasse in that it does not offer a common framework for understanding a similar experience with racism. When Huaynoca references the *q'ara*, as he frequently does, it is typically followed by a revision of that history. "Before, Indigenous people didn't even know how to read," he said during his opening speech at the second hearing. "No one remembers how it was. Before they saw us as animals, and they scared us; even children were beaten with stones," he said, imitating a rock smacking down into his fist. "Whack! There are stories, my dear brothers." This presented a framework for understanding shared experiences of oppression in order to organize against them, similar to Reinaga's *racismo indio*.

In the present-day context, the impasses of the conflict between Sopocari and Titiamaya call for a more nuanced understanding of oppression. Huaynoca's use of *q'ara* oriented the community members toward their internal divisions. But also, he often combined narratives of oppression with those of betrayal. During the on-site inspection, for example, he made this explicit by referencing accusations of paying off judges to complete fraudulent land sales. "Now we are the deceitful ones, brothers," he said. "People always like to lie, look to give *plata*, to give money to the authorities, brothers." He then placed this back in the framework of intergenerational colonial oppression. "Since our grandparents, and their parents, they've made us bait for the fish, for the tiger, for the lion; they made us swallow ourselves [nos han hecho de caranda al pescado, al tigre, al león a ese nos hacian tragar, a nosotros]," adding, "Now we are the grandchildren."

Huaynoca spoke after an on-site inspection of the disputed area of land, and a final hearing the following week would end with as much, if not more, uncertainty than the first. Once again, representatives from Sopocari were absent, and the leaders rushed to complete full documentation of the hearings to support their resolution, which favored Titiamaya (by reasoning that Sopocari had forged documents and therefore acted as the guilty party). Within a month, there were reports that the Sopocareños had returned to the sector to plant their fields, which, although not provoking a conflict, certainly signaled that they would not respect the resolution, even if it had been sent to the court.

Despite the impasse, Tata Basilio concluded the on-site inspection by outlining a common framework for reimagining hope. In his closing words to both communities, he shared, "Sometimes we get advice from a lawyer. Lawsuits are the lawyer's farm, from which they can sustain themselves [hacerse aguantar] two, three years. Just like we harvest the land to keep our bellies full, their farm does the same. They give the orders, and you all keep going back over and over again to check [on your cases]; it's their work, their office. But the communities, it would be better if there was no decision. We have to straighten all of this out, brothers." Using the allegory of the farm, Basilio reframed what was at stake in the case—an ethical imperative to reorient their exhaustive search for justice toward their own social projects. Extending this analogy of the farm to Nuijten's hope-generating machine, we can see how the lawyer's farm is sustained by bureaucratic logics that send the "message that everything is possible, that cases are never closed, and that things will be different from now on" (Nuijten 2003, 91). By extension, their energies could be invested into imagining a project not of liberal state justice but of the Mixed Tribunal as an institution for Indigenous self-determination.

Conclusions

The day before the final hearing, we interviewed Tata Basilio to get his personal reflections on the potentiality and legacies of the Mixed Tribunal. Already aware that the Sopocari would not be present, he was visibly concerned and also exhausted from the long, ten-hour trip from his community to Quime. Yet despite the seemingly disappointing outcome of all of their efforts, he still spoke with the same inspiring and determined tone he had always taken when reflecting on the potential of the Mixed Tribunal. Indeed, it was at the beginning of this interview that he explained his vision of its emancipatory potential. For nearly an hour and a half, Basilio centered this potentiality in a story of the Mixed Tribunal that was largely punctuated by moments of ongoing uncertainty and impasse. In closing, he offered an amended version of his definition of Indigenous justice: "Indigenous justice is taking a step forward in [addressing one's] problems [dar un paso en los problemas]. When one has problems, when there is no justice, people don't sleep or work, and half of the family gets abandoned. They have to manage their own economies, and getting justice also becomes an issue. So when we talk about justice, what we mean is that we want to live free in the territory that we possess." From this perspective, injustice stems from having to abandon one's own social project—work, family, the land, and so on—to cover the costs of an extractive, ordinary justice system. By extension, "dar paso en los problemas" can be understood as a project of Indigenous reparations in that it seeks to free up the materials that can create social projects from the sedimented landscapes in which they have been entangled. Only when the knots of injustice driving communities apart are undone can meaningful repairs begin.

The case underscores the limits of liberal legal frameworks in addressing collective and systemic harms. While such frameworks often prioritize individual restitution, they struggle to account for broader legacies of colonial violence. For Sopocari and Titiamaya, land disputes were not merely legal disagreements but expressions of deeply rooted histories of dispossession, identity politics, and uneven reparations policies. Addressing these entangled harms required the Mixed Tribunal to balance reliance on state recognition with the pursuit of culturally informed practices of repair. Yet indeterminacy did not foreclose imagination of a more just future.

This brings us back to a focus on the different meanings of hope illustrated throughout the chapter. As mentioned in the introduction, early discussions of chapters for this volume drew our attention to conflicting meanings of the verb *esperar*: to wait, as impasse of hope for a justice that may never come, on the one hand, and to hope for better futures as a form of optimism that produces new knowledge of alternative forms of justice on the other. Piergiorgio Di Giminiani first drew our attention to thinking about these different meanings of hope in his comments on Natasha Zaretsky's research on ongoing mobilizations against impunity for violence committed by the military dictatorship in Argentina. Rather than seeing these different meanings of hope as separate and irreconcilable, Di Giminiani asked, How might we better understand what gets produced at their intersections as a space engendered by reparations that leads to new ways of knowing?

In the case of the Mixed Tribunal, focus on the intersections of impasse and hope draws our attention to a notion of repair that does not exhaust itself in state-centered legal performances of justice. In the wake of recognition, leaders were pressed to rethink the meaning of Indigenous justice in ways that could better diagnose and respond to the overlapping harms affecting both communities. In contrast to the "hope-generating machine" (Nuijten 2003) of state reparations, the vision of hope articulated by leader Tata Basilio in his definition of Indigenous justice implied a form of repair that did not require one to abandon the very social world of moral obligation and collective belonging that such politics seek to repair. Uncovering pathways to a restorative future first and foremost entails creating the conditions for alternative social projects that can "strive" (Povinelli 2011).

By grounding their collective search for justice within the site in question, the actual land, Tata Basilio offered a decolonial option that articulated Mixed Tribunal leaders' visions of the court ruling's emancipatory potential as an alternative means for Federation members to access justice. From this perspective, Indigenous justice is an intermediary space for reparations and belonging that can emerge as a place of dispute, allowing for the reimagining of new forms of belonging by inhabiting the cracks of dominant social projects and expanding them by exposing their underlying impasses and contradictions.

Notes

1   Piergiorgio Di Giminiani first drew our attention to thinking about different meanings of the Spanish verb *esperar* in his comments on Natasha Zaretsky's research on escraches in Argentina during our initial Wenner-Gren seminar on March 5, 2021. As we discuss in the conclusion of this chapter, we found the questions Di Giminiani raised for thinking about the intersections of different notions of waiting and hope extremely helpful to think about ideas of justice that go beyond state-centered legal frameworks of reparations.

2   Following the *colonato* system of hacienda labor implemented throughout the region, where peasants were obligated to work for hacienda owners in exchange for a small plot of land for subsistence farming. In Bolivia and throughout Latin America, colonos were also commonly referred to as *pongos* (see Rivera 1984).

3   Archivo de la Paz / Expedientes Prefecturales (ALP/EP), 1923, box 257, file 15.
4   ALP/EP, 1923, box 257, file 15.
5   ALP/EP, 1923, box 257, file 15.
6   APE/EP, 1924, box 266, file 44.

References

Barragán, Rossana. 2007. "De la reforma agraria a las tierras comunitarias de origen." In *Los nietos de la Reforma Agraria: Tierra y comunidad en el altiplano de Bolivia*, edited by Miguel Urioste, Rossana Barragán, and Gonzalo Colque, 81–112. La Paz: Fundación Tierra.

Cannessa, Andrew. 2012. *Intimate Indigeneities: Race, Sex, and History in the Small Spaces of Andean Life*. Durham, N.C.: Duke University Press.

Copa Pabón, Magalí Vienca. 2017. *Dispositivos de ocultamiento en tiempos de pluralismo jurídico en Bolivia*. MA thesis, Universidad Autónoma de San Luis Potosí.

Gotkowitz, Laura. 2007. *A Revolution for Our Rights*. Durham, N.C.: Duke University Press.

Mendieta, Pilar. 2010. *Entre la alianza y la confrontación: Pablo Zárate Willka y la rebellión indígena de 1899 en Bolivia*. La Paz: Plural.

Miyazaki, Hirokazu. 2004. *The Method of Hope: Anthropology, Philosophy, and Fijian Knowledge*. Stanford, Calif.: Stanford University Press.

Moore, Donald. 2005. *Suffering for Territory: Race, Place, and Power in Zimbabwe*. Durham, N.C.: Duke University Press.

Nuijten, Monique. 2003. *Power, Community and the State: The Political Anthropology of Organisation in Mexico*. London: Pluto Press.

Postero, Nancy G. 2013. "Introduction: Negotiating Indigeneity." *Latin American and Caribbean Ethnic Studies* 8 (2): 107–121.

Postero, Nancy G. 2017. *The Indigenous State: Race, Politics, and Performance in Plurinational Bolivia*. Oakland: University of California Press.

Povinelli, Elizabeth. 2011. *Economies of Abandonment: Social Belonging and Endurance in Late Liberalism*. Durham, N.C.: Duke University Press.

Schavelzon, Salvador. 2012. *El nacimiento del Estado Plurinacional de Bolivia: Etnografía de una Asamblea Constituyente*. La Paz: CEJIS–Plural.

Simpson, Audra. 2014. *Mohawk Interruptus: Political Life Across the Borders of Settler States*. Durham, N.C.: Duke University Press.

Soliz, Carmen. 2021. *Fields of Revolution: Agrarian Reform and Rural State Formation in Bolivia, 1935–1964*. Pittsburgh: University of Pittsburgh Press.

Spedding, Alison, and David Llanos. 1999. *No hay ley para la cosecha*. La Paz: PIEB.

Unidad de Descolonización (UD). 2017. *Informe técnico sobre el conflicto de linderos entre las comunidades Titiamaya y Sopocari, Segunda Sección Quime, Provincia Inquisivi, Departamento de la Paz*. Report prepared by Víctor Alanes. Unidad de Descolonización, TCP, Sucre.

7

Engendering Repair

•••••••••••••••••••••••

Mapuche Women Elders'
Life Histories, Violence, and
the Future

PATRICIA RICHARDS AND
MILLARAY PAINEMAL

> You never forget the bad stuff. The people end up
> traumatized. Torture is not forgotten. Many people
> say [it happened] because God wanted it that way.
> [But] those people are the guilty ones.
> —Luisa

> The hope we talk about with our sons [is that]
> someday the Mapuche will be free.
> —Ambrosia

Luisa and Ambrosia were two Mapuche women elders, both of whom have now
passed on to the *wenu mapu*.[1] Their life history narratives, like those of others,
disclose lives informed by the intersections of racism, sexism, classism, and colonialism, revealing harms that have accrued at multiple levels. Yet they also provide a record of women's everyday forms of resistance, creativity, and survival,

despite a state that fails to recognize them and others who do not acknowledge their full humanity. What can these narratives—recalling Mapuche women's lives as individuals, members of their communities, and part of a sovereign people—teach us about reparations?

In this chapter, I am interested in exploring that question.[2] The five life histories analyzed here are part of a collaborative project with Mapuche historian/social activist Millaray Painemal, in which we seek to document Mapuche women elders' knowledge and how it might inform efforts to envision alternative visions for the future. Thus, I am also interested in how the question of reparations relates to decolonization—the undoing or disruption of settler colonialism. As Tuck and Yang (2012, 1) define it, "Decolonization brings about the repatriation of [I]ndigenous land and life." Decolonization, they point out, is about Indigenous futurities—not settler ones. Decolonization needs to be *for* Indigenous people and their thriving into the future, which, as I show later, stands in tension with how reparations are often conceived. The narratives analyzed in this chapter point to several insights regarding decolonization and the content of reparations for Indigenous women and their communities. First, harms at multiple and intersecting levels require reparations that address these complexities based on an ethics of consent, healing, and self-determination. Second, while recognizing the state as a necessary actor in creating them, reparations should decenter the state and focus on Indigenous futurities. This does not imply that the state and settler citizens/bystanders are irrelevant; any process of reparations is necessarily relational. However, centering Mapuche futures shifts the focus from compensating for past harms to recognizing their ongoing effects. And third, Mapuche women's own creative vitality is central to collective and individual repair and the imagining of these futures. Together, these insights highlight the urgent need and real possibility of building forms of belonging very different from those that have governed state-settler-Indigenous relations in Chile up until today and suggest that to the extent that decolonial reparations are possible, they must be rooted in both individual and collective consent and foster healing for minds, bodies, and territories, with the objective of enhancing Indigenous futures.

This chapter is organized into six sections. After discussing methods and providing some background on the Mapuche struggle, I reflect on my own dilemmas and hesitancies about reparations and my concerns about writing about Indigenous women as survivors of violence. Then I turn to the women's narratives to show the intersecting forms of violence within them, following that with a discussion of what reparations that address these harms might look like. In the last section, I turn back to the narratives, exploring what the women's agency and "survivance" might tell us about the possibilities for reparations and Indigenous futurities. Throughout the chapter, I use the work of Indigenous scholars and activists from across the Americas to inform my analysis; their writings have been critical in thinking through the issues addressed in this chapter.

Methods

Of the five narratives that form the basis for this chapter, four were collected in 2013–2014 and one in 2017. Four of the women lived in rural Mapuche communities and the fifth in a small southern city. Millaray and I conducted two life histories together, and she conducted the other three on her own. Interviews took place over multiple sessions, in Spanish with a smattering of Mapudungún, the Mapuche language. Millaray transcribed the interviews, and I coded them, immersing myself in the texts and identifying emerging themes, which I then discussed with Millaray. Given the sensitive nature of aspects of their testimonies, the women have been assigned pseudonyms.

Life histories are narratives coproduced by the interviewee and interviewer (Shopes 2002). We view the women we interviewed not as objects of analysis but as producers of knowledge. Aware that dominant epistemological positions are often privileged over Indigenous ones (Tuhiwai Smith 1999), we came to the interviews with questions of interest but ultimately allowed the women themselves to guide the direction. The narratives are not definitive historical records but socially produced ones; the women were making meaning and sense of their lives in conversation with us, the interviewers. They are, as García (2017, 17, 37) puts it, "microhistories," "voices that name the silence." An archive of sorts was created as the women delivered these narratives; indeed, as this project continues, it is our hope to create a collection of life histories that others can add to and that might be of use to Mapuche communities and organizations interested in the connections between the recent past and the creation of new futures.

Background

Before colonization, the *Wall Mapu*, the vast Mapuche domain, encompassed significant portions of what we now call Chile and Argentina.[3] Although parts of this original territory were lost over time, the Mapuche were one of the last large Indigenous nations in the Americas to remain free and sovereign. It was only in the 1880s that, in a war known as the Pacification of the Araucanía, the Chilean government fully conquered Mapuche lands just as Argentines had done across the Andes a few years earlier. Mapuche survivors in Chile retained a small fraction of their original territory, divided into isolated communities called reductions. Chilean and European settlers, in contrast, were granted prime lands where they established profitable *fundos* (medium to large farms; Bengoa 2004). The resulting rural economy both relied on and exacerbated distinctions of race and culture, imprinting on the region the clear character of a colonial society.

Although some Mapuche benefited from agrarian reform in the 1960s and 1970s, neoliberal policies put in place during the Pinochet dictatorship (1973–1990) primarily served the interests of local elites and large timber corporations in ancestral Mapuche territory, whose operations were heavily subsidized by the dictatorship. From that point on, many Mapuche communities have been surrounded by pine and eucalyptus plantations. The plantations have resulted in reduced biodiversity, degraded soil, and polluted and diminished water sources, contributing to high levels of outmigration and socioeconomic suffering among those who remain (Haughney 2006). Politically persecuted, economically exploited, and racially oppressed, the Mapuche were now facing the environmental consequences of national development as well.

Toward the end of the 1990s, conflicts erupted between Mapuche communities and private and state actors over territorial claims and development projects, including the construction of hydroelectric dams and the massive expansion of the timber industry. Some of these encounters involved arson, equipment sabotage, raids on Mapuche communities, and charges of terrorism, recalling the worst days of the dictatorship (Pairican 2014). At the same time, long-standing aspirations for sovereignty, autonomy, and self-determination gained political traction among significant sectors of the Mapuche (Mariman 2012).

Hesitancies and Ambivalences

When first asked to contribute to this volume, I was hesitant for several reasons. Although I have dedicated much of my career to studying Indigenous rights, policies, and programs in Chile, I am new to thinking about them in the context of reparations (see Richards 2004, 2013). Apart from a few cases that have gone to the Inter-American Court of Human Rights, it was uncommon over the course of my fieldwork to hear direct mention of reparations for Indigenous peoples in Chile (despite the reparations that have been delivered to victims of the Pinochet dictatorship and their families). In an early document prepared for this project, editors Di Giminiani, Risør, and Vanthuyne (n.d.) wrote, "As memory devices, reparations work not only to forecast what forms of life and citizenship belong to the future, but also to situate events and sufferings in a discrete finite past, a feature particularly clear in governmental projects of reconciliation in Latin America inspired by the image of *deuda*, debt to be repaid to past victims as a way to leave the past permanently behind" (3).

In my experience in southern Chile, the notion of a historical debt is indeed more common than reparations, but reading this passage made me apprehensive. As Bacigalupo (2018, 230) writes, "For the Mapuche, past events are never only or entirely in the past. . . . Mapuche understand state violence as existing simultaneously in the past, present, and future." To the extent that they relegate harms to the past, do reparations let the state (and citizens) off the hook for *ongoing* harms? How do we ensure that reparations account for underlying, systemic, and ongoing injustices and inequalities (Sharp 2007)?

Indeed, as Di Giminiani, Risør, and Vanthuyne note in the introduction to this volume, it is not actually possible for reparations to close off the past.

But as Corntassel and Holder (2008) observe, by locating harms in the past, official apologies can give more power to states, enabling settler colonialism to continue unquestioned. For reparations to be effective, then, they must address the underlying (and usually ongoing) structural inequalities that led to the violations in the first place. While the state plays a role in processes of reparation, if, from the perspective of the state (and many settler citizens as well), reparations are designed to place the violence of the past definitively in the past, it seems imperative that reparations both recognize and address the ongoing damages of settler colonialism and include the resources and reforms necessary to put Indigenous nations at the center of change (Deer 2015). And indeed, although the women we interviewed spoke about the past, their motivations for sharing their narratives generally focused on what they could do for future generations. They recognized the need for past debts to be repaid, but they also were clear about the ongoing harms done to their people and desperately hoped for a better world for their grandchildren. Their narratives suggest that effective reparations would recognize the ongoingness of harm—that the harms that have been done are not dead and in the past at all. To repair, in this sense, would be to ensure better futures.

Then there is the related question of how reparations position victims/survivors: As noted in the introduction of this volume, the ambivalences of belonging observed in reparation politics are ultimately predicated upon the twofold position of subjects of reparations as passive recipients of state or corporate support, and as politically engaged citizens demanding rights. Based on my work in the region, I feel these ambivalences deeply. The Comisión Verdad Histórica y Nuevo Trato (Historical Truth and New Deal Commission) during the Lagos government in the early 2000s is a case in point. Initially, the project had a vision for some sort of reckoning at its core. In the end, however, most of the commission's recommendations that might have contributed to greater autonomy for Indigenous peoples were ignored by the administration. For example, the administration rejected proposals to officially recognize Indigenous peoples, demarcate their ancestral territories, and guarantee their rights to natural resources, instead investing primarily in already existing programs focused on "development with identity" in education, economic production, and other realms. Other projects, such as Programa Orígenes, a development program also initiated under Lagos, kept Indigenous leaders busy doing bureaucratic paperwork, one leader told me, which distracted them from the "real" work of fostering self-determination (Richards 2013). It is worth noting, too, that the sorts of programs and policies that might be considered "reparations" for the Mapuche thus far have not only functioned to alleviate settler colonial guilt without addressing ongoing structural harms but also likely disproportionately benefited settlers and the state. Indeed, Mapuche historian Sergio Caniuqueo has emphatically insisted that the Mapuche "conflict" has economically sustained the region of the Araucanía through, for example, land buyback programs that allow non-Indigenous landowners to sell to the state at high prices and development projects that enrich the livestock sellers, lumber mills, hardware suppliers, and others who sell the goods used in these projects (in Richards 2013). So I am hesitant as well about how reparations might contribute to a politics of distraction and commodification that works against decolonizing aims.

Another dilemma involves the callousness with which reparations put a price tag on irreparable harm. Colonialism has been built on the assault against women's bodies as well as their social and political roles (Barker 2008; Calfío 2016; Tzul 2013). As Renya Ramirez (2004) notes, "Colonial representations tied women's bodies to the land and viewed both as open, 'rapeable,' inviting male penetration and exploration" (107). If, as she and others have pointed out, colonialism has involved the exercise of power and control over Indigenous women and land alike, how can we even begin to put a price tag on the damage endured? Yet even as it is impossible to talk about reparations without addressing the damage incurred, there is a risk of reinscribing harm when we focus overwhelmingly on it. As Annita Lucchesi (2019) writes of her work with Indigenous survivors of sexual trafficking and other violence and as a survivor herself, survivors must be recognized as experts on their own lives, capable of establishing solutions and processes for healing. This is especially important lest reparations contribute to building up what she calls an "Indigenous trauma industry." For her, "We are not voiceless or silent; we are being suppressed by the very voices that aim to speak for us. This colonial fantasy—of a violated Indigenous woman or girl incapable of speaking for herself—is created by, and supports, economies of trauma that marginalize victims of violence while positioning settlers to benefit from commodification of continued violence" (55). Lucchesi's words bear witness to ongoing colonial harms and affirm the necessity of centering Indigenous perspectives on healing. She writes that "trauma becomes weaponized to legitimize invasive colonial state intervention in the daily lives of Indigenous peoples. . . . This view of Indigenous people allows the legitimacy of the settler state to go unquestioned and casts it as benevolent rather than genocidal" (57). Settler colonial states (and citizens) avoid accountability and, again, fail to address how these forms of colonialism are ongoing, even in the presence of reparations. These "economies of trauma," Lucchesi suggests, function as "centuries-old extractive industries" (64). They also operate at both individual and collective levels.

I do not want this work on the multiple forms of violence experienced by Mapuche women to be what Eve Tuck (2009) refers to as "damage-centered research." As Silvia Rivera Cusicanqui has observed, reducing Indigenous women to mere victims is itself a colonial exercise (in Mora 2015). It is hard, though, to talk about reparations without highlighting damage. Still, I think Tuck's point is to not *only* focus on damage and, moreover, to be careful not to naturalize it, instead drawing attention to the structural and systemic—settler colonialist—causes of harm. I therefore also attempt to center the women's "narratives of desire," as Tuck (2009) calls them, which speak to Indigenous futurities. She writes, "A framework of desire recognizes our sovereignty as a core element of our being and meaning making; a damage framework excludes this recognition" (423). I hope my efforts to focus on the women's "narratives of desire," their creativity, care work, resistance, and survival, can perhaps clue us in to what reparations centered on Mapuche futurities might entail. A future-oriented politics of reparation is itself a disruptive politics.[4]

Finally, the life histories we carried out might not facilitate talking about reparations as much as specific events or occurrences would (e.g., massacres, disappearances, removal, environmental damage). The women we interviewed referred to many such events but ultimately spoke about whole lifetimes and communities shaped by settler colonial, state, environmental, and interpersonal violence and trauma. Their stories also reveal how the private sphere hides much of the violence that shapes women's lives. As shall be seen, these betrayals are not disconnected from the settler colonial context. As Das (2006) points out in her work on the Partition of India, the violence of the past is "folded into everyday relations" (75). It shapes the present and invades lifeways and relationships in unanticipated ways. By the same token, though, the women's stories show the "everyday work of repair," care, and healing they have undertaken on behalf of themselves and their communities (Das 2006, 62). Again, this work is seldom considered in political discussions of reparation. Above all, the women's narratives indicate the importance of recognizing harm as a *social process* rather than just an event. How might this wider view and recognition of women's work help repair toward Indigenous futures?

Together, these hesitancies lead me to the importance of a future-oriented view of repair and to the question "What might decolonial reparations (if I can call them that)—reparations that foster healing for minds, bodies, and territories, with the objective of enhancing Indigenous futures—look like?" And indeed, despite all these apprehensions, I am not willing to give up on the idea of repair, either in terms of debt or in terms of healing, even if healing is necessarily incomplete (Bacigalupo 2018).

The Narratives

The women's narratives draw attention to the multiple and intersecting processes of violence that have shaped their lives, families, and the communities and territories of which they are a part. Indeed, to the extent that life history narratives reveal how people make sense of the world and their place in it, the fact that violence and suffering play such a formative role in these women's narratives is compelling (Richards and Painemal 2018). These processes are related to all three factors identified in the introduction to this volume: colonialism, the political violence of the 1970s and 1980s, and environmental/territorial damage rooted in neoliberal economic activities in the region, as well as to interpersonal violence. Importantly, however, no life narrative is *only* about suffering and violence, and as reported later in the chapter, the women's stories also draw attention to the seeds of resurgence, survivance, and the creation of better futures for generations to come. Violence and harm, on the one hand, and self-making, repair, and the future, on the other, function as a sort of dialectic in the women's narratives, a dialectic that is usefully suggestive of what future-oriented reparations should consider: both the multiple harms that have been inflicted and also the women's own strategies of individual and collective repair. I present the women's stories here integrally, rather than separating out different processes or instigators of violence, to make clear the interrelations between these processes in their lived experiences.[5]

Luisa was in her early eighties in 2013. Asked about her childhood, she replied, "I don't have an experience of childhood. Childhood of the poor, that's all. . . . I almost don't have any [happy memories]." Her earliest memories were of work and poverty. Speaking of one of the many challenges in her life, she reflected, "I just had to accept it. I just had to live. You must live the situation that presents itself. You have to adapt."

Luisa's great-grandfather was the non-Mapuche secretary to an important *lonko* (literally "head"; leader) during the war with Chile. She told stories that have been passed down to her: "The women were always hard working. The men always had to dedicate themselves to fighting with the Spanish [Chileans], always preparing themselves to defend their land." She was suspicious of religion: "They wanted to make us more stupid to take away our land. There are Mapuche who realized that." Her father was literate and dedicated himself to helping other Mapuche navigate local courts and government offices and defend their property during an era in which, as Luisa described, "Whoever paid more got justice."

When she was about twelve years old, she went to school for a while, but her studies were cut short by poverty. She was fourteen when her parents agreed for her to be married, against her will. She gave birth to fourteen babies, ten of whom survived to adulthood. Many of her children were active on the political left, motivated by hope for what Salvador Allende's brand of Marxism might offer the Mapuche. "It seemed like a war" in the campo when the coup came; they could hear shots whistling at the bridge down the road all night long. Their house was raided time and again, turned upside down by soldiers. Her husband, a political activist, was jailed twice. Two of her sons were tortured and imprisoned—one for two years, one for longer. Other children of hers went into exile.

Luisa worried, though, that I would add too much color to the story. She worried about the hurt that could come to her children when they read these words. Talking about solidarity during the dictatorship and working with women academics and NGOs from Santiago, she offered a caution to the academic sitting before her: She had felt taken advantage of sometimes; those anthropologists were surely paid, while the Mapuche received nothing. "Because of me, you have this movement," she told one. "Without me, who would have taken you in?" Luisa initiated her passage to the *wenu mapu* in 2023.

"At the time [of my childhood], there was already a lot of injustice, [related to] defense of our territory, of our land. I can't tell another story because I, my growing up, was full of suffering. It almost makes it very painful to tell." So began the narrative of Emiliana, a Williche (Southern Mapuche) woman from the island of Chiloé who was in her early seventies in 2014.

When Emiliana was about seven, the government tried to take her community's land, accusing them of not paying the fees and taxes associated with ownership. This was a ruse to take the land away from them. When the people refused to abandon their land, the soldiers shot at them, injuring several, including her father. Emiliana's parents, along with other community members, were jailed for several months. Her mother took her fifteen-day-old baby with them; the baby later died. Each day they were in jail, her mother said, they were lined up and told they were going to be killed. Soldiers, meanwhile, had burned down their house, and Emiliana fled into the bush with her younger brother and an aunt. This was a time of suffering, hunger, and the loss of collective routines. When she was in her twenties, her family endured yet another government attempt to take their land, and Emiliana herself spent time in jail.

Emiliana got married at the age of thirty. In retrospect, it seemed unclear even to her why she married this man—she swore she never liked him much. She was already mothering a son born to a sister who was too young to take care of a child. As it turned out, Emiliana was unable to have children of her own, which made her husband very angry. He was a drunk and beat her often, but she did not leave him because their house was on land her father had given her. "My husband [was] not going to take it from me," she explained. He was hit by a car and died when Emiliana was about fifty. Like Luisa, Emiliana worried for the future of her people. People need to change, she said, "to return to their own mentality from before, but I think it will be difficult."

We interviewed Perla, a Lafquenche (Mapuche from the seaside) woman, in 2013, when she was in her mid-sixties. Perla's father was a *werken* (spokesman) and her grandfather, an important *lonko*. Perla, too, referred to her childhood as one of suffering. Perla and her sister took care of their mother after she became paralyzed when Perla was five. She died when Perla was just eleven.

Perla had very little schooling, and her biggest regret was never having learned to read. After her mother died, she attended school for a few months, but her father was suspicious because she regularly came home late. (The teacher had asked her to help with the cleaning.) He accused her of messing around and beat her. She stopped going to school. She described her father's frequent abuse: "Sometimes my dad was waiting for me with a whip. He didn't listen to reason. He simply arrived and punished me."

When she was nineteen, marriage provided her with an escape. Her husband was very active in Allende's campaign and politics on the left. She wasn't involved herself. When the coup happened, he went into hiding. She was placed under house arrest. Their home was raided several times and eventually taken away from them. After eight months, she found her way to Santiago. There, she and her husband lived in hiding together, moving around from house to house. After four years, her husband escaped into exile. Perla went to work as a live-in maid, and four and a half years later, a solidarity group offered her a plane ticket to be reunited with her husband in Eastern Europe. "What was it like to see your husband after so much time?" I asked. "He was gray and old. It made me sad. We hugged, we cried together."

After the return to democracy, her husband wanted to return to Chile. She did not share his wishes but eventually agreed. Their return was not auspicious; as she described it, they stayed here and there, "begging again." As before, their home community was overcrowded, with very little land for each family. Around 2002, some of them bought land through CONADI (Corporación Nacional de Desarrollo Indígena), the National Indigenous Corporation, forming a "new community," far from their original homeland. It wasn't an easy transition; twelve years on, she, her husband, and their two children were still sleeping in one room, and the community had no access to water. Perla lamented the loss of culture and language among the younger generations, an issue made more complex by the physical split of her community.

Marisa, a Williche woman, was in her early sixties in 2014. Her father died when she was around two years old. The family's home belonged to the mill where her father had worked, and Marisa and her mother were kicked out upon his death. Her mother, not Mapuche herself, ended contact with her husband's family after he died.

Marisa's mother eventually remarried, and her new husband was physically and emotionally abusive toward Marisa. The abuse was often racialized; he called Marisa ugly, lazy, and a host of other racist epithets. Her mother did nothing to defend her and in fact made her drop her Mapuche last name. At school, Marisa was nevertheless discriminated against for being Mapuche. Eventually, she had to quit to care for her siblings. She had been a good student and was deeply saddened to leave.

As Marisa grew into her teens, her stepfather attempted to rape her several times. She ran away at sixteen and went to work for a farm manager, who raped her. Pregnant, she returned to live with her mother and stepfather. Her relationship with them did not improve, and in 1970 she left for Santiago. There, she met a much older man, with whom she had several more children. She describes the agony of birthing child after child into poverty. The children were malnourished, and the relationship with her partner wasn't good. Things got worse with the coup in 1973. Many people were killed in her neighborhood, and the dictatorship meant other daily abuses as well—she found herself begging for food. After that relationship ended, she fell in love with another man, with whom she had her sixth child. This man was jealous, despite her love for him. He beat her. In her mid-thirties, she left him, returning south once more.

Ambrosia, from the northern part of Mapuche territory, was in her late sixties in 2017. She began, "My parents were very poor, so I was born that way." Hunger and work are the themes of her interview. As the oldest child, she was "superexploited," working from a young age. She cooked, cleaned, and tended the garden. "I had to help raise my siblings, to wash the diapers, walk with the babies on my shoulder, help my dad [in the fields]." She was a good student but struggled to complete her studies, initially leaving after the fourth grade. She spoke of the cultural knowledge lost because her mother's family was evangelical. Her parents did not want to speak Mapudungún and did not teach their children because their church prohibited it. Her father was an alcoholic and beat her mom. "It made me feel horrible. I said, 'I will never get married, I will never look for a man, I will never have children.'" When she confronted her father, he sent her to live with her paternal grandparents. Later, when she was around twelve, her father took her with him to do some work at a *fundo* in the mountains. He left her alone there with an older man, who assaulted her. Her father had always threatened to kick her out if she got pregnant, so she didn't say anything about what had happened.

The family didn't have the oxen and tools they needed to work their land, so they worked a half share for a neighboring *fundo*. This went on until they received land through agrarian reform in the 1960s. It was an *asentamiento*[6] first, which they organized as a cooperative. "Then we were able to eat better. . . . We lived in a better house; the situation got better." The kids helped a lot at the *asentamiento*, earning work credit for the family. Later, Ambrosia was able to continue her education, eventually going to school to become an agricultural technician. It was during her internship that she met her future husband. He was violent when he drank, but she told him, "You hit me, I am going to hit you back, or grab your things and go." She eventually had five children; the only girl died as an infant.

By the time of our interview, the land surrounding Ambrosia's community was full of pine and eucalyptus. "The water is going to dry up. We don't have land, the people have nowhere to work, [our community] is like a *población*[7]— the people are living on top of each other." She and her husband used to keep bees, but all fifty of their hives were destroyed when the owners of neighboring timber plantations fumigated without warning them. Ambrosia served as the community's president for eight years and tried to get land for the community through CONADI. The process was slow and ended when Ambrosia got sick and was bedridden for a year. At the time of the interview, her sons were among about a dozen young people working to reclaim land from neighboring *fundos* through extralegal means. They had faced threats as a result, including from members of their own community. The owners of one of the *fundos* hired a Chilean, whose family has lived on the community's land for generations, to shoot up the houses of the people active in reclaiming land and set fire to some of them, including Ambrosia's. She worried about the repression and violence, even as she believed their struggle was just. Ambrosia went to meet the ancestors in 2024.

That violence has shaped these women's lives in so many ways compels us to consider the relationship between patriarchal and colonial power. In North and South America alike, Indigenous women scholars have written extensively about the links between colonization and the destruction of ways of life that valued and protected women (Cumes 2012; Deer 2015; Tzul 2013; among others). "Settler colonialism as a structure and logic is ongoing," Shannon Speed (2019) observes, and "gender and sexual violence remain crucial to the colonial process" (35). This also means that "state violence cannot be extricated from other forms of violence because it is state discourse and practice that set the context and generate the conditions in which such violence can be enacted" (40). As the women's narratives illustrate, colonial violence; ongoing dispossession; failure to recognize Mapuche rights to resources, territory, and self-determination; everyday racism; intimate partner violence; and rape are all interconnected. For Indigenous women and their communities, repair must entail addressing patriarchy *and* ongoing colonialism, as well as the ways they sustain one another.

My prior research indicates a failure to integrate a critique of patriarchy with a critique of colonialism into policies intended to address Mapuche women's concerns (Richards 2004). Often, Mapuche women have been lumped into (already inadequate) gender policies designed for all women without consideration for how colonialism and racism have shaped their experiences. And almost never are issues like land/territory, development, dislocation, or the environmental damage wrought by hydroelectric dams or timber plantations seen as the gender issues they are, insofar as they have imperiled women's familial, social, and cultural roles and their very communities (Cosgrove 2019).

One emblematic case demonstrates how, even when they claim to reckon with the mutually constituting character of patriarchy and colonialism, policies, programs, and laws can instead reinforce both. The case, involving the application of ILO Convention 169 to court proceedings regarding intimate partner and sexual violence against Mapuche women, draws attention to the importance of centering survivors rather than national or even international law in the process of working toward repair. In March 2013, SERNAM, the National Women's Service, publicly denounced defense attorneys' successful use of two articles of the convention to excuse Mapuche men who had perpetrated domestic violence against Mapuche women in at least twelve unique cases. The defense attorneys used articles 9 and 10, which state that Indigenous peoples' own methods of conflict resolution and allocation of punishment should be respected, to argue that in Mapuche culture, all that was necessary in cases of violence against women was for the men to apologize. As the National Association of

Rural and Indigenous Women (Asociación Nacional de Mujeres Rurales e Indígenas, ANAMURI) noted in a public declaration, the extent to which this was ever a cultural practice is doubtful, and "*machista* violence" inherited from "the patriarchal system" was not part of ancestral Mapuche culture. The organization lamented the misuse of a "valuable international instrument" against Indigenous women's interests.

In this case, the courts did not consider Mapuche women as subjects who were protected by its terms. This application of the convention was simultaneously colonialist and patriarchal. It was colonialist in the sense that a dubious assertion of "ancestral custom" was accepted as fact and patriarchal in the sense that "Mapuche rights" seemed to have been taken to mean only men's rights. This combination serves, as Wallmapuwen, then a Mapuche political party in formation, pointed out in its own declaration, to "naturalize violence against Mapuche women" and to reinscribe it through the legal process (2013). The rights, voices, and wishes of the survivors were completely elided in these legal processes.

All told, the narratives in this section display how multiple forms of violence have shaped these women's lives. Colonial, state, and political violence; economic and environmental violence; interpersonal violence—none of these can be isolated from the other, and all must be addressed in conceptualizing repair.

Consent and Sovereignty as Starting Points for Multilevel Repair

How might reparations attend to these multiple and intersecting forms of violence? The first step would be to acknowledge and address the harms that have occurred and are occurring. For some of the harms described by the women earlier, this has happened, however inadequately, as in the case of reparations for victims of torture during the dictatorship. But much in their experiences has not been addressed—or has been actively dismissed, as in the case of the land claims of Emiliana's and Ambrosia's communities. And certainly, the interpersonal violence suffered by these women is generally considered unrelated to colonialism and its ongoing effects.

In thinking through what decolonized repair might look like, I draw from Indigenous feminist approaches that link collective and individual struggles. As Gladys Tzul (2013) has asserted, Indigenous women must engage in a simultaneous decolonial struggle for individual subjectivity and collective liberation. Related to this, the Women's Earth Alliance and Native Youth Sexual Health Network (WEA and NYSHN 2014) have advanced a praxis-based analysis that connects bodily and territorial consent "from an Indigenous reproductive justice framework—examining issues of land and body as intimately connected" (6). They see "solutions to violence as coming from a resurgence of self-determination and consent for people over their bodies and the lands of which they are a part" (6), relating consent of women regarding what happens to their bodies to the collective "free, prior and informed consent" addressed in the U.N. Declaration on the Rights of Indigenous Peoples and other international documents. These organizations also draw attention to the need to challenge the structures that facilitate continued violence. They explain, "Traditional cultures of consent have been impacted by entrenched colonial governance systems in Indigenous communities, by patriarchal and paternalistic solutions to issues around their bodies, and by the intense invasion of their lands and bodies themselves" (16), concluding that "the only way that we will address violence on Indigenous lands and Indigenous peoples themselves is to support these two issues coming together and mobilizing responses" (17).

What might things look like if we used the concept of consent as the starting point for thinking about reparations? A document by Sacred Circle, an organization in South Dakota focused on domestic and sexual violence against Indigenous women, provides some useful starting points. It draws parallels between the sovereignty of Tribal Nations and the sovereignty of Native women. For example, it argues that all Tribal Nations have inherent rights to "a land base [wherein] possession and control is unquestioned and honored by other nations [and the right] to exist without fear, but with freedom," and that, likewise, all Native women have an inherent right to "their body and path in life [in which] the possession and control is unquestioned and honored by others [and the right] to exist without fear, but with freedom" (2012, 2). The organization draws similar parallels between collective and individual rights to self-governance and decision-making, economic well-being and resources, and language, history, and cultural identity. These parallels and connections are helpful for thinking about multilevel reparations for Mapuche women and their communities.

Indigenous feminists have also drawn attention to healing, an objective that should be central to how reparations are imagined (Ramirez 2007; WEA and NYSHN 2014). Healing implies an active, holistic, and ongoing approach to repair. To prioritize healing would mean recognizing how violations continue over time in the form of mental health issues, post-traumatic stress, alcoholism, and intergenerational trauma (NARF 2013). WEA and NYSHN (2014) recognize the utility of local, federal, and international laws and policies as "critical tools" in the healing process but emphasize Indigenous-designed, "culturally-safe and community-based" (3) solutions for reducing harm. This suggests again that keeping Indigenous peoples, their worldviews, and their priorities (rather than the state, its actors, and its priorities) at the center is of the essence for building decolonial reparations. Indigenous futurities, rather than the relegation of damages to a mythical, closed-off past, not only can but must be the goal of reparations.

Reparations for the intersecting forms of violence suffered by the women we interviewed would need to address multiple levels or spheres of their existence. Territorial dispossession, political violence, the extension of the carceral state into ancestral Mapuche territory, and environmental damage are harms in and of themselves. However, if we understand collective and individual consent and sovereignty as connected in the ways the organizations previously discussed lay out, we can see how these forms of violence are also gendered, disrupting women's social and cultural roles, routines, and family lives. Moreover, they create conditions that undermine respect for women's autonomy and contribute to intimate partner and sexual violence. As Speed (2019) writes, "Individual or interpersonal gender violence cannot be understood outside the historical and ideological structures that give rise to it and in which it is enacted" (43). Decolonial reparations would address all of these intersections and lines of causality.

What would have happened if, instead of centering on the "law," ILO 169 focused on Mapuche women's self-determination, consent, healing, and repair? Deer (2015) has written about the problems with relying on "peacemaking" in such circumstances, and she and other Indigenous feminists have emphasized the importance of centering survivors in the healing process as well as relying on Indigenous institutions. Lucchesi (2019) calls for "survivor leadership" (59) and stresses understanding experiences of sexual violence as "credentials that enhance capacity to design creative and effective efforts to account for and address violence" (56). In the Chilean context, Millaray Painemal and Andrea Alvarez have made a valuable contribution in this regard with the 2015 publication of a manual about the prevention of intrafamilial violence designed specifically for Mapuche women and their communities. The manual places gender violence in the context of the other forms of violence that shape Indigenous women's lives—institutional, structural, environmental, spiritual, political, and so on. It also calls for both centering and recuperating Mapuche norms and protective mechanisms (such as harmony, being upstanding, and living well) that have been damaged by colonial domination.

Reparations for Mapuche women would also include reparations for their communities—whatever this means in their individual circumstances. Later I address what the women's narratives suggest these reparations might involve. Here, though, I want to propose a few things. Starting with the recognition of sovereignty and consent would mean territorial reparations, of course, but it would also mean halting the extension of the carceral state (and state terrorism) in Mapuche territory. It would mean reconceptualizing the markers of belonging and unbelonging, which for so long have been determined by national discourses and policies that have explicitly refused to recognize the right to self-determination of the Mapuche and other Indigenous nations and official practices like the application of antiterrorist laws against Mapuche making land claims. A new vision of belonging would center mutual care, plurinationality, and the relationship between people and nature.[8]

I am reminded of a man I spoke with in southern Chile in the early 2000s. His community's sacred spaces had been enveloped by a timber plantation. He told me he understood why people left for the cities and didn't come back—that the harm to their sense of place and, by extension, their sense of self had become too much to bear. In thinking about land or territorial reparations, it is imperative to recognize that, as Tuck puts it, "the collective extends beyond human life" (in Simpson 2016, 25). Barker (2018) and Di Giminiani (2018) similarly emphasize that Indigenous territory/land is a mode of relationality, not property. Decolonial reparations would need to foster that. As Barker (2018) has written, demanding "rights [is] a tactic and not the strategy of lived responsibility to the land" (209). Decolonial reparations ought to foster a healing of the territory, the individuals and communities within it, and this sense of relationality and lived responsibility.

Survivance/Resurgence and Future-Looking Reparations

The women's narratives we heard weren't just about violence. They also told stories that evoked their own agency, creativity, tenacity, and survival in the face of forces aimed at obliterating them and their people. I turn to these stories now to see what ideas they contain for reparations with an eye toward Mapuche futures.

Gerald Vizenor's (1999) concept of survivance is useful for thinking about this aspect of the narratives. He writes, "Survivance is an active sense of presence, the continuance of native stories. . . . Native survivance stories are renunciations of dominance, tragedy and victimry" (vii). In asserting their active presence, protesting the annihilation of their people, and constructing their lives in community with others, the elders' narratives embody survivance. Survivance could also be understood as the seeds of what other Indigenous scholars and activists refer to as "resurgence." According to Snelgrove, Dhamoon, and Corntassel (2014), resurgence is about centering Indigenous futurities rather than settler apprehensions or the state itself. Corntassel (2012) references a conversation with Taiaiake Alfred in which Alfred suggests that the goal of resurgence should be that "our children should have the opportunity to live more Indigenous lives than we do" (99). These concepts, along with Tuck's "narratives of desire," are a departure from colonial visions of the future focused on "progress" in Western terms, even as they keep us looking forward, thinking about reparations as they might contribute to better Indigenous futures.

I turn now to the women's stories of action, creation, and survival to think about reparations, healing, sovereignty, and belonging. These stories draw attention to individual and community-level repair. They also speak to Natasha Zaretsky's chapter 4 in this volume, which addresses what it means to desire repair, to hope for justice, even if it never comes. These are narratives of everyday lives that contain the seeds of better everyday lives for future generations. Indeed, the women's hopes for a better world for their grandchildren, their desire to fulfill their role as *kimches* (sages, imparters of cultural knowledge), motivated much of their participation in this project. Their narratives demonstrate (and again, I'm drawing from Zaretsky) the will to create something that endures and other ways of being and belonging despite many past and contemporary losses.

When it comes to much of her family life and experiences during the dictatorship, Luisa simply didn't want to revisit them. Her refusal should be understood as a means of taking ownership over the interview, preemptively rejecting the possibility of being reduced to a victim (Simpson 2014). What she did want to talk about was the history of her family and her people, the values her parents passed down. She spoke of the need to ask for pardon before killing an animal and the importance of respecting plants. She recalled *mingas*, collective work events, where someone might be paid to tell jokes and make the workers laugh so they wouldn't get so tired. She remembered the women making *mudai*,[9] grinding the wheat with their feet, singing as they worked. Her grandmother was a bonesetter and a midwife. She passed on sacred practices for dealing with chronic stillbirths and children dying young.

Her parents modeled solidarity. Her father taught her, "In spite of their poverty, the poor, when they want to learn, they learn. He always said to walk with a clean conscience. . . . We are people before God. We are all human beings." Her father helped people negotiate the legal system for free, feeding people who came from afar. He taught his children not to deny their race, to speak Mapudungún, but not to be prideful, to respect everyone. "The more you have, the simpler you should be; the more you learn, the nicer you should be. Some people learn a little and become stupid. That is not good." He left land to his daughters. He was very clear that they had the same rights to land as men, a belief that is not universal among Mapuche communities today.

Overall, Luisa said, things aren't great now, but they are calmer than before. "To eat and sleep tranquilly, that is important." She reveled in hearing her young granddaughter speak Mapudungún, when most of her own children were not taught the language because her husband feared they would be discriminated against. She seemed to recognize the role of epistemic privilege in justifying colonization: "You can call the Mapuche backward," she mused, "but they had their own way of thinking."

Emiliana, like Luisa, reflected on the lessons transmitted by her elders. They taught the importance of hard work and defending the land. They explained how the mountain, the sea, and the rivers have spirits. She, too, recalled *mingas*, the women held for spinning and knitting. In the time of *chicha*, she shared, they held a *minga*, and they drank *chicha* and ate meat and abundant bread. These practices were interrupted when her parents went to jail (and the island in general was in crisis), but they were recovered when they were released. "Later the good times returned and the great bitterness passed," Emiliana explained, not because her family had great resources but because they were able to live and work together again, planting and reaping wheat and potatoes and harvesting lumber.

After her husband died, Emiliana was initiated as a Maestra de la Paz, a Teacher of Peace, an important spiritual and ceremonial role in her community. For her, spirituality is about fomenting harmony, good health, and a good way of life: "Only God gives us a good mentality and makes us aware of how we can live in this world. To have love and care, to keep working on Mother Earth, because that is what gives us the fruit to live our days." If the Williche can be guided by the mentality of before, she said, if they have strength and work together, they will be able to face the world and find justice.

Despite her father's abuse, Perla recalled the love and adoration of her grandparents. She spent as much time with them as possible, and they taught her "to speak Mapuche, to make food, how to live, how to share." Her memories of greatest happiness and abundance, however, centered on the nearly ten years she spent in exile. It was hard to learn the language, but she did, and after a couple of months, she went to work, mending clothes in a laundry. She remembers a wonderful life there; her house was furnished, and she had a TV, refrigerator, and washing machine. "When would I have had those things? Never," she mused. Her relative happiness in exile may seem contradictory, but it underscores the insufficient reparation paid to Mapuche people, above and beyond any reparations she and her husband received after the dictatorship and the impoverishment to which they returned, despite their hopes for better.

Racism and gender oppression shaped Marisa's young life, but so did a thirst to know more about her Mapuche roots. When she was a teen, an uncle helped her secretly meet her father's sister, who guided her over the years. During her years in Santiago, Marisa began learning more about Mapuche history and language. After returning south, she met a kind and caring man to whom she remains married today. She went back to school and finished the eighth grade at the age of forty-five. After her kids were grown, Marisa joined a Mapuche organization. There she learned about traditional medicine and came to the realization that she carried a lot of that knowledge inside of her. Cures had come to her in dreams: "Many times I cured my children with natural remedies, but it just came to me. . . . I didn't grow up with my people." By the time of our interview, she had become known as a *lawentuchefe*, a traditional healer. She thought of her garden, her chicken coop, as her sovereignty. "I feel happy when I take a bird from my corral and I make a *cazuela* [stew]. I add in beans, potatoes, carrots, everything . . . that is mine, that is sovereign." She was sad when she recalled her life before and worried about the loss of Mapuche medicine caused by the timber industry but had come to proudly identify as Mapuche-Williche.

Despite a childhood shaped by hunger and work, Ambrosia was grateful for the lessons her parents taught her, such as being honorable: "[They taught me] I had to work hard, that I shouldn't say 'I can't do that,' [but rather, should] do what must be done." When she lived with her paternal grandmother, she said, she was able to learn more about Mapuche lifeways than she had at home, lessons she valued throughout her life.

She was very active during the governments of Alessandri, Frei, and Allende, attending rallies and protests. The women in the *asentamiento* organized, and she made Mapuche clothes to barter or sell to buy things that she could then resell in the *campo*. Eventually, she earned the right to study agriculture in the province of Santiago. During the dictatorship, she joined with other women in her area to form an organization of women artisans—they wanted an organization composed of only Mapuche and only women: "Because in the mixed organizations, the men paid little attention to women and their opinions, and we as women wanted to fight for our rights, as women to have the right to apply for something, to have a piece of land, that they respect you as a woman, to defend your values." The organization became a way for women to provide for their families by selling their weavings and to pass down cultural knowledge literally woven into their work.

By the time of our interview, her sons and their comrades had successfully reclaimed a neighboring *fundo*. An earlier owner had harvested all the pine and eucalyptus before he left, and the young people were removing the new sprouts, replacing them with native trees, and trying to restore the watershed:

> Hopefully it will be possible to reclaim a little bit of land . . . even just a little so our brothers and sisters can live tranquilly and so the children that are [yet to be] born feel that they have rights, not just to their name, but to their culture, with their people, their territory. . . . Hopefully my grandchildren and great-grandchildren will be able to reclaim their lands and the Mapuche will be the owners of our territory and we will be able to be free from the timber plantations, free of all these things, and be able to breathe tranquil, clean air, and nature returns. . . . And hopefully my sons will know and be able to drink the waters.

Ambrosia was battling a serious illness when we interviewed her, and of her own life, she reflected, "My view of death is that one doesn't die. We are of the earth, the Mapuche are of the earth. If we die, we will return to the earth. I am always going to return . . . to build the earth anew." Ambrosia's story shows the individual, family, community, and territory all as potential sites of reparation; all were integral to her imaginings of better futures.

These elements of the women's narratives show a decolonized determination, survivance, and resurgence in action. The women's focus on historical memory and cultural values and practices demonstrates a desire to pass down lifeways they fear are dying away. We can read Marisa's act of becoming a medicinal healer, Ambrosia's family's involvement in reclaiming land, Emiliana's induction as a Maestra de la Paz, and Luisa's many lessons as a decolonized praxis, and we can see them as seeds for what reparations with an eye to Indigenous futurities might look like. What if reparations put elders like these women at the center, saw them as experts in individual and cultural survival, and created the conditions for passing on their language skills and historical and cultural knowledge to future generations?

These reparations would certainly entail a reckoning about past and ongoing harms and dedication of the resources necessary for the development of Indigenous-led initiatives that could help generate the sort of resurgence Alfred described—for future generations of Mapuche to live more Mapuche lives than their forebears. Importantly, they also would entail recognizing the authority and expertise of the intended beneficiaries of reparations. I imagine this to be not an essentialist project based on romanticized notions of what it meant to be Mapuche before colonization and dispossession but rather a dynamic process, full of contradiction (as any relational process is) and based on sovereignty and consent. The elders we spoke with asserted themselves creatively and persistently as subjects. They were already envisioning and desiring more Indigenous futures, forms of endurance greater than mere potentiality, and the ability to "persist in the being they find proper to the world" in modes that allow them to thrive (Povinelli 2011, 129). They were, on their own and with others, engaged against the odds in self-, community, and nation healing. They were living forms of belonging that ran counter to official forms of citizenship based on dispossession and denial. The seeds of decolonial reparations are already planted, nourished in the everyday lives and actions of women like Luisa, Marisa, Emiliana, Ambrosia, and Perla.

Conclusion

The act of valuing elder Indigenous women's generative experiences, practices, and knowledge offers a more complete understanding of the *ongoing* implications of colonialism and thus provides a more complex image of what repair can and should look like. Not merely a philosophical exercise, the women's narratives here have material implications for how we think about reparations. In this conclusion, I therefore draw from them to summarize some possible directions for (decolonial) reparations.

First, reparations should be designed with Indigenous futures in mind rather than locating harms in the past. The women made clear that their goal in putting their life histories down was to contribute to better futures for their grandchildren and communities. In their narratives, the idea of a "better" future signals not assimilation or progress on colonial terms but rather a future that is both more Mapuche and less violent. The women's desire to impart Mapuche ways of knowing to younger generations, the delight Luisa displayed at being able to speak Mapudungún with her young grandchildren, Ambrosia's sense of sovereignty in her garden—all of this is Indigenous futurity in action. For some, things had become calmer than they once were, but this was not true for all, and each also spoke of her desire for their people and lands to be free of discrimination, territorial conflicts, state violence, environmental suffering, and poverty. These desires, too, are Indigenous futurity in action.

Undoubtedly, focusing on Indigenous futures necessarily requires starting from Indigenous rather than Chilean/Eurocentric viewpoints. Efforts to repair cannot be, as Deer (2015) writes, "entrenched in abusive colonial power" (24). In describing the values instilled in them by their own elders, values like harmony, reciprocity, being upstanding, and living well, the women offer a sense of the principles that should structure how reparations take shape. Even as engagement with the state may be necessary in this process, reparations must not prioritize the state or settlers. They must instead center Indigenous experiences, perspectives, expertise, and desire, and they should recognize how humans are connected to nonhuman life and the territory itself—repair also entails repair for relations beyond the human form. As Ambrosia stated in the epigraph to this chapter, the hope is that the Mapuche will one day be free.

Second, reparations must take into consideration the multiple and interlocking forms of domination and their gendered effects. Reparations rooted in self-determination and consent require addressing specific instances of violations experienced by the women and their families, such as territorial dispossession, torture and political upheaval, and environmental damage. However, they also require addressing the structures of oppression that enabled those violations, including ongoing colonialism, racism, capitalism, and patriarchy, all of which intersected in the lives of Perla, Ambrosia, Marisa, Emiliana, and Luisa and disrupted their social and cultural responsibilities as well as what was possible for them. Relatedly, the women's lives also reveal the need for repair at multiple scales: minds, bodies, communities, and territories. Reparations should consider how ongoing colonial systems have undermined self-determination and consent at the collective and individual levels and make possible alternate futures. Ambrosia's hopes for healing for the water, the territory, her community, her family, and herself perfectly encapsulate this point.

And finally, any reparations should recognize and value the work of repair and healing already (and long) underway. Recall Luisa's stories of women working to sustain community in the face of war and oppression, how women have consistently worked to protect and sustain community, both Emiliana's and Luisa's recollections of collective work events, Ambrosia's example of keeping culture and community alive through weaving, and Marisa becoming a *lawentuchefe*. This is the everyday work of sustaining and taking care of life, community, and culture. These acts contain the possible; they instruct us that repair is a lived process. Thus, reparations should recognize the active work of repair that Indigenous women engage in throughout their lives, acknowledging how, despite everything, they have actively survived and have continued to create and nurture the future of their people.

Notes

1 When the Mapuche die, they are said to travel on to the *wenu mapu*, the land above, where they are reunited with their ancestors. Sometimes simply referred to as *el más allá* (the beyond), this Mapuche afterlife is understood as another dimension of reality (Quidel 2020), "unspecified and unknown" (Course 2027, 79).
2 The coauthorship of this chapter recognizes that Richards and Painemal carried out the research for this project together, as described in the "Methods" section. Richards wrote this chapter independently, and as such, it is written in the first person.
3 This section draws from Richards (2013).
4 I thank Helene Risør for this observation.
5 The stories of Marisa, Luisa, and Emiliana appear in similar form in Richards and Painemal (2018).
6 A settlement on an expropriated estate, usually occupied through struggle before official expropriation.
7 *Población* is the Chilean term for a shantytown or informal urban settlement.
8 The 2021 constitutional convention generated similar discussions. Unfortunately, the majority of Chileans voted to reject the resulting document.
9 A lightly fermented beverage, akin to *chicha*.

References

Asociación Nacional de Mujeres Rurales e Indígenas (ANAMURI). 2013. "Carta pública: 'La violencia machista no forma parte de la cultura ancestral de los pueblos originarios.'" March 2013. Accessed June 10, 2021. https://www.movimientos.org/es/content/%E2%80%9Cla -violencia-machista-no-forma-parte-de-la-cultura-ancestral-de-los-pueblos-originarios%E2 %80%9D.

Bacigalupo, Ana Mariella. 2018. "The Mapuche Undead Never Forget: Traumatic Memory and Cosmopolitics in Post-Pinochet Chile." *Anthropology and Humanism* 43 (2): 228–248.

Barker, Joanne. 2008. "Gender, Sovereignty, Rights: Native Women's Activism Against Social Inequality and Violence in Canada." *American Quarterly* 60 (2): 259–266.

Barker, Joanne. 2018. "Decolonizing the Mind." *Rethinking Marxism* 30 (2): 208–231.

Bengoa, José, ed. 2004. *La memoria olvidada: Historia de los pueblos indígenas de Chile.* Santiago: Cuadernos Bicentenario (Presidencia de Chile).

Calfío Montalva, Margarita. 2016. "Cuerpos marcados: Comunidades en construcción." In *Kyanq'ib'il Xu'j b'ix Kyanq'ib'il Qxe'chi, Tuwün Pu Zomo, Mujeres y Pueblos Originarios: Luchas y Resistencias hacia la descolonización,* edited by Andrea Alvarez and Millaray Painemal, 33–38. Santiago de Chile: Pehuén Editores.

Corntassel, Jeff. 2012. "Re-Envisioning Resurgence: Indigenous Pathways to Decolonization and Sustainable Self-Determination." *Decolonization: Indigeneity, Education & Society* 1 (1): 86–101.

Corntassel, Jeff, and Cindy Holder. 2008. "Who's Sorry Now? Government Apologies, Truth Commissions, and Indigenous Self-Determination in Australia, Canada, Guatemala, and Peru." *Human Rights Review* 9 (4): 465–489.

Cosgrove, Serena. 2019. "Who Will Use My Loom When I Am Gone? An Intersectional Analysis of Mapuche Women's Progress in Twenty-First Century Chile." In *Bringing Intersectionality to Public Policy,* edited by Julia Jordan-Zachery and Olena Hankivsky, 529–545. New York: Palgrave Macmillan.

Course, Magnus. 2007. "Death, Biography, and the Mapuche Person." *Ethnos* 72 (1): 77–101.

Cumes, Aura Estela. 2012. "Mujeres indígenas, patriarcado y colonialismo: Un desafío a la segregación comprensiva de las formas de dominio." *Anuario de Hojas de WARMI* 17:1–16.

Das, Veena. 2006. *Life and Words: Violence and the Descent into the Ordinary*. Berkeley: University of California Press.

Deer, Sarah. 2015. *The Beginning and End of Rape: Confronting Sexual Violence in Native America*. Minneapolis: University of Minnesota Press.

Di Giminiani, Piergiorgio. 2018. *Sentient Lands: Indigeneity, Property, and Political Imagination in Neoliberal Chile*. Tucson: University of Arizona Press.

Di Giminiani, Piergiorgio, Helene Risør, and Karine Vanthuyne. n.d. "Proposal for Wenner-Gren Workshop: The Futures of Reparation in Latin America: Imagination, Translation and Belonging in Restorative Politics." Unpublished manuscript.

Forbis, Melissa, and Patricia Richards. 2016. "Teoría y praxis de las mujeres indígenas: Descolonización y los límites de la ciudadanía." In *Kyanq'ib'il Xu'j b'ix Kyanq'ib'il Qxe'chi, Tuwün Pu Zomo, Mujeres y Pueblos Originarios: Luchas y Resistencias hacia la descolonización*, edited by Andrea Alvarez and Millaray Painemal, 83–94. Santiago de Chile: Pehuén Editores.

García Mingo, Elisa, ed. 2017. *Zomo Newen: Relatos de vida de mujeres Mapuche en su lucha por los derechos indígenas*. Santiago, Chile: LOM.

Haughney, Diane. 2006. *Neoliberal Economics, Democratic Transition, and Mapuche Demands for Rights in Chile*. Gainesville: University Press of Florida.

Lucchesi, Annita Hetoevéhotohke'e. 2019. "Indigenous Trauma Is Not a Frontier: Breaking Free from Colonial Economies of Trauma and Responding to Trafficking, Disappearances, and Deaths of Indigenous Women and Girls." *American Indian Culture and Research Journal* 43 (3): 55–68.

Mariman, José. 2012. *Autodeterminación: Ideas políticas mapuche en el albor del siglo XXI*. Santiago: LOM.

Mora Robles, David. 2015. "El colonialismo es una cadena de opresiones que nos hemos metido dentro." *Semanario Universidad* (San José, Costa Rica), May 13.

Native American Rights Fund. 2013. "Let All That Is Indian Within You Die!" *Native American Rights Fund Legal Review* 38 (2): 1–11.

Painemal Morales, Millaray, and Andrea Alvarez Díaz, eds. 2015. *Caminando juntas hacia la recuperación del kvme mogen y el azmapu*. Santiago: FACSO Ediciones.

Pairican, Fernando. 2014. *Malon: La rebelión del movimiento mapuche, 1990–2013*. Santiago: Pehuén.

Povinelli, Elizabeth A. 2011. *Economies of Abandonment*. Durham, N.C.: Duke University Press.

Quidel Lincoleo, José. 2020. "La noción mapuche de che (persona)." PhD diss., Instituto de Filosofía y Ciencias Humanas, Universidad Estadual de Campinas, São Paulo, Brazil.

Ramirez, Renya. n.d. "Healing, Violence, and Native American Women." *Social Justice* 31 (4): 103–116.

Ramirez, Renya. 2007. "Race, Tribal Nation, and Gender: A Native Feminist Approach to Belonging." *Meridians* 7 (2): 22–40.

Richards, Patricia. 2004. *Pobladoras, Indígenas, and the State: Conflicts over Women's Rights in Chile*. New Brunswick, N.J.: Rutgers University Press.

Richards, Patricia. 2013. *Race and the Chilean Miracle: Neoliberalism, Democracy, and Indigenous Rights*. Pittsburgh: University of Pittsburgh Press.

Richards, Patricia, and América Millaray Painemal Morales. 2018. "The Life Histories of Mapuche Women Elders as Protest." *Women's Studies Quarterly* 46 (3–4): 31–48.

Sacred Circle. 2012. "From the Roots Up: An Overview of Shelter and Advocacy Program Development Supporting Women's Sovereignty." https://www.niwrc.org/sites/default/files/images/resource/From_the_Roots_Up.pdf.

Sharp, Susan. 2007. "The Idea of Reparation." In *Handbook of Restorative Justice*, edited by Gerry Johnstone and Daniel W. Van Ness, 24–40. Portland, Ore.: Willan.

Shopes, Linda. 2002. "Making Sense of Oral History." *History Matters: The U.S. Survey Course on the Web*, February. http://historymatters.gmu.edu/mse/oral/.

Simpson, Audra. 2014. *Mohawk Interruptus: Political Life Across the Borders of Settler States.* Durham, N.C.: Duke University Press.

Simpson, Leanne Betasamosake. 2016. "Indigenous Resurgence and Co-Resistance." *Critical Ethnic Studies* 2 (2): 19–34.

Snelgrove, Corey, Rita Dhamoon, and Jeff Corntassel. 2014. "Unsettling Settler Colonialism: The Discourse and Politics of Settlers, and Solidarity with Indigenous Nations." *Decolonization: Indigeneity, Education & Society* 3 (2): 1–32.

Speed, Shannon. 2019. *Incarcerated Stories: Indigenous Women Migrants and Violence in the Settler-Capitalist State.* Chapel Hill: University of North Carolina Press.

Tuck, Eve. 2009. "Suspending Damage: A Letter to Communities." *Harvard Educational Review* 79 (3): 409–428.

Tuck, Eve, and K. Wayne Yang. 2012. "Decolonization Is Not a Metaphor." *Decolonization: Indigeneity, Education & Society* 1 (1): 1–40.

Tuhiwai Smith, Linda. 1999. *Decolonizing Methodologies: Research and Indigenous Peoples.* London: Zed Books.

Tzul Tzul, Gladys. 2013. "Mujeres indígenas: Ideas y liberaciones plurales." Paper presented at Primer Congreso Internacional de Pueblos Indígenas de América Latina, October 30, Oaxaca, Mexico.

Vizenor, Gerald. 1999. *Manifest Manners: Narratives on Postindian Survivance.* Lincoln: University of Nebraska Press.

Wallmapuwen. 2013. "Wallmapuwen rechaza mal uso de Convenio 169 para justificar violencia contra la mujer." March 19. https://oge.cl/wallmapuwen-rechaza-mal-uso-de-convenio-169-para-justificar-violencia-contra-la-mujer/.

Women's Earth Alliance and Native Youth Sexual Health Network. 2014. *Violence on the Land, Violence on Our Bodies: Building an Indigenous Response to Environmental Violence.* Berkeley, Calif.: Women's Earth Alliance and Native Youth Sexual Health Network. http://landbodydefense.org/uploads/files/VLVBReportToolkit2016.pdf.

8

Involuntary Resettlement Resulting from Mining Operations in Peru

• •

The Illusion of
Commensuration,
State Responsibility, and
Corporate Reparations

GUILLERMO SALAS CARREÑO

This chapter analyzes how themes that emerge in discussions on reparations also relate to the process of involuntary resettlement by looking specifically at the case of the Antamina mine and the resulting resettlement process in Ancash, Peru, in the late 1990s. This type of resettlement, in contrast to those resulting from disasters and wars, tends to be justified through ideologies of development and a cost-benefit analysis in which the national is prioritized over the local (Oliver-Smith 2009, 4). Similar to the way in which many extractive industries have turned spaces associated with natural deposits into sacrificial landscapes (Black 2000), the populations living near mines have historically been sacrificed in the name of national progress. Paradoxically, this peculiarity and its current association with corporate social responsibility tend to frame involuntary resettlement resulting from mining projects in relatively positive ways.

According to the International Finance Corporation's (IFC) Performance Standard 5, involuntary resettlement due to mining and infrastructure projects "refers both to physical displacement (relocation or loss of shelter) and to economic displacement (loss of assets or access to assets that leads to loss of income sources or other means of livelihood) as a result of project-related land acquisition and/or restrictions on land use" (2012, 1). While this definition and most discussions on resettlement rely heavily on economic rationale, nonetheless, "resettlement is fundamentally a political phenomenon, involving the use of power by one party to relocate another" (Oliver-Smith 2009, 5). Power imbalances not only are a condition that makes resettlement possible but also help explain why these processes often provoke much damage and suffering to the resettled populations. Guidelines that aim to remove negative outcomes for people facing involuntary resettlement are relatively recent. The World Bank's (WB) Operational Directive 4.30 (OD 4.30), its first policy for protecting people displaced by the projects it finances, was introduced in 1980 and applied until 2001. Since 2002, resettlements related to these projects have been regulated by the Operational Policy and Bank Procedure 4.12 (OP/BP 4.12; Clark 2009; World Bank 2004).[1]

The IFC, which is the branch of the WB that provides credit to private corporations, has developed similar policies. Its Performance Standard 5, cited earlier (IFC 2012), has become the most important guideline for mining corporations regarding land acquisition and involuntary resettlement processes, while the eight IFC performance standards on environmental and social sustainability, as a whole, "are generally regarded as the guiding standard in the extractive sector, with the expectation that companies comply with them or model their own corporate standards on them" (ICMM 2015, 9).

The Performance Standard 5, similar to the OP/BP 4.12, seeks to avoid or minimize displacement and to prevent forced evictions (IFC 2012, 1). When that is not possible, it aims "to minimize adverse social and economic impacts from land acquisition or restrictions on land use by (i) providing compensation for loss of assets at replacement cost and (ii) ensuring that resettlement activities are implemented with appropriate disclosure of information, consultation, and the informed participation of those affected" (IFC 2012, 1–2).

Additionally, these guidelines aim "to improve living conditions among physically displaced persons through the provision of adequate housing with security of tenure at resettlement sites" (IFC 2012, 2). Unfortunately, the record of processes carried out using the WB and IFC guidelines shows that they have largely failed to achieve this objective. There is considerable research that points to this somber panorama (see León 2017; Oliver-Smith 2009, 2010). Indeed, the literature shows that "the majority of people who are uprooted in the name of development do not easily recover, much less improve, their previous standards of living" (Clark 2009). Moreover, "although states and international financial institutions have, for years, accepted the proposition that resettlement projects must be development projects in their own right, the record of dismal failures and concomitant pain and suffering for the displaced continues with depressing regularity" (Oliver-Smith 2009, 17).

Given this panorama, how can involuntary resettlement be thought in relation to reparations? According to Johnston (2009), reparations are "those efforts to voice social injustice, demand accountability, and seek remedy not only for violations of international human rights and humanitarian law that occur during the time of war but also for those violations that occur as a result of state-sponsored violence against its own citizens in the name of colonial expansion, economic development, and national security" (13). Certainly, the WB and IFC guidelines involve measures that are forms of reparations. Ensuring the same or better living standards after resettlement involves *restitution*—that is, to "restore the victim to his or her original situation"—and oftentimes these processes include *compensation*, or "economic payment for any assessable damage" (Johnston 2009, 14). Hence current international regulations around involuntary resettlement are strongly related to the logics of reparations. Further, both restitution and compensation involve forms of commensuration—that is, "the transformation of different qualities into common metric . . . [as in,] qualities into quantities, difference into magnitude" (Espeland and Stevens 1998, 314, 316). Certain forms of commensuration are fundamental for constructing legitimacy (Li 2011; Povinelli 2001), evident both in involuntary resettlement processes and with certain forms of reparations.

Typically, involuntary resettlement processes are conceived of, planned, and executed according to economic logics that are grounded in Western presuppositions surrounding issues such as property, value, and rights over resources. Such "economicism" not only helps hide the political nature of these processes but is also central to the emergence of what I call the "illusion of commensuration," which requires that particular, usually Indigenous, socionatural assemblages be reduced into quantifiable, Western, economic categories that conceal their complexity. This illusion of commensuration is deeply related to commodity fetishism, which renders invisible intricate social relations transforming complex socionatural assemblages into commodities isolated from their producers.

An important aspect of reparations is that they tend to be pursued only after a regime change, when the state is able to recognize the damage done. However, as the Peruvian state has strongly promoted large multinational mining investments since the neoliberal reforms of the 1990s and is therefore coresponsible for the damages involuntary resettlement has caused, it is unlikely that it will start a conversation about reparations or regulations for resettlement while its development agenda built around extractive industries remains central.

Finally, resettlement processes and reparations are closely related in the way they spark the reimagining of futures. As a result of the drastic changes experienced through these processes, in particular the tensions and consequences they involve, they can encourage forms of belonging and exercises of citizenship that inevitably point to the state's responsibility for outcomes and repair.

Antamina Resettlement Process

At the time it began in the late 1990s, Antamina was the largest mining investment in Peruvian history, a $2.3 billion project in the highlands of Ancash. As part of the conditions of a commercial bank loan, Antamina had to comply with the World Bank Operational Directive for Involuntary Resettlement (OD 4.30). When Antamina representatives arrived in the San Marcos District in 1997, with the then novel discourse of corporate social responsibility, they presented the company as a good neighbor and partner who would actively contribute to local development. The community received this news with enthusiasm, and expectations about the project were lifted based on this initial social contract proposed by Antamina—a partnership involving the acceptance and belonging of the mining company in the locality and founded on the imagination of a future of mutual benefit.

Upon completion of my BA in 1998, I began work as a research assistant for GRADE (Grupo de Análisis para el Desarrollo), an NGO that launched a research project on Antamina as it was completing its land acquisition process. In December 1998, due to my research experience in the area, Antamina hired me as part of a team carrying out a detailed survey in order to build a socioeconomic baseline for the resettlement process. However, as a result of miscommunications and tensions within the company, this survey was never carried out, and I was reassigned to a team in charge of community relations in the construction of the main access road. Two months after the Accelerated Resettlement Plan concluded, I was reassigned again to the postresettlement team in charge of receiving, systematizing, and proposing solutions for the many grievances that the land acquisition and resettlement processes had created. Hence my understanding of the resettlement process benefits from the research I carried out with the NGO previous to the resettlement itself as well as from working as a member of the postresettlement team.

After leaving the company, I analyzed the resettlement process and published my findings in a book (Salas Carreño 2008),[2] using various sources of information, including the data I produced in the research prior to the resettlement, several surveys produced by company officials, and notes from meetings and conversations with resettled families, authorities, members of the broader community, and company officials that emerged in my daily work with the postresettlement team.[3] These experiences gave me the ability to directly observe daily life both before and after these families left the high pasturelands of Yanacancha. The available data did not include interview recordings or detailed notes of these conversations, and as such, I cannot include direct

FIG. 8.1 Part of Yanacancha pasturelands previous to the resettlement process. *Source:* Author, 1998.

testimonies from resettled families. All the data referenced in the following pages comes from my 2008 book, which can be consulted for additional details.

The Assemblages of the Sheep Flocks of Yanacancha

The high pasturelands of Yanacancha (San Marcos District, Huari Province, Ancash region)—4,600 hectares, 3,250 of which compose pasturelands at an altitude of approximately 4,300 meters—were occupied by roughly fifty Indigenous Quechua households in 1996 when the Antamina mining concession was acquired by a consortium of Rio Algom and Inmet, two Canadian mining companies,[4] in the privatization process of Centromin Perú, the largest state mining company. The new Antamina Mining Company initiated its presence in these highlands in 1997, occupying a small exploration camp next to what was then Lake Antamina.

Before Antamina moved in, these lands had two types of proprietors. While two *comunidades campesinas* had collective land titles for roughly half of these pasturelands as a result of the 1969 agrarian reform, the other half were maintained by several smaller properties, none of which had proper legal titles. The majority of these properties' many legal heirs lived elsewhere in lower agricultural areas, the district capital, coastal cities, or in Lima, and had never organized to obtain titles for lands largely considered worthless in monetary terms. Those few heirs who remained relied heavily on subsistence gift economies.

FIG. 8.2 House of Yanacancha before the resettlement process. *Source:* Author, 1998.

The Indigenous families living in Yanacancha were mainly sheepherders who cared for animals that belonged directly to them but also to their siblings and extended families who had moved out of the highlands once they married. Those who left kept their sheep through multiple reciprocity agreements with the family members who remained in Yanacancha. In this way, each flock of sheep articulated a network of relatives that lived in the pastures of Yanacancha, in lower-altitude agricultural villages (most around 3,200 meters), in the district capital town (at 2,900 meters), or in faraway coastal cities, including Lima. Thus, all of these participants accessed the highland pastures' resources in different ways and played various roles in each family's economy.

The families living in Yanacancha sometimes also had agricultural land at lower altitudes and therefore alternate homes in a lower village. The heterogeneous combination of sizes and locations of plots and homes that each family had depended on the particular histories of marriages, inheritances, and decisions that a couple and their elders had made. Hence a sheep flock in Yanacancha was the core of a broader assemblage that also included houses, agricultural plots, pasturelands, crops, cows, horses, other animals, and humans, as well as sentient plains and mountains.[5] The complexity of these assemblages involved many actors co-constituting each other beyond the nature-culture divide (Blaser 2019; Latour 2007).

These assemblages were grounded in gift economies but participated, to different degrees, in monetary economies as well. While the family members who permanently lived in the pasturelands used monetary exchanges in marginal ways, those living on the coast were more fully involved in them while only minimally engaged in the gift economy of Yanacancha. These assemblages also supposed heterogeneous practices and categories. They involved Quechua and Spanish monolingualism as well as different degrees of Quechua-Spanish bilingualism, across gender and generational lines. Categories, emerging from one language or the other, were part of a wide array of technologies through which people engaged with multiple production cycles on these agricultural plots spanning different altitudes, pasturelands, vegetables, animals, and sentient places.

Antamina's Resettlement Plans and Practices

The Antamina Mining Company started its land acquisition process in 1997, with a small team led by a Peruvian engineer with neither experience in these processes nor knowledge of Antamina's commitments to the WB guidelines. It involved a strong logistical support to state officials of the Programa Especial de Titulación de Tierras (PETT, a state program for land titling). Through this, the local population saw that state institutions were clearly at the service of Antamina rather than its citizens. PETT expedited the process despite that just a small minority of those who were potentially legal owners of the land lived in the pastures themselves. The social complexity and the speed of the land acquisition left many complaints unsolved. Antamina had bought all the lands necessary for the project by September 1998, while the families occupying them remained.

During the land acquisition, explanations around what the resettlement process would entail were unclear. For instance, Antamina's environmental impact assessment did not include a resettlement plan with the details necessary for actual implementation. In 1998, Antamina contracted a small, new, local NGO with no experience in resettlement to design the resettlement program. The NGO's plan did not consider the complexity of the networks articulated by the sheepherders and mistakenly assumed that *land-for-land* replacement was appropriate, without input from these families. When a small team of Antamina negotiators—engineers without training in the company's obligations to follow OD 4.30—attempted to start the resettlement process in November 1998, it became obvious that the plan was unviable. The families claimed that they were promised resettlement in lands that included planted pastures (as opposed to natural ones) and new houses following the scale model displayed in the Antamina office in the district capital, "with all the services" that were absent in Yanacancha: electricity, running water, a sewage system, and good education and health services.

In January 1999, Antamina contracted Bechtel[6] to carry out the construction process. When Bechtel took charge, they demanded that all lands be cleared of occupants immediately, and Antamina responded by expediting the task. The reasons behind this abrupt change of plans were complex but related to what

FIG. 8.3 Yanacancha during the construction of the camp and the mining facilities. *Source:* Author, 1999.

Gerritsen and MacIntyre (1991) call the mining projects' logic of capital—that is, how the structure of financial fluxes, investment schedules, construction bonuses, and legal commitments with the state and investment banks end up prioritizing a particular schedule over social commitments to the local population. Between February and April 1999, Antamina carried out the Accelerated Resettlement Plan, which involved a payment of $33,000 to each household, an offer to buy their animals, and their immediate move to the place chosen by the family.

While most families received checks for this amount, it was not universal, as the criteria used to consider qualification varied according to different Antamina representatives. Since Antamina only gave this resettlement compensation to permanent residents, sometimes one compensation ended up divided between a nuclear family that alternated between the high pasturelands and lower agricultural zones and another that stayed permanently in the highlands. In other cases, families that had recently moved out of the pasturelands to lower houses were not compensated, even though their economies relied heavily on their highland sheep. In still more cases, where nuclear families were in the process of becoming independent from one another, two nuclear families were considered to be one and received only one set of compensation. Other families were in charge of sheep without being landowners and thus were not compensated (or, in other cases, the sheep owners were not compensated). Additionally, families considered to have no legal rights to the land (those not members of *comunidades campesinas* or not recognized as proprietors by PETT), despite

FIG. 8.4 Resettled family's house under construction in a village at lower altitude (3,200 meters). *Source:* Author, 2000.

having lived there for decades, were not fully compensated. Each of these situations went against the OD 4.30 guidelines. Even beyond all of these inconsistencies, the stark contrast between the promises made and the abrupt evictions implemented provoked suffering, deep resentment, and distrust among these families and the broader local community.

Promises, Evictions, and Imagining Futures

While Antamina representatives were purchasing these lands, they also made vague promises of *land-for-land* resettlements (as prioritized by OD 4.30). According to several testimonies from the families involved, these promises offered a move to land with cultivated pastures and ample homes "with all the services." Although it was never clear where these pastures would be located, the testimonies emphasized the presentation of utopian pasturelands. Maintaining cultivated pastures for sheep requires a greater investment of labor than local herding practices do. Embracing the necessary technologies would have implied an intense process of adaptation and change as well as taking on the risk of there being a market guaranteeing the economic viability of these new assemblages, none of which was considered in the compensation plans. Nonetheless, this uncertainty over a future tinted with utopian promises was shattered by the Accelerated Resettlement Plan.

Indeed, the abrupt change led to the sudden breaking apart of existing assemblages and their radical reconfiguration. Almost half of the animals living in Yanacancha were bought by Antamina, and the families that decided to sell all or part of their herds did so because they were not able to relocate them to alternate pasturelands. However, the animals that were kept were relocated to other highlands through kinship networks and reciprocity arrangements. While this put extra pressure on pastures already being grazed, it is important to note that this was possible as a result of the flexibility of Indigenous technologies for managing these complex ecosystems. With four exceptions, all families requested a move to their alternate house or the house of a relative in one of the lower villages. In this way, these networks were not dismantled but were able to reconfigure themselves when the Yanacancha pasturelands were suddenly taken from them. The ingrained logic around organizing relationships with both kin and land at different altitudes was crucial for rearranging the possibilities of these families' futures.

Nonetheless, these families' forced evictions were violent and traumatic. They quickly had to decide whether to sell or take their animals with them and then immediately had to pack their belongings onto a truck. Without assistance or time to consider, they had to sign documents in exchange for a piece of paper with a promise of $33,000. Most of these families did not have enough experience with the monetary economy to be able to assess what that amount was worth. Certainly, trading their lives in the highlands for a bit of paper meant to represent an indiscernible amount of money added a sense of confusion to these sudden and rushed evictions.[7]

The many actors that made up these assemblages, many of which were (in) Yanacancha, constituted these people. Thus, suddenly removing Yanacancha from them radically shattered who they were. This was particularly clear among seniors for whom the highlands and animals there were fundamental elements of themselves. When moved to the lower agricultural areas and villages, they felt out of place, with no clear "things to do" without their animals to tend to. One of the ways they expressed this disruption was by emphasizing their dislike for these lower spaces by describing them as too hot, too crowded with people, too noisy, and full of flies and bad smells.

The heterogeneity of these assemblages could also be seen in how they related to the resettlement processes and imagined their futures. Generational and gendered tensions marked not only different ways of relating to the lost pastures but also a variety of ideas around what to do with the monetary compensation. For the young adults used to coming and going between the highlands and coastal cities who desired the opportunities of urban life, the money meant the possibility of starting a life in the city. In contrast, the seniors did not see their futures as involving the acquisition of a minivan to work in transportation or an urban plot on the coast to support their new lives. While some families chose to buy agricultural land at lower altitudes, others, sometimes siblings or parent and child members, were not able to come to an agreement on what to do. These differences and tensions that arose in the context of abrupt eviction also caused mental health issues, as seen, for example, through an increase in alcohol abuse (see Kedia 2009). These families inevitably faced overwhelming uncertainty about their futures, risked losing the compensation money or spending it poorly, feared being deceived, and experienced tensions within the family.[8] All of these conditions acted to put these assemblages under extraordinary pressure from these multidimensional forms of stress that have commonly been witnessed in resettlement processes (Scudder 2009).

When Antamina completed the Accelerated Resettlement Plan, its local development initiatives fell short of meeting local expectations. Local hiring and purchasing were almost entirely absent, and the announced development projects had not arrived yet. As such, Antamina's partnership with and belonging to the local community were put into question. The resettlement thus marked a distinct change to Antamina's presence and perception in the region, leading to local disappointment and distrust as well as new concerns regarding a common future shared with the mining presence and its potential environmental consequences.

Translation and the Illusion of Commensuration

Some scholars have argued that resettlement processes often fail because they are inherently extremely complex interventions. Resettlement is a "'totalizing' phenomenon, affecting virtually every aspect of life" (Oliver-Smith 2009, 3). There are too many factors, both internal and external to the affected population, working at the same time and involving multiple actors, making the possible outcomes largely unpredictable and full of risks (De Wet 2006).

Typically, the viability of a mine is calculated through a cost-benefit analysis in which the well-being of the population to be displaced is given less weight than the purported economic benefits (De Wet 2009). This is not explicitly stated and is rather hidden by the explicit provision of the WB and IFC guidelines as well as practices of corporate social responsibility. The economicism of cost-benefit analysis is also at the core of the design and implementation of resettlement processes and, to some extent, explains much of their failures. Certainly, in the planning and execution of involuntary resettlements, all of the complexity that cannot be reduced or translated into economic quantifications tends to be dismissed as immaterial and unimportant (Oliver-Smith 2010). In particular, resettlement plans typically fail to incorporate or attempt to understand Indigenous notions and logic. Such plans also often discount the extent of the necessities and losses that resettled people face (Cernea 2009). Hence it is not surprising that "projects are often unrealistic about time and resources required to undertake land access and resettlement negotiations properly and successfully" (ICMM 2015, 23) and that compensatory schemes constructed in these ways end up being inadequate (Johnston 2009, 21).

The original *land-for-land* compensation in the Antamina resettlement plan did not consider the complexity of these assemblages that included lower lands, crops, and other homes and people. Instead, it followed a logic of replacement of the pastures without taking into consideration the broader networks involved or the logics structuring life in these pasturelands. When this attempt failed, the $33,000 compensation and the unevenness with which it was assigned made clear that this was an emergency approach taken by the company as a means to resolve the issue as quickly as possible. The underlying logic of the *land-for-land* and monetary compensations presupposed that all things and relations making up these assemblages could have equivalents and that money could replace the value of these assemblages. The possibility that these assemblages involved inalienable things typically associated with ancestry, sacredness, and identity (Godelier 1999) was out of question from the beginning, revealing the strong power imbalance at play.

The assemblages that involved permanent residents of Yanacancha as well as those alternating between the agricultural valley and the high pasturelands were grounded in the reciprocity arrangements of a gift economy. The forms of commensuration assumed in the *land-for-land* resettlement plan and, more clearly, in the monetary compensation simply ignored how these particular gift economies worked. As is well understood by economic anthropologists, the basic logics at play in gift economies cannot be translated or reduced to those of capitalist economies. That is, gift economies and capitalist economies are inherently incommensurable to each other (Godelier 1986; Graeber 2001).

The alien logic of capitalist exchange mediated by commodity fetishism was expressed by the resettled families faced with rebuilding their lives from a mere payout (see Taussig 1980). All of this was dramatically marked by the receipt of a piece of paper promising a monetary sum before having their belongings thrown into a truck and being taken away forever from their gift-grounded lives in Yanacancha. Phrases used by these families in the months following resettlement, such as "Money is quickly gone; it escapes like when trying to hold water in your hands" or "Money does not reproduce like sheep do," express this incommensurability well.

Within these Quechua lifeworlds, sheep reproduce due to the goodwill of the *hirkas*, the sentient mountains that oversee the pasturelands and are crucial participants in, as well as the ultimate owners of, these assemblages (Salas Carreño 2002, 2016; Venturoli 2011). If Antamina resettlement plans did not consider the gift economy built on the continuity between humans and nonhumans, it goes without saying that practices treating nonhumans as sentient beings and owners of fertility, far exceeding Western ontological presuppositions, were totally out of consideration.

As Marx (1978) explained long ago, the most basic notion of exchange value is only possible through an extreme abstraction of use value. Commodity exchange can only occur through a process of abstraction of the actual practices and assemblages from which a particular thing emerges, which is deeply related to commodity fetishism, the assumption that there is no continuity between things that become commodities and the people who produce them. Commodity fetishism is clearly unthinkable within the most basic logics of gift economies (Mauss 1990), as it sees assemblages of people and things that become commodities as separate from one another.[9] However, these assumptions make possible ideas about the commensuration of lifeworlds—that people can be detached from them and successfully resettled elsewhere. While the International Council on Mining and Metals acknowledges that "finding adequate replacement land for displaced people is often a major challenge" (ICMM 2015, 21), this recognition reproduces the idea that the land can actually be successfully replaced. While the IFC Performance Standard 5 aims "to improve, or restore, the livelihoods and standards of living of displaced persons" (IFC 2012, 2), it is not clear how it is possible to measure the new situation in relation to the predisplacement one or which criteria must be privileged in order to make such a measure. As Li (2011) explains, "In the context of mining, commensuration makes it possible to compare (and ultimately reconcile) different forms of value, such that, for example, water pollution can be offset with monetary compensation, or a company's water usage can be measured against the needs of agriculturalists downstream from the mine" (62). Resettlement plans work as tools for legitimizing the displacement of populations through the use of what I call the "illusion of commensuration" of the inherently complex and unpredictable resettlement scenarios. Here, I am not claiming that commensuration is necessarily illusory. In fact, commensuration is a crucial form of practice at the core of multiple forms of constructing reality, as it "creates new things, new relations among disparate and remote things, changes the meanings of old things" (Espeland and Stevens 1998, 324), making it deeply political. Further, it "constructs relations of authority, creates new political entities, and establishes new interpretive frameworks. . . . It is not a neutral or merely technical process" (Espeland and Stevens 1998, 323).

What then is the illusory aspect of commensuration in relation to mining resettlement processes? The forms of commensuration present in resettlement processes are key to legitimizing the idea that there are ways of accurately measuring and quantifying a particular lifeworld's complexity and that this can be done in such a way that it is possible to resettle a population and ensure that their life will be better than or similar to what it was before resettlement. However, in practice, these forms of commensuration fail to apprehend these complexities, and the resettlements typically end up failing and causing damage to the resettled population.

Resettlement plans entail forms of commensuration that create the illusion of the feasibility of properly restituting the assemblages affected by displacement. Clearly the assumptions legitimizing resettlement processes are inscribed in broader frameworks governing them—such as the WB guidelines, Peruvian national legislation, and property regimes—that, like those in Chile, "imply the translation of land from a qualitative, topological, and agential subject into a quantitative and standardized object" (Di Giminiani 2015, 491). These broader frameworks only strengthen the illusion of commensuration, legitimizing the actions of mining companies.

As the Antamina case shows, monetary compensation ends up being a privileged way of constructing equivalences. Money gives the illusion that there is always the possibility of compensating for whatever kind of negative impacts a mining project might have (Li 2011, 65). Even though Antamina's implementation of the Accelerated Resettlement Plan caused suffering, resentment, and a break from the initial framing of its presence in San Marcos, the monetary compensations allowed it to maintain its claim of being a socially responsible company (see Li 2011, 70).

Any assemblage enacting its ontological particularities through practices that are alien or only marginally related to the capitalist economy is incommensurable and beyond monetary (or other types of) commensuration that only partially acknowledge its intricacies.[10] The conceptual apparatus used in resettlement plans constructs an illusion of commensuration of a particular assemblage situated in the margins of the capitalist market by deploying what Viveiros de Castro (2004) calls uncontrolled equivocations. An uncontrolled equivocation entails explaining another world using categories of the translator's world without awareness of how the very translation deforms and even causes violence to what is being translated. Referencing Walter Benjamin's (1968) claim that translation is always treason, Viveiros de Castro points out that translation through uncontrolled equivocations is a betrayal to the world being translated, as it constructs a version of the other world "as though it were an illusory version of our own, unifying the two via a reduction of one to the conventions of the other" (Viveiros de Castro 2004, 16). Notice that forms of commensuration work structurally as uncontrolled equivocations. They are technologies for "discarding information and organizing what remains into new forms. In abstracting and reducing information, the link between what is represented and the empirical world is obscured and uncertainty is absorbed" (Espeland and Stevens 1998, 317). All the complexity that cannot be explained or reduced to forms of commensuration constitutes the excess that is discarded, and the illusion of commensuration makes this excess momentarily invisible. However, when the resettlement plan is confronted with the actual complexities of assemblages, it falls apart and fails because the excess that was temporarily hidden never actually disappeared.

This clearly does not mean that Indigenous peoples in the Andes or elsewhere are passive agents or that their worlds preclude them from being acquainted with the dominant worlds ingrained in the state and corporate practices that affect their lives. They have become acquainted with these worlds and have sought to use them to their advantage as much as possible, on their own terms, from early colonial times (Stern 1993) until now (De la Cadena 2015). This fact, however, does not make the violence imposed by illusions of commensuration less real.

While some families resettled by Antamina were able to carry on and adapt relatively quickly to their new conditions, this was due not to the monetary compensation received but rather to the complexity and reach of the displaced peoples' networks that extended beyond Yanacancha. The logic and possibilities of these assemblages, which Antamina failed to consider or understand, were in the end what saved them.

Resettlement, State Responsibility, and Reparations

According to Peruvian law, people who occupy a property without a legal title or an agreement with the landowner are precarious occupants and, as such, can be evicted through a judicial process. Given that this framework also applies in cases such as the Antamina project, current laws are clearly insufficient to guarantee the livelihoods of families living under arrangements such as those in Yanacancha. The payments that Antamina provided for the purchase of this land did not allow these families the possibility of rearranging their lives elsewhere. Some families, who were members of the *comunidades campesinas* that owned the land but not landowners themselves, did not receive any part of the payments. In other cases, families recognized as private owners by PETT received very little money, as it had to be shared between so many coproprietors. There were other families living in Yanacancha without legal rights to the land they kept, even though they had occupied it for more than thirty years. If Antamina had strictly followed Peruvian law, it would have evicted all these families with no further compensation.

When the state carried out mining projects, it did so in the name of national development, overlooking and sacrificing the needs of those families affected by them, as is typical in displacement due to mining or infrastructure projects (Oliver-Smith 2009, 4). For instance, Tintaya, the last state mining project of the 1980s in the Cusco region, displaced eighty-six families of the *comunidad campesina* Antaycama. The state expropriated the land at a low price and evicted these families without compensation (De Echave 2005; León 2015).

As in many other countries, there is currently no national legal framework regulating involuntary resettlement due to mining projects (for Peru, see León 2017, 22; for Chile, see Li 2011, 65; for Papua New Guinea, see Kirsch 2006, 127; for a general characterization, see ICMM 2015, 8).[11] In the 1990s, neoliberal reforms introduced a legal framework to promote foreign mining investments, which involved such instruments as the environmental impact assessment to ensure alignment of national regulations with international environmental standards. However, the reforms did not introduce any social standards for mining practices. The state largely allowed mining companies to directly negotiate with communities regarding the social impacts of their projects, as though these actors had the resources required to successfully negotiate with large corporations.

This is particularly important to understand involuntary resettlement in relation to reparations. Typically, the state participates in reparations to address suffering it has directly or indirectly caused, but where the context in which violence took place has been superseded by a more democratic regime. However, in Peru today, the state actively promotes mining, and so any associated resettlements are an indirect responsibility of the state. Given the lack of legislation regulating these processes, it is impossible for the state to oversee them, and as such, the state has left the citizens affected by forced displacement in the hands of multilateral institutions (Bury 2005; Revesz and Diez 2006).

From the local community's perspective, the institutions of the central government were more concerned with Antamina's agenda than the community's rights. This was first made clear through the association between Antamina representatives and PETT officials in charge of titling the lands to be purchased by Antamina. And then, when Antamina began the Accelerated Resettlement Plan, the first family they evicted was also the most vocal in their opposition to the resettlements. Here, Antamina called in assistance from the provincial justice of peace to expedite the eviction order and also requested police presence to carry it out. Thus, Antamina made active use of national laws and state institutions in order to force these families to move out of Yanacancha and accept the monetary compensation.

In February 2000, toward the end of Fujimori's second term, some Yanacancha families organized themselves as the Asociación de Campesinos de Yanacancha and sent complaints regarding Antamina's Accelerated Resettlement Plan to the presidency of the Republic, Congress, the Ombudsman (Defensoría del Pueblo); the Canadian Embassy; and the World Bank. The local municipality, together with most of the district institutions, sent further letters to these organizations complaining about Antamina's unfulfilled promises of development. However, the only institution to respond to the letters was the Multilateral Investment Guarantee Agency (MIGA), a member of the World Bank Group.[12] Due to the conditions of a Japanese commercial bank loan, Antamina had to comply with World Bank OD 4.30 (involuntary resettlement) and OD 4.20 (Indigenous peoples). MIGA sent a mission to San Marcos in May 2000, where their members remained for a month, listening to those who wanted to be heard. However, there was never any response from the state authorities that had been contacted.

This lack of action surrounding social issues associated with mines was also witnessed when the Tintaya operation was privatized in the 1990s. After massive protests led to negotiations, BHP Billiton (the private Australian corporation that owned Tintaya) carried out its own reparations in 2002 and agreed to resettle those families displaced by the state in the 1980s as well as a new group of families that were recently affected by the mine's expansion. It is notable that Australia's Ombudsman intervened in and facilitated the negotiations, in stark contrast to the absence of Peruvian central government institutions as in the Antamina case (De Echave 2005; León 2015; Scurrah 2008).

Through this inaction, the state silently leaves local communities and Indigenous peoples unprotected from corporate mining practices and relinquishes its duty to protect them. As such, the state tends to emerge in these contexts as a foreign and hostile set of institutions uninterested in the well-being of its own Indigenous citizens.

However, this lack of mediation between mining companies and local communities transforms itself when the local community, frustrated by unresponsive institutions, turns to protest in order to have their complaints heard. Socioenvironmental conflicts have been by far the most common type reported by the Peruvian Ombudsman since it began producing conflict reports in 2004. For example, in April 2021, the Ombudsman reported that 64.4 percent of the 191 registered conflicts were of a socioenvironmental nature (Defensoría del Pueblo 2021). When these become large protests, the state turns its inaction into an alarming level of police violence that has led to many deaths: During President García's tenure (2006–2011), eighty people died in protests. The corresponding number of Humala's government (2011–2016) was fifty-two (Montaño 2020).[13]

Instead of regulating mining activity, legislative changes have focused on allowing for the intervention of the army as a means to control protests and granting immunity to police using firearms during them (Saldaña and Portocarrero 2017). None of the police accused of causing protesters' deaths since 2001 have been found guilty (Montaño 2020). TV journalists, central government officials, and even corporate representatives have boldly labeled protesters as "antimining terrorists" who fanatically oppose national progress (Gestión 2015). Given the recent history of political violence in the country, accusing someone of terrorism without substantiation (a phenomenon that has been coined *terruquear*) equates to an absolute moral disqualification and a negation of human rationality and dignity.

This scenario reinforces the inability of these communities to fully exercise their fundamental constitutional rights. This was seen, for example, through the continuous extension of a "preemptive" state of exception in the so-called Southern Mining Corridor that spans several provinces of the Apurímac and Cusco regions, including the one where Tintaya was located (IDL 2020; Red Muqui 2021). It was further witnessed through claims made by then-president Alan García in response to mobilization against further liberalization of Indigenous territories in the Amazon region in 2016: "These people are not first-class citizens. Four hundred thousand natives cannot say to twenty-eight million Peruvians, 'You have no right to come here.' No way. That is a very serious mistake. Whoever thinks that way wants to lead us to irrationality and primitivism" (SPDA Actualidad Ambiental 2016; my translation).

There is a somber and wider pattern within which the violence that took place in the internal armed conflict, the victims' disillusionment with state reparations programs,[14] the negative impacts of displacement and involuntary resettlement processes due to state and corporate mining projects, and the state violence used against communities protesting mining projects have a common denominator: The majority of the victims of these abuses are Indigenous (Bajak and Briceno 2012; Bowyer 2019; CVR 2003; León 2017). The pattern is consistent. Whether violent state interventions in the internal armed conflict or social protests or lack of action in repairing the wounds of the internal conflict and regulating and implementing social standards for mining projects, these cases involve racial-ethnic discrimination, Indigenous exclusion from citizenship, and the reinscription of a racialized geography (Orlove 1993).[15]

The combination of dominant ideologies of racial-ethnic hierarchies that reproduce these exclusions of Indigenous populations from fully belonging in the nation and a weak state that only reacts when the protests affect the fluidity of highways has been eroding the image of large-scale mining as fundamental to the nation's prosperity. While the state has approved the National Action Plan for Enterprises and Human Rights (MINJUS 2021), which aims to implement the U.N. Guiding Principles on Business and Human Rights—one being that "business enterprises should avoid causing or contributing to adverse human rights impacts through their own activities, and address such impacts when they occur" (U.N. 2011, 14)—there still remains a lack of regulation related to involuntary resettlement and other social aspects of the relationship between mines and local communities.[16]

Having all these elements in mind, it is difficult to propose paths toward improving the performance of involuntary resettlement due to mining projects. Rather, the history of failures of resettlement processes points toward a radical solution: stop implementing them. However, given that this seems an overtly unrealistic expectation in the current Peruvian context, a rereading of Performance Standard 5 reveals that an actual and strong adherence to its conditions could prevent, as much as possible, damage and suffering due to resettlement. The direct, substantial, and long-term participation from the population involved is crucial to reduce a resettlement's harm. This also supposes the necessary time and resources and a highly qualified team able to understand the local culture and practices and with real power within the company to carry it out. All this and many other crucial aspects are clearly stated in Performance

Standard 5. The problem lies in the application of these guidelines. Why do resettlement processes fail to properly apply these guidelines? The answer is straightforward: This is due to the strong and even extreme power disparity between mining corporations and local communities preexisting the displacement and making it possible. While the WB OD 4.30 and the IFC Performance Standard 5 do help improve involuntary resettlement processes, these institutions cannot ensure their strict implementation, which usually contradicts the project's logic of capital.

An obvious actor that should intervene to balance the power disparity between mining corporations and local communities is the state. However, the state's macroeconomic interests are also shaped by the logic of capital in such ways that it ends up failing to protect its vulnerable citizens. Rather than protecting them, it is prone to repressing their protests with extreme violence. If things stay the way they are now, the state institution's performance regarding mining might rather end up needing its own plan for reparations—that is, a plan to reconstruct forms of peaceful coexistence and interrelationality—in contrast with the current lack of regulation and extremely excessive and illegal use of state force.

Notes

1 According to some analysts, the review that produced OP/BP 4.12 has led to a weakening of the WB's guidelines and fewer protections for people facing resettlement (Clark 2009; Oliver-Smith 2010).
2 This process was also discussed by Szablowski (2007), Gil (2009), and Damonte and Glave (2019), among others.
3 I was able to use this data thanks to Antamina's transparency policy.
4 Currently, Antamina is owned by BHP Billiton (33.75 percent), Glencore (33.75 percent), Teck (22.5 percent), and Mitsubishi (10 percent). For more information, see https://www.antamina.com/quienes-somos/.
5 On sentient plains and mountains in the region, see Venturoli (2011) and Salas Carreño (2002), and for a broader discussion, see De la Cadena (2015) and Salas Carreño (2016).
6 Bechtel is a large construction corporation. According to their website, "Since 1898, we have helped customers complete more than 25,000 projects in 160 countries on all seven continents"; https://www.bechtel.com/about-us/.
7 These events encapsulate the incommensurability of gift economies and capitalist ones (Godelier 1986; Graeber 2001), as will be discussed later.
8 On risk and uncertainty in resettlement processes, see Dwivedi (1999).
9 I do not claim that these assemblages are constituted by people who are absolutely alien to the worlds mediated by commodity fetishism. Rather, their acquaintance with it is part of their very complexity that I seek to convey.
10 This is a particular consequence of lifeworlds being always only partially connected, always excessive from one another (De la Cadena 2015).
11 Peru signed ILO 169 (Indigenous and Tribal Peoples Convention) in 1993. Article 16 mentions general safeguards regarding relocation. The state incorporated this

convention in the national legislation only after the 2009 Bagua massacre with the Ley 29785 (Ley de Consulta Previa a los Pueblos Indígenas) of 2011.

12 MIGA's "mandate is to promote cross-border investment in developing countries by providing guarantees (political risk insurance and credit enhancement) to investors and lenders"; https://www.miga.org/about-us.

13 This chapter was written before December 2022. The death of forty-nine civilians by state forces' live ammunition in the context of social protests between December 2022 and March 2023, under the presidency of Dina Boluarte, only confirms the extremely alarming use of lethal and unpunished state violence (see Amnesty International 2024; Comisión Interamericana de Derechos Humanos 2023).

14 For example, by the beginning of 2021, the results of state efforts to find and return the remains of the 21,334 registered disappeared persons between 1980 and 2000 were telling: only 12.5 percent of the cases had ended with the restitution of remains and a dignified burial, 3.1 percent of cases were being investigated, and an overwhelming 84.4 percent were pending investigation (RENADE 2021).

15 This is consistent with a broader pattern in which a "lack of consideration for the human rights of the people being affected and ignorance of the complexity and gravity of development-forced displacement and resettlement's impacts characterized the arrogance of authorities in many countries of both the developed and the developing worlds" (Oliver-Smith 2009, 8).

16 To add complexity to this scenario, there is a notable expansion of illegal mining that does not follow environmental standards, is far from having any social ones, is becoming associated with criminal organizations, and has a clear influence and support within the national congress (see Chávez and Haro 2023; Sierra 2024).

References

Amnesty International. 2024. "Who Called the Shots? Chain of Command Responsibility for Killings and Injuries in Protests in Peru." https://www.amnesty.org/en/wp-content/uploads/2024/07/AMR4682492024ENGLISH.pdf.

Bajak, Frank, and Franklin Briceno. 2012. "Peru's Anti-Riot Tactics Unmatched in Lethality." *The New York Times*, July 14, 2012.

Benjamin, Walter. 1968. "The Task of the Translator." In *Illuminations*, 69–82. New York: Harcourt Brace Jovanovich.

Black, Brian. 2000. *Petrolia: The Landscape of America's First Oil Boom*. Baltimore: Johns Hopkins University Press.

Blaser, Mario. 2019. "On the Properly Political (Disposition for the) Anthropocene." *Anthropological Theory* 19 (1): 74–94.

Bowyer, Timothy James. 2019. *Beyond Suffering and Reparation: The Aftermath of Political Violence in the Peruvian Andes*. Cham: Springer.

Bury, Jeffrey. 2005. "Mining Mountains: Neoliberalism, Land Tenure, Livelihoods, and the New Peruvian Mining Industry in Cajamarca." *Environment and Planning* 37:221–239.

Cernea, Michael M. 2009. "Financing for Development: Benefit-Sharing Mechanisms in Population Resettlement." In *Development and Dispossession: The Crisis of Forced Displacement and Resettlement*, edited by Anthony Oliver-Smith, 49–76. Santa Fe: School for Advanced Research Press.

Chávez, Rosa, and Gonzalo Haro. 2023. "Pataz: La violencia criminal del oro ilegal en los Andes peruanos." *Ojo Público*, December 10, 2023. https://ojo-publico.com/sala-del-poder/crimen-organizado/pataz-la-violencia-criminal-del-oro-ilegal-los-andes-peruanos.

Clark, Dana. 2009. "An Overview of Revisions to the World Bank Resettlement Policy." In *Displaced by Development: Confronting Marginalisation and Gender Injustice*, edited by Lyla Mehta, 195–224. New Delhi: SAGE India.

Comisión Interamericana de Derechos Humanos. 2023. "Situación de derechos humanos en Perú en el contexto de las protestas sociales." https://www.oas.org/es/cidh/informes/pdfs/2023/Informe-SituacionDDHH-Peru.pdf.

CVR. 2003. *Informe Final*. Lima: Comisión de la Verdad y Reconciliación.

Damonte, Gerardo, and Manuel Glave. 2019. "Reasentamiento involuntario: Políticas y prácticas en los Andes." *Mundo Agrario* 20 (45): 1–15.

De Echave, José. 2005. *Los procesos de diálogo y la administración de conflictos en territorios de comunidades: El caso de la mina de Tintaya en el Perú*. Lima: CooperAcción.

Defensoría del Pueblo. 2021. *Reporte de Conflictos Sociales 206, Abril 2021*. Lima: Adjuntía para la Prevención de Conflictos Sociales y la Gobernabilidad.

De la Cadena, Marisol. 2015. *Earth Beings: Ecologies of Practice Across Andean Worlds*. Durham, N.C.: Duke University Press.

De Wet, Chris. 2006. "Risk, Complexity and Local Initiatives in Forced Resettlement Outcomes." In *Development-Induced Displacement: Problems, Policies and People*, edited by Chris De Wet, 180–202. New York: Berghahn Books.

De Wet, Chris. 2009. "Does Development Displace Ethics? The Challenge of Forced Resettlement." In *Development and Dispossession: The Crisis of Forced Displacement and Resettlement*, edited by Anthony Oliver-Smith, 77–96. Santa Fe: School for Advanced Research Press.

Di Giminiani, Piergiorgio. 2015. "The Becoming of Ancestral Land: Place and Property in Mapuche Land Claims." *American Ethnologist* 42 (3): 490–503.

Dwivedi, Ranjit. 1999. "Displacement, Risks and Resistance: Local Perceptions and Actions in the Sardar Sarovar." *Development and Change* 30:43–78.

Espeland, Wendy Nelson, and Mitchell L. Stevens. 1998. "Commensuration as a Social Process." *Annual Review of Sociology* 24 (1): 313–343.

Gerritsen, Rolf, and Martha MacIntyre. 1991. "Dilemmas of Distribution: The Misima Gold Mine, Papua New Guinea." In *Mining and Indigenous Peoples in Australasia*, edited by John Connell and Richard Howitt, 35–53. South Melbourne: Sydney University Press.

Gestión. 2015. "Tía María: Southern Copper reitera denuncia de 'terrorismo antiminero' contra proyecto." March 28. https://gestion.pe/economia/tia-maria-southern-copper-reitera-denuncia-terrorismo-antiminero-proyecto-83198-noticia/.

Gil, Vladimir. 2009. *Aterrizaje Minero: Cultura, conflicto, negociaciones y lecciones para el desarrollo desde la minería en Ancash, Perú*. Lima: Instituto de Estudios Peruanos.

Godelier, Maurice. 1986. *The Mental and the Material: Thought, Economy and Society*. London: Verso.

Godelier, Maurice. 1999. *The Enigma of the Gift*. Chicago: University of Chicago Press.

Graeber, David. 2001. *Toward an Anthropological Theory of Value: The False Coin of Our Own Dreams*. New York: Palgrave Macmillan.

ICMM (International Council on Mining and Metals). 2015. *Land Acquisition and Resettlement: Lessons Learned*. London: International Council on Mining and Metals.

IDL (Instituto de Defensa Legal). 2020. "Gobierno decreta nueva declaratoria de emergencia en el corredor vial minero del sur que se superpone a la declaratoria de emergencia sanitaria por COVID-19." May 13, 2020. https://www.idl.org.pe/gobierno-decreta-nueva-declaratoria-de-emergencia-en-el-corredor-vial-minero-del-sur-que-se-superpone-a-la-declaratoria-de-emergencia-sanitaria-por-covid-19/.

IFC (International Finance Corporation). 2012. "Performance Standard 5: Land Acquisition and Involuntary Resettlement." International Finance Corporation. https://www.ifc.org/ps5.

Johnston, Barbara Rose. 2009. "Waging War, Making Peace: The Anthropology of Reparations." In *Waging War, Making Peace: Reparations and Human Rights*, edited by Barbara Rose Johnston and Susan Slyomovics, 11–30. Walnut Creek, Calif.: Left Coast Press.

Kedia, Satish. 2009. "Health Consequences of Dam Construction and Involuntary Resettlement." In *Development and Dispossession: The Crisis of Forced Displacement and Resettlement*, edited by Anthony Oliver-Smith, 97–118. Santa Fe: School for Advanced Research Press.

Kirsch, Stuart. 2006. *Reverse Anthropology: Indigenous Analysis of Social and Environmental Relations in New Guinea*. Stanford, Calif.: Stanford University Press.

Latour, Bruno. 2007. *Reassembling the Social: An Introduction to Actor-Network-Theory*. Oxford: Oxford University Press.

León, Camilo. 2015. "Reubicación de poblaciones por proyectos mineros en el Perú: Diferencias por género y edad." In *Desigualdades en un mundo globalizado*, edited by Narda Henríquez, Gerardo Damonte, Marianne Braig, and Barbara Göbel, 201–214. Lima: CISEPA PUCP.

León, Camilo. 2017. "Reasentamiento de poblaciones en el Perú por proyectos mineros y de infraestructura: Diálogo entre prácticas y teoría social." *Debates en Sociología* 44:5–30.

Li, Fabiana. 2011. "Engineering Responsibility: Environmental Mitigation and the Limits of Commensuration in a Chilean Mining Project." *Focaal* 60:61–73.

Marx, Karl. 1978. "Capital, Volume One." In *The Marx-Engels Reader*, edited by Robert C. Tucker, 2nd ed., 294–438. New York: W. W. Norton.

Mauss, Marcel. 1990. *The Gift: The Form and Reason for Exchange in Archaic Societies*. London: Routledge.

MINJUS (Ministerio de Justicia y Derechos Humanos). 2021. *Plan Nacional de Acción sobre Empresas y Derechos Humanos 2021–2025*. Lima: Ministerio de Justicia y Derechos Humanos.

Montaño, Fiorella. 2020. "En 18 años, 159 personas murieron en protestas sociales y ningún policía acusado recibió sanción." *Convoca*, July 12, 2020. http://convoca.pe/agenda-propia/en-ocho-anos-159-personas-murieron-en-protestas-sociales-y-ningun-policia-acusado.

Oliver-Smith, Anthony. 2009. "Introduction: Development-Forced Displacement and Resettlement; A Global Human Rights Crisis." In *Development and Dispossession: The Crisis of Forced Displacement and Resettlement*, edited by Anthony Oliver-Smith, 3–23. Santa Fe: School for Advanced Research Press.

Oliver-Smith, Anthony. 2010. *Defying Displacement: Grassroots Resistance and the Critique of Development*. Austin: University of Texas Press.

Orlove, Benjamin S. 1993. "Putting Race in Its Place: Order in Colonial and Postcolonial Peruvian Geography." *Social Research* 60:301–336.

Povinelli, Elizabeth A. 2001. "Radical Worlds: The Anthropology of Incommensurability and Inconceivability." *Annual Review of Anthropology* 30:319–334.

Red Muqui. 2021. "Apurímac: TC desarrolla criterios para decretar Estados de Emergencia a partir del caso del corredor minero." *Red Muqui*, January 8, 2021. https://muqui.org/noticias/apurimac-tc-desarrolla-criterios-para-decretar-estados-de-emergencia-a-partir-del-caso-del-corredor-minero/.

RENADE (Registro Nacional de Personas Desaparecidas y de Sitios de Entierro). 2021. "Reporte Estadístico N° 01." https://www.gob.pe/institucion/minjus/informes-publicaciones/1666390-reporte-estadistico-n-01-renade.

Revesz, Bruno, and Alejandro Diez. 2006. "El triángulo sin cúpula (o los actores desregulados en los conflictos mineros)." In *Perú Hoy, nuevos rostros en la escena nacional*, edited by Eduardo Toche, 49–88. Lima: DESCO.

Salas Carreño, Guillermo. 2002. "Jóvenes, animales y monstruos en las punas sanmarquinas: Algunos motivos de la tradición oral de Conchucos." *Anthropologica* 20:333–350.

Salas Carreño, Guillermo. 2008. *Dinámica social y minería: Familias pastoras de puna y la presencia del proyecto Antamina (1997–2002)*. Lima: Instituto de Estudios Peruanos.

Salas Carreño, Guillermo. 2016. "Places Are Kin: Food, Cohabitation, and Sociality in the Southern Peruvian Andes." *Anthropological Quarterly* 89 (3): 813–840.

Saldaña, José, and Jorge Portocarrero. 2017. "La violencia de las leyes: El uso de la fuerza y la criminalización de protestas socioambientales en el Perú." *Derecho PUCP* 79:311–352.

Scudder, Thayer. 2009. "Resettlement Theory and the Kariba Case: An Anthropology of Resettlement." In *Development and Dispossession: The Crisis of Forced Displacement and Resettlement*, edited by Anthony Oliver-Smith, 25–48. Santa Fe: School for Advanced Research Press.

Scurrah, Martin. 2008. *Defendiendo derechos y promoviendo cambios: El Estado, las empresas extractivas y las comunidades locales en el Perú*. Lima: IEP, Oxfam International.

Sierra, Yvette. 2024. "Pese a críticas, Congreso peruano busca aprobar ley que favorece a minería ilegal." *Mongabay*, February 12, 2024. https://es.mongabay.com/2024/02/congreso-peruano-busca-aprobar-ley-que-favorece-a-mineria-ilegal/.

SPDA Actualidad Ambiental. 2016. "No son ciudadanos de primera clase." https://youtu.be/m67Tkfh70j4.

Stern, Steve J. 1993. *Peru's Indian Peoples and the Challenge of Spanish Conquest: Huamanga to 1640*. Madison: University of Wisconsin Press.

Szablowski, David. 2007. *Transnational Law and Local Struggles: Mining, Communities and the World Bank*. Oxford: Hart.

Taussig, Michael T. 1980. *The Devil and Commodity Fetishism in South America*. Chapel Hill: University of North Carolina Press.

United Nations. 2011. *Guiding Principles on Business and Human Rights: Implementing the United Nations "Protect, Respect and Remedy" Framework*. New York: United Nations, Human Rights, Office of the High Commissioner. https://digitallibrary.un.org/record/720245?ln=es.

Venturoli, Sofia. 2011. *Los hijos de Huari: Etnografía y etnohistoria de tres pueblos de Ancash*. Lima: Fondo Editorial PUCP.

Viveiros de Castro, Eduardo. 2004. "Perspectival Anthropology and the Method of Controlled Equivocation." *Tipití: Journal of the Society for the Anthropology of Lowland South America* 2:3–22.

World Bank. 2004. *Involuntary Resettlement Sourcebook: Planning and Implementation in Development Projects*. Washington, D.C.: World Bank.

Afterword

• •

The Politics of Reparations

NANCY POSTERO

By extending reparations beyond their traditional usage as tools of transitional justice in postconflict societies, this volume considers the larger domain of societal repair. How do societies rebuild fractured political and environmental communities? The authors in this volume examine the harms caused by civil wars and dictatorships, which have been the focus of traditional human rights approaches, but they also go further to think about the harms caused by centuries of colonialism and racism as well as neoliberal extractivism across Latin America. The contributors here use the frame of reparations to encompass a wide range of responses, from formal state compensation and resettlement projects to forms of resistance and collective protest as well as efforts to foster healing completely outside of formal channels. The cases show the many ways people across the region are repairing their communities: victims and survivors of genocides, torture, and disappearances calling for accountability; Indigenous people building futures based on their traditional knowledge and practices; social movements struggling against extractive development; psychologists helping people remember and heal; and archives documenting the existence and contestation of those erased by state violence. These stories demonstrate inspiring activism, as people engage their memories, their bodies, and their voices to construct new forms of coexistence.

However, the chapters also show the limits of these reparations practices. People cannot be brought back from the dead, suffering cannot be forgotten, and ecosystems and socionatural relations cannot be revived. Thus, a central question in all of the chapters is what kinds of repair are actually possible. Given the impossibility of true justice, can processes of reparation restore shattered societies? Recognizing that formal processes of reparation are often molded by languages and technologies of psychotherapy in which healing is the ideal end-point of intervention, the authors instead look to processes that escape or exceed this temporal determinacy, seeing societal repair as a nonlinear, contested, and always unfinished process. Moreover, the authors do not overstate their arguments for reparations. Instead, they show the enormous efforts necessary to overcome fear and suffering so as to be able to take small steps toward repair. Through great sacrifice, survivors remake their worlds both from the depths of their shattered everyday lives and through heroic acts of public protest.

The editors suggest that reparations are "best understood as a set of material and ideological practices through which multiple futures are imagined and anticipated, past harm is translated into symbolic or material acts of repair, and emergent forms of belonging to the nation or other social collectivities are forged." This definition focuses on three themes—imagination, translation, and belonging—each of which is developed in the insightful introduction. In this afterword, I want to push these themes a bit, emphasizing the politics at play in each. This move reflects not only my own continuing obsession with politics but also, and more importantly, the politics that emerge in the chapters. The editors are keenly aware of the political nature of reparations. They rightly claim that reparations "have the potential to reactivate political processes of world making." Here, I merely highlight the ways in which power, politics, and governance are central to the work of reparations.

Imagination, Governance

The first theme the editors discuss is imagination, explaining that most traditional reparations projects rely on an imagined temporality of justice as moving forward. As Robert Meister (2010) and others have made clear, transitional justice mechanisms such as truth and reconciliation commissions (TRCs) and memory museums promise to put the evil of human rights violations and civil conflict in the past, ushering in a new future of justice. State mechanisms of reparation rely on these same temporal discourses, promising to make victims whole, thus ending social or political conflicts and bringing into being the imagined healed society. The flaws in this discourse have been widely documented. Meister argues that it creates binary subjects of individual "perpetrators" and individual "victims" and fails to recognize the "bystanders" who benefited and the structures of inequality that made violence possible in the first place (Meister 2010). Moreover, everyone in the newly constituted society is asked to show their "affiliation" to this discourse by declaring, "Never again!" demonstrating their agreement with closing the door on the evils of the past. Those who complain or point out the ongoing structural foundations of violence are accused of being "unreconciled" to the forward-looking plan and, by extension, obstacles to progress (Meister 2010).

As the chapters show, such discourses have great power, especially accompanied as they are by institutions (TRCs, state resettlement programs), technologies (archives, psychosocial healing exercises, new constitutions), and performances (museums of memory, official apologies). Here, I want to emphasize the utility of such practices as forms of governance. While imagination can certainly be a means of contesting governance, as I discuss later, it is also an essential element of governing. In their insightful work on Andean states, Christopher Krupa and David Nugent argue that the state is best thought of as an imaginary construct (2015). They describe the fantastical process by which certain groups of actors exert domination over others in the name of the state and in the name of democracy. This process is made almost invisible because the idea of the state is so hegemonic that the underlying processes of state formation become hidden by what appears to be "politically real" (Krupa and Nugent 2015, 4). What is relevant for our discussion here is their assertion that a central way state power is constructed is through emotions, fantasy, and imagination—that is, what people think, feel, and fear about the state and the makeup of the nation. The force of imagination is as critical to our understanding of violent states as it is to our understanding of liberal ones; postconflict states also operate by engaging imagination, hope, fear, and desire.

Thus, a central challenge for the politics of reparation is making visible the governmental effects such discourses have and questioning them even when this governance takes the form of a seemingly progressive, democratic, and "healing" state. One important mechanism of governance through imagination is what Nuijten (2003) calls the "hope-generating machine" of the state: the way that hope is inspired by a liberal state's promises of redemption and restitution. As Kennemore and Copa Pabón show in chapter 6, which deals with legal pluralism in plurinational Bolivia, when the state promises to enact justice—in their case by establishing Indigenous legal processes to untangle historic knots of violence and dispossession—it can lead people to wait for a promised justice that never arrives. This is a form of governance, as it disables alternative visions of justice and sows discord among those calling for reparations for past harms. This is governing by impasse.

It is essential to ask how the imagined process of moving "beyond evil," as Meister (2010) puts it, acts to govern and discipline subjects but also to inquire about how this can be challenged. In chapter 1, Bernasconi describes how archives act as a "space of appearance" (Butler 2015, 59–60), where the voices of victims and witnesses make visible the acts of terror that the state sought to erase, first by coercion and then by relegating them to the past. The forms of "enunciation" she draws attention to in reports, documents, photos, and so on belie efforts to close off the past. Instead, they contain a latency that keeps the past open, subject to new interpretations in the present. I would argue that these voices make up a kind of agentive "disagreement" challenging the speakers' erasure. This is what Jacques Rancière would term "politics," or the creation of political subjectivity through litigation (1999). In chapter 2, dealing with psychosocial healing processes, Ronsbo argues for the importance of autobiographical reflections of victims, whose fear, remembrances, forgetting, and hope make clear that violence is not a matter of past trauma but is present in everyday life. This kind of reparations ethnography pushes back against the assumed linearity and stability of the healing process, noting instead how fears of violence and death return in repetitive patterns in the present. Again, here we see disagreement. By refusing to be swept cleanly into the past through healing technologies offered by NGOs, memory and fear remain steadfastly in the present, braided into the mundane.

Translation, Incommensurability, Harms

The second theme identified by the editors and clearly visible in the chapters is the question of translation and incommensurability. How can lost lives, relationships, and ecosystems be compensated? How can the value of these material and social things be translated into economic and political terms? Particularly given the hegemony of neoliberal values and logics across the region, the impetus to translate all damage into economic terms raises concern for those seeking reparations. The authors point out the critical issue of "equivocation," using Viveiros de Castro's (2004) notion, showing that there is a fundamental mistranslation between social and cultural values and relationships, what Marx ([1867] 2007) would call "use value," and purely economic or monetary appraisals, or "exchange value." In chapter 8, about projects to resettle rural herders displaced by mining activities in the Peruvian Andes, Salas Carreño describes what he calls the "illusion of commensuration." In the case he presents, villagers are part of complex socionatural assemblages made up of sheepherders, their kin in other ecological niches, their animals, and the land. Salas Carreño argues that the state and mining corporations' efforts to compensate them are impossible because the relationships and networks of care upon which the villagers rely are invisible to the state. They certainly cannot be accounted for in the state's materialist calculus that translates land and animals into commodities.

What Salas Carreño's chapter and others make clear, however, is that this is not merely equivocation. More specifically, this is not merely an ontological failure. Instead, this equivocation is an artifact of unequal power relations. Embodying and enacting colonial principles that dismiss the value of rural Indigenous peoples, the state and the mining corporation are unable to understand the villagers' relationships to the land. To use Rancière's terms (2019) again, Indigenous peoples here are not visible political actors. They are seen as outside the political sphere, "the part without a part," and thus their voices are considered "noise." Focusing on this power differential leads us to see that the deeper question for reparations is that of the definition of the harm to be repaired. What is the harm? Who are the harmed? And most importantly, who gets to decide? This is the politics of reparations: understanding who sets the terms of the debates.

Salas Carreño makes the critical point that the equivocation starts not during the reparation process but at the point of the harm. Ongoing colonial power relations mean that dominant elites continue to consider Indigenous people as savages standing in the way of progress and not as citizens whose rights must be protected. Thus, harms to their "backward" ways of life are not considered harms that the state needs to repair. This raises the important question, How can we trust the state to repair what it does not see as a problem? Of course, the state is often the source of the harm. In the case of state violence, like the disappearances and torture that occurred in Chile under the dictatorship, described by Bernasconi in chapter 1, the state is invested in denying or hiding the harm. Bernasconi argues that one of the most significant achievements the Chilean archive made was documenting and making visible the damage caused, thereby defining the harm. While many of the materials in the archive were produced for more immediate needs, such as trying to find lost loved ones at the moment of crisis, the accumulated data produced patterns of violence—repertoires of terror that are visible to history. This visibilization also extends to defining those harmed. Where the state argued that activists were merely missing or in exile, these accumulated records challenged the erasure of victims, survivors, and witnesses, clearly declaring who was harmed.

Even in the process of reparation, however, the contestation over harms and harmed continues. Chapter 3 by María Eugenia Ulfe demonstrates how political the very act of categorizing victims is. Thinking through two different cases in Peru, those disappeared through state violence and those impacted by an oil spill, she argues that the category of victim is a construction that results from the reparations efforts themselves. But these categories are disputed. Are all people who suffered violence during a conflict victims? Should this include members of armed groups? As Rothschild (2017) has shown in the case of East Timor, post–civil war accountings always happen in particular political contexts, where certain actors from the conflict have gained power. Thus, the process of truth making is anything but neutral; instead, it takes place in power-laden institutions operating in societies sedimented with narratives about in-groups and out-groups.

For instance, in chapter 5 by Karine Vanthuyne on Indigenous activists protesting mining in Guatemala, the state official sent to oversee reparations failed to acknowledge the harms the mine had wrought on the lands and waterways, even though the Inter-American Human Rights Commission had already made a ruling determining the damage. Instead, he blamed the Indigenous people themselves, reproducing racist tropes and neoliberal discourses of individual responsibility. Without concrete state buy-in regarding the harm, activists are left to endure in limbo, suffering exhaustion in the case Vanthuyne describes or having to remake their own socioenvironmental networks in the case Salas Carreño describes. In both examples, the state is deeply implicated in the harms resulting from its extractive natural resource development model and is unable or unwilling to pursue repair.

The state's refusal to identify harms can be altered once there is a regime change, since the succeeding government can blame the evils of the past on a prior administration and justify its power on the basis of being "reconciled" to "never again" cause such harms. But this does not always happen. In chapter 6 by Kennemore and Copa Pabón on legal pluralism in Bolivia, we see another way the state can refuse to identify and resolve the harm. In the case they describe, the seemingly progressive plurinational state granted jurisdiction to Indigenous tribunals to resolve intercommunity conflict. This appeared to be a move to overcome colonial harms and decolonize justice. Yet uncertainties over what the harms actually were continued to undermine the possibilities for reparations. The complex sedimentation of colonial dispossession, legal corruption, market forces, and conflicting schemes of local organizing all combined to make it nearly impossible to identify the harms or the perpetrators. The Indigenous tribunal did not have the tools necessary to repair five centuries of violence. Yet by recognizing Indigenous legal pluralism, the state was able to wash its hands of the conflict, claiming to have passed responsibility to identify and resolve the harms onto the local people. The Aymara leaders Kennemore and Copa Pabón follow struggled to disentangle the harms, returning in the end to their own culturally informed social projects and their own relations to the land as avenues of repair. Whereas liberal legal definitions of harm focus on individual loss, the leaders' search for justice turned to collective belonging and moral obligations.

Identifying the harm is also the critical issue for the Indigenous Mapuche women in Chile whom Richards and Painemal interviewed for chapter 7. They describe their lives as subject to intersecting and ongoing violence: colonial and neoliberal dispossession, racialized discrimination, economic violence and poverty, state violence during and after the dictatorship, and gendered and domestic violence. This intersecting violence, what Speed (2019) calls "multi-criminality," cannot be easily parsed; moreover, it is ongoing. These women, like the women Kimberly Theidon (2007) documented in her reports from post-conflict Peru, point not just to individual acts of violence with a single perpetrator or victim but to an ongoing social and political structure of discrimination and oppression that impacts women in particular ways. Much of the harm they have suffered occurred in what might be called the "private sphere," hidden by its characterization as interpersonal, interfamilial, or domestic violence. Therefore, Richards and Painemal call for intersecting reparations that take this multiplicity into account.

Belonging, Citizenship, Futurities

The final theme the editors highlight is belonging. They rightly situate repara-tions in the relation between the state and its citizens. A central goal of tran-sitional justice is to recognize the societal fractures—both those that underlie conflict and those that result from war and violence—and then to restore those relationships. This act of repair is intended to suture the wounds, bringing about healing to a society so that all its members, including those excluded Others victimized by past harms, can be included as legitimate and valued. This liberal story of redemption through a healed and inclusive polis reveals the promise that liberalism makes to its followers: that liberalism can always be repaired and improved. As Povinelli (2002) has suggested, the seeming perfectibility of liber-alism is a central mechanism of its ability to govern. For those agentive modern subjects who align with liberalism, errors such as colonialism can be placed in the past, with an apology and an assurance that society will be ever more per-fect in the future. Those nonmodern Others (read: Indigenous peoples) who have suffered from these errors are told they may be redeemed by performing a certain kind of indigeneity that acknowledges this future perfection. That is, according to the liberal state, their pain "will have been" worth it, as they are included in the perfected liberal state (Povinelli 2011, 3).

Here we return to the hope-generating mechanism of liberal states, where reparations produce a certain kind of future healing administered by and imag-ined by liberal institutions and those who govern them. There is no doubt that many of the people seeking reparations want to be reincluded in the state com-munity as defined by liberal citizenship. In chapter 4 by Zaretsky on Argen-tina, for example, we see efforts by survivors to revive their citizenship. After the bombing of a Jewish community center, Jewish survivors and witnesses fol-low the embodied repertoires of human rights activists, like those made famous by the Mothers of the Plaza de Mayo, in order to weave themselves back into the national imaginary. Despite the slim chances of achieving justice, one survivor explains that she continues her activism because the most important thing is to "hold space as a citizen" to dispute impunity through her actions. The antimin-ing activists Vanthuyne describes in Guatemala also have limited expectations of state action or repair, yet she describes them as "performing their belonging" to the state, enacting a kind of citizenship they can only hope will be realized.

Yet one of the most inspiring lessons of the chapters for me was the fact that for many of those seeking repair, the site of that repair was outside of, or bypass-ing, the state. Bernasconi documents the ways that the Chilean archive carried out repair in part through what she calls its "affiliative" effects. She suggests that by restoring the identities of the victims and bringing together people united in making the harms visible, the archive engendered new affiliations of belong-ing, new collectivities "working through" the past together. For Zaretsky as well, the Argentine activists working together to bring back the disappeared "with life" found themselves taking responsibility for one another and creating new spaces of belonging. Zaretsky calls this "symbolic repair," but I think it is more. I would call this a form of politics. These communities of belonging come into being by declaring themselves and asserting their presence. Rancière (1999) suggests that politics is in a profound sense the dispute about the "distribution of the sensible," by which he means the ways certain people are not seen or heard. It is by disagreeing with the exclusions of the dominant ordering of society that this order can be changed and new political subjectivities can emerge (Rancière 1999).

For the Indigenous people discussed by Kennemore and Copa Pabón and Richards and Painemal, reparations require more of a restoration of Indigenous sovereignty than an inclusion in a state project. Even in their flawed efforts to untangle centuries of violence and harm, the Aymara leaders Kennemore and Copa Pabón describe imagine that they can find some form of repair that doesn't exhaust itself in the legal machinery of the state. They work to push back from the state in order to enhance their own "world-making" social projects—their relations with kin, land, and ancestors. Thinking alongside Indigenous feminists, Richards and Painemal argue for a notion of restoration centering on the creativity and "survivance" of Mapuche women, to use Vizenor's (2009) term. Indigenous women are the experts in Indigenous cultural survival, they argue, so the repair they seek is to be able to experience the full resurgence of Indigenous life so that they may pass on their language and cultural knowledge to future generations. Thus, they call for reparations that decenter the state and focus on Indigenous futurities. Thus, she calls for reparations that decenter the state and focus on Indigenous futurities. The rich literature on futurities (see, e.g., Harjo 2019; Simpson 2017) describes a radically different approach to the future than the discourse of transitional justice with which I began. Instead of dwelling on past harms or promising a particular future, a focus on Indigenous futurity recognizes the actions in the present necessary to enable an imagined future. It also links to the past, drawing upon the knowledge and practices of ancestors that provide the basis for future generations to live fully. This is an intergenerational belonging that exceeds citizenship and provides a holistic form of healing. However, it is important to remember that all such world making is profoundly political, whether the site of healing and belonging or the space of contestation and disagreement (Postero and Elinoff 2019).

Conclusion

This book makes important contributions to the scholarship and practice of transitional justice, expanding our notions of reparations beyond the legal formal spheres to a wide variety of other avenues of social repair. The chapters provide important critiques of the reparation framework that understands violence as an eventful exception rather than one part of a continued experience of injustice and suffering—feelings of hate, racism, fear of the Other, and despair—that are part of society. These critiques raise a number of questions for future research.

First, the question of temporality suffuses the chapters, as survivors and societies attempt to grapple with the past in the present in order to influence the future. One critical goal of the reparations scholarship in this book is to open rather than close the past, enabling those working to build just social futures. This is an ongoing contested political process that will benefit from the constant rethinking of what and who counts (Nelson 2015). Because it entails an ongoing rewriting of history, future research would benefit from the inclusion of a diachronic perspective. We call on historians to join this endeavor to document the ways that history and memory change over time, creating new hegemonies and sites of contestation.

Second, can restorative policies facilitate mechanisms that enable people to live with and control the harmful practices and feelings described earlier? That is, to what extent can the reparation of past harms prevent future ones? If we see reparations as a "temporally loaded form of governance," as the editors so concisely put it, who is benefiting from the repaired social relations? How do those who continue to be excluded respond? Repair can only function to prevent future violence if it restructures society in ways that preclude the colonial, patriarchal, and racist othering that allowed some people to be valued and protected and others to be cast aside. So what policy implications do these chapters have? How can the illuminating analyses presented here intervene to prevent continuing harm? Here, I call attention to the relations between scholarship and advocacy, urging reparations scholars to build on the profoundly political nature of their work.

Finally, if reparations are inherently suspect or just not enough, what other dimensions and languages for constructing and contesting social order and social contracts are available, and what horizons would they allow? In Latin America, there is a long tradition of practical political intervention that is worth emulating, from Paolo Freire's ([1970] 2018) popular education model to performance-based organizing like the *teatro del oprimido* (theater of the oppressed; Boal 2013). In Bolivia, the Indigenous majority took another tack: It acquired state control, electing Indigenous leaders and then passing a new constitution that recognized the martyrs of the past and then promised to decolonize society. While the "Indigenous state" did not fulfill all its promises, Indigenous self-determination and plurinationality remain inspiring horizons for addressing past harms (Postero 2017). As I mentioned earlier, Indigenous scholars are increasingly using the language of resurgence and futurities, arguing that Indigenous communities "already have what they need to live, shape, and imagine many modes of futurity" (Harjo 2019, 46). Moving away from a trauma-based paradigm of repair might entail recognition of forms of healing and collective sociality that fundamentally challenge liberal (and neoliberal) forms of governance.

References

Boal, Augusto. 2013. *Teatro del oprimido*. Barcelona: Alba Editorial.

Butler, Judith. 2015. *Notes Toward a Performative Theory of Assembly*. Cambridge, Mass.: Harvard University Press.

Freire, Paulo. (1970) 2018. *Pedagogy of the Oppressed*. London: Bloomsbury.

Harjo, Laura. 2019. *Spiral to the Stars: Mvskoke Tools of Futurity*. Tucson: University of Arizona Press.

Krupa, Christopher, and David Nugent, eds. 2015. *State Theory and Andean Politics: New Approaches to the Study of Rule*. Philadelphia: University of Pennsylvania Press.

Marx, Karl. (1867) 2007. *Capital: A Critique of Political Economy*. Vol. 1, part 2. New York: Cosimo.

Meister, Robert. 2010. *After Evil: A Politics of Human Rights*. New York: Columbia University Press.

Nelson, Diane M. 2015. *Who Counts? The Mathematics of Death and Life After Genocide*. Durham, N.C.: Duke University Press.

Nuijten, Monique. 2003. *Power, Community and the State: The Political Anthropology of Organisation in Mexico*. London: Pluto Press.

Postero, Nancy. 2017. *The Indigenous State: Race, Politics, and Performance in Plurinational Bolivia*. Berkeley: University of California Press.

Postero, Nancy, and Eli Elinoff. 2019. "Introduction: A Return to Politics." *Anthropological Theory* 19 (1): 3–28.

Povinelli, Elizabeth A. 2002. *The Cunning of Recognition*. Durham, N.C.: Duke University Press.

Povinelli, Elizabeth A. 2011. *Economies of Abandonment*. Durham, N.C.: Duke University Press.

Rothschild, Amy. 2017. "Victims Versus Veterans: Agency, Resistance and Legacies of Timor-Leste's Truth Commission." *International Journal of Transitional Justice* 11 (3): 443–462.

Simpson, Leanne Betasamosake. 2017. *As We Have Always Done: Indigenous Freedom Through Radical Resistance*. Minneapolis: University of Minnesota Press.

Speed, Shannon. 2019. *Incarcerated Stories: Indigenous Women Migrants and Violence in the Settler-Capitalist State*. Chapel Hill: University of North Carolina Press.

Theidon, Kimberly. 2007. "Gender in Transition: Common Sense, Women, and War." *Journal of Human Rights* 6 (4): 453–478.

Viveiros de Castro, Eduardo. 2004. "Perspectival Anthropology and the Method of Controlled Equivocation." *Tipití: Journal of the Society for the Anthropology of Lowland South America* 2 (1): 1.

Vizenor, Gerald. 2009. *Native Liberty: Natural Reason and Cultural Survivance*. Lincoln: University of Nebraska Press.

Acknowledgments

Identifying a clear starting point for this volume is difficult. Bits and pieces of ideas and reflections for this anthology have emerged over coffees, in teaching contexts, and at conferences over the past years. Our inspiration is manifold, and even if we wanted to list all the situations, people, and communities who have inspired us, it would be impossible. Whether we focus on human rights violations and new formations of politics and citizenship, Indigenous peoples' incessant struggles for rights and self-determination, or, in recent decades, struggles around environmental degradation and the effects of climate change, the concern with reparation has emerged as a relevant category—because it is deeply relevant to the people and communities with and among whom we conduct our work. Anyone who lives and works in Latin America knows of its diversity and the many (at times contradictory) demands for change. Yet it seems that these demands share a concern with how to continue living and how to restore a world that often appears damaged. In its broadest sense, this anthology thus stems from an attempt to ask what it means to live in a damaged world and engage in its reparation. What kinds of futures emerge when we approach politics as a matter of reparations?

In more concrete terms, this volume originates from a Wenner-Gren Foundation workshop initially scheduled for 2020 in Santiago, Chile, and then turned into an online version consisting of shorter sections spread over three days in 2021. We thank the Wenner-Gren Foundation for their support and understanding during the heyday of the COVID-19 pandemic. Editing and copyediting of this book were supported by grants provided by the University of Ottawa (Fonds Finisseur du Collabzium 2022), Instituto Milenio para la Investigación en Violencia y Democracia VioDemos (ANID, Millennium Science Initiative Program, ICS2019_025), Center for Indigenous and Intercultural Research (CONICYT/FONDAP/1522A0003), and project Fondecyt Regular 1230912

After Harm. We thank Kristin Glenn and Owen Gurrey for their patience and generosity in the revision of the manuscript. We are indebted to the amazing editorial team at Rutgers University Press—in particular, Peggy Solic—and to the editors of the Genocide, Political Violence, Human Rights Series, Alexander Laban Hinton, Nela Navarro, and Natasha Zaretsky, for guiding us through the entire book project. This book is dedicated to the memory of Paula Vásquez Lezama, who accompanied us in the early stages of this project before her passing in 2021.

Notes on Contributors

ORIANA BERNASCONI is a sociologist and associate professor at the Institute of Applied Ethics, Pontifícia Universidad Católica de Chile. Her research focuses on how societies confront state violence and its enduring impacts. Over the past decade, she has conducted interdisciplinary studies in Chile, Argentina, Mexico, and Colombia, focusing on how the documentation of human rights violations, archives, and knowledge infrastructures influence how societies address the legacies of violence. She is the editor of four special issues on this subject and of the book *Resistance to Political Violence in Latin America: Documenting Atrocity* (Palgrave, 2019).

MAGALÍ VIENCA COPA PABÓN is a lawyer and Aymara activist. She holds a master's degree in human rights from the Universidad Autónoma de San Luis Potosí and a bachelor's degree in law from the Universidad Mayor de San Simón and is currently a doctoral candidate in socioenvironmental law at the Pontifícia Universidade Católica do Paraná, Brazil. She is a former student leader (2000–2003) and previously worked with the Decolonization Unit of the Plurinational Constitutional Tribunal (2012–2014), the Office of the Ombudsman (2015), and the Mayor's Office of El Alto (2021–2022). Her work focuses on social movements, legal pluralism, and socioenvironmental conflicts in Latin America.

PIERGIORGIO DI GIMINIANI is an associate professor of anthropology at the Pontifícia Universidad Católica de Chile. He is the author of *Sentient Lands: Indigeneity, Property, and Political Imagination in Neoliberal Chile* (University of Arizona Press, 2018) and *Alterhumanism: Becoming Humans on a Conservation Frontier* (University of Arizona Press, 2025). His research interests concern land politics, conservation, entrepreneurship, and Indigenous rights.

AMY KENNEMORE holds a PhD in anthropology from the University of California, San Diego. Her main areas of research are legal pluralism, decolonization, and Indigenous justice. She has conducted ethnographic research in Bolivia to explore rights as a tool for critique and political action. Her recent publication, coauthored with Nancy Postero, *Collaborative Ethnographic Methods: Dismantling the "Anthropological Broom Closet"?*, examines the contributions of collaborative research in Latin America.

MILLARAY PAINEMAL is a founding member of ANAMURI (Asociación Nacional de Mujeres Rurales e Indígenas), where she has carried out several projects and held various roles. She also founded and coordinated the Indigenous Mapuche women's network Trawun pu Zomo, based in the town of Cholchol, Chile. She holds an undergraduate degree in history from the Patrice Lumumba Peoples' Friendship University in Russia and a master's degree in social sciences from the gender and development program of FLACSO (Facultad Latinoamericana de Ciencias Sociales), Ecuador.

NANCY POSTERO is a professor emerita of anthropology at the University of California, San Diego. She is the author of *Now We Are Citizens: Indigenous Politics in Postmulticultural Bolivia* (Stanford University Press, 2007); *The Indigenous State: Race, Politics, and Performance in Plurinational Bolivia* (University of California Press, 2017); and numerous edited volumes and articles on Indigenous rights, multiculturalism, and state power in Latin America. Her most recent publication is a coedited volume focusing on Indigenous futurities, called *The Routledge Handbook of Indigenous Development* (Routledge, 2023).

PATRICIA RICHARDS is a professor of sociology and women's and gender studies at the University of Georgia. She is the author of *Pobladoras, Indígenas, and the State: Conflicts over Women's Rights in Chile* (Rutgers University Press, 2004) and *Race and the Chilean Miracle: Neoliberalism, Democracy, and Indigenous Rights* (University of Pittsburgh Press, 2013), among other books and articles. Her work focuses on gender, social movements, and Indigenous rights in Latin America.

HELENE RISØR is an associate professor of anthropology at the Pontifícia Universidad Católica de Chile and director of the Millennium Institute on Violence and Democracy. She has written extensively on insecurity, citizenship, violence, and social movements in Bolivia and Chile.

HENRIK RONSBO is an anthropologist currently serving as director of the Dignity Lab at the Danish Institute Against Torture. He has published on the psychosocial effects of torture, civil war, and genocide, with a particular focus on

Indigenous populations in Latin America. He coedited the volume *Histories of Victimhood* (Pennsylvania University Press, 2014).

GUILLERMO SALAS CARREÑO is a professor of anthropology at the Pontifícia Universidad Católica del Perú. His latest book, *Lugares Parientes: Comida, cohabitación y mundos andinos* (Fondo Editorial PUCP, 2019), explores Indigenous Andean forms of sociality that exceed humans and their articulations with state and mining practices. He has also published articles on social impacts and conflicts around mining, implicit indigeneity, and ontological multiplicity in the Peruvian Andes.

MARÍA EUGENIA ULFE is a senior professor and researcher of anthropology at the Pontifícia Universidad Católica del Perú, where she is a member of the Interdisciplinary Research Group on Memory and Democracy. She is the author of *Reparando mundos: Víctimas y Estado en los Andes peruanos* (Fondo Editorial PUCP, 2021) and *¿Y después de la violencia qué queda? Víctimas, ciudadanos y reparaciones en el contexto post-CVR en el Perú* (CLACSO, 2013), among other manuscripts and edited volumes.

KARINE VANTHUYNE is a full professor of anthropology at the University of Ottawa. She is the author of *La présence d'un passé de violences: Mémoires et identités autochtones dans le Guatemala de l'après-génocide* (Presses de l'Université Laval, 2014) as well as coeditor of *Power Through Testimony: Residential Schools in the Age of Reconciliation in Canada* (University of British Columbia Press, 2017). Her work focuses on Indigenous rights movements in Guatemala and Canada.

NATASHA ZARETSKY is a clinical associate professor at New York University and a visiting scholar at the Center for the Study of Genocide and Human Rights at Rutgers University, where she leads the Truth in the Americas Initiative. Her latest book, *Acts of Repair: Justice, Truth, and the Politics of Memory in Argentina* (Rutgers University Press, 2021), examines transitional justice and memory in Argentina.

Index

Page numbers in italics refer to figures.

Irina Silber, *Everyday Revolutionaries: Gender, Violence, and Disillusionment in Postwar El Salvador*

Amy Sodaro, *Lifting the Shadow: Reshaping Memory, Race, and Slavery in U.S. Museums*

Samuel Totten and Rafiki Ubaldo, eds., *We Cannot Forget: Interviews with Survivors of the 1994 Genocide in Rwanda*

Eva van Roekel, *Phenomenal Justice: Violence and Morality in Argentina*

Anton Weiss-Wendt, *A Rhetorical Crime: Genocide in the Geopolitical Discourse of the Cold War*

Kerry Whigham, *Resonant Violence: Affect, Memory, and Activism in Post-Genocide Societies*

Timothy Williams, *The Complexity of Evil: Perpetration and Genocide*

Ronnie Yimsut, *Facing the Khmer Rouge: A Cambodian Journey*

Natasha Zaretsky, *Acts of Repair: Justice, Truth, and the Politics of Memory in Argentina*

Julien Zarifian, *The United States and the Armenian Genocide: History, Memory, Politics*